Matrix Calculus and Zero-One Matrices

This book presents the reader with mathematical tools taken from matrix calculus and zero-one matrices and demonstrates how these tools greatly facilitate the application of classical statistical procedures to econometric models. The matrix calculus results are derived from a few basic rules that are generalizations of the rules of ordinary calculus. These results are summarized in a useful table. Well-known zero-one matrices, together with some new ones, are defined, their mathematical roles explained, and their useful properties presented.

The basic building blocks of classical statistics, namely, the score vector, the information matrix, and the Cramer–Rao lower bound, are obtained for a sequence of linear econometric models of increasing statistical complexity. From these are obtained interactive interpretations of maximum likelihood estimators, linking them with efficient econometric estimators. Classical test statistics are also derived and compared for hypotheses of interest.

Darrell A. Turkington is Professor in the Department of Economics at the University of Western Australia, Perth. He is coauthor with Roger J. Bowden of the widely cited work *Instrumental Variables* (1984) in the Econometric Society Monographs series published by Cambridge University Press. Professor Turkington has published in leading international journals such as the *Journal of the American Statistical Association*, the *International Economic Review*, and the *Journal of Econometrics*. He has held visiting positions at the University of California, Berkeley, the University of Warwick, and the University of British Columbia.

Matrix Calculus and Zero-One Matrices

Statistical and Econometric Applications

DARRELL A. TURKINGTON
University of Western Australia

CAMBRIDGE
UNIVERSITY PRESS

CAMBRIDGE UNIVERSITY PRESS
Cambridge, New York, Melbourne, Madrid, Cape Town, Singapore, São Paulo

Cambridge University Press
The Edinburgh Building, Cambridge CB2 2RU, UK

Published in the United States of America by Cambridge University Press, New York

www.cambridge.org
Information on this title: www.cambridge.org/9780521807883

First published 2002
This digitally printed first paperback version 2005

A catalogue record for this publication is available from the British Library

Library of Congress Cataloguing in Publication data

Turkington, Darrell A.

Matrix calculus and zero-one matrices : statistical and econometric applications / Darrell A. Turkington.

p. cm.

Includes bibliographical references and index.

ISBN 0-521-80788-3

1. Matrices. 2. Mathematical statistics. I. Title.

QA188 .T865 2001

512.9′434 – dc21 2001025614

ISBN-13 978-0-521-80788-3 hardback
ISBN-10 0-521-80788-3 hardback

ISBN-13 978-0-521-02245-3 paperback
ISBN-10 0-521-02245-2 paperback

To Sonia

Contents

Preface

This book concerns itself with the mathematics behind the application of classical statistical procedures to econometric models. I first tried to apply such procedures in 1983 when I wrote a book with Roger Bowden on instrumental variable estimation. I was impressed with the amount of differentiation involved and the difficultly I had in recognizing the end product of this process. I thought there must be an easier way of doing things. Of course at the time, like most econometricians, I was blissfully unaware of matrix calculus and the existence of zero-one matrices. Since then several books have been published in these areas showing us the power of these concepts. See, for example Graham (1981), Magnus (1988), Magnus and Neudecker (1999), and Lutkepohl (1996).

This present book arose when I set myself two tasks: first, to make myself a list of rules of matrix calculus that were most useful in applying classical statistical procedures to econometrics; second, to work out the basic building blocks of such procedures – the score vector, the information matrix, and the Cramer–Rao lower bound – for a sequence of econometric models of increasing statistical complexity. I found that the mathematics involved working with operators that were generalizations of the well-known vec operator, and that a very simple zero-one matrix kept cropping up. I called the matrix a shifting matrix for reasons that are obvious in the book. Its basic nature is illustrated by the fact that all Toeplitz circulant matrices can be written as linear combinations of shifting matrices.

The book falls naturally into two parts. The first part outlines the classical statistical procedures used throughout the work and aims at providing the reader with the mathematical tools needed to apply these procedures to econometric models. The statistical procedures are dealt with in Chap. 1. Chapter 2 deals with elements of matrix algebra. In this chapter, generalized vec and devec operators are defined and their basic properties investigated. Chapter 3 concerns itself with zero-one matrices. Well-known zero-one matrices such as commutation matrices, elimination matrices, and duplication matrices are defined and their properties listed. Several new zero-one matrices are introduced in this chapter. Explicit expressions are given for the generalized vec and devec of the commutation matrix, and the properties of these matrices are investigated in several theorems. Shifting matrices are defined and the connection among these matrices and Toeplitz and circulant matrices is explained. Moreover, the essential role they play in time-series processes is demonstrated. Chapter 4 is devoted to matrix calculus. The approach taken in this chapter is to derive the matrix calculus results from a few basic rules that are generalizations of the chain rule and product rule of ordinary calculus. Some of these results are new, involving as they do generalized vecs of commutation matrices. A list of useful rules is given at the end of the chapter.

The second part of the book is designed to illustrate how the mathematical tools discussed in the preceding chapters greatly facilitate the application of classical statistical procedures to econometric models in that they speed up the difficult differentiation involved and help in the required asymptotic work.

In all, nine linear statistical models are considered. The first three models (Chap. 5) are based on the linear-regression model: the basic model, the linear-regression model with autoregressive disturbances, and the linear-regression model with moving-average disturbances. The next three models (Chap. 6) are based on the seemingly unrelated regression equations (SURE) model: the basic model, the SURE model with vector autoregressive disturbances, and the SURE model with vector moving-average disturbances. The final three models (Chap. 7) are based on the linear simultaneous equations (LSE) model. We consider the basic LSE model and the two variations that come about when we assume vector autoregressive or vector moving-average disturbances.

For each model considered, the basic building blocks of classical statistics are obtained: the score vector, the information matrix, and the Cramer–Rao lower bound. Statistical analysis is then conducted with these concepts. Where possible, econometric estimators of the parameters of primary interest that achieve the Cramer–Rao lower bound are discussed. Iterative interpretations of the maximum-likelihood estimators that link them with the econometric estimators are presented. Classical test statistics for hypotheses of interest are obtained.

The models were chosen in such a way as to form a sequence of models of increasing statistical complexity. The reader can then see, for example, how the added complication changes the information matrix or the Cramer–Rao lower bound. There are, in fact, two such sequences in operation. We have in Chap. 5, for example, the basic linear-regression model followed by versions of this model with more complicated disturbance structures. Second, between chapters, we have sequences of models with the same characteristics assigned to the disturbances: for example, the linear-regression model with autoregressive disturbances followed by the SURE model and the LSE model with vector autoregressive disturbances.

It is assumed that the reader has a good working knowledge of matrix algebra, basic statistics, and classical econometrics and is familiar with standard asymptotic theory. As such, the book should be useful for graduate students in econometrics and for practicing econometricians. Statisticians interested in how their procedures apply to other fields may also be attracted to this work.

Several institutions should be mentioned in this preface: first, my home university, the University of Western Australia, for allowing me time off from teaching to concentrate on the manuscript; second, the University of Warwick and the University of British Columbia for providing me with stimulating environments at which to spend my sabbaticals. At Warwick I first became interested in matrix calculus; at British Columbia I put the finishing touches to the manuscript.

Several individuals must also be thanked: my teacher Tom Rothenberg, to whom I owe an enormous debt; Adrian Pagan, for his sound advice; Jan Magnus, for introducing me to the intricacies of zero-one matrices; my colleagues Les Jennings, Michael McAleer, Shiqing Ling, and Jakob Madsen for their helpful suggestions and encouragement; Helen Reidy for her great patience and skill in typing the many drafts of this work; finally, my family, Sonia, Joshua, and Nikola, for being there for me.

1 Classical Statistical Procedures

1.1. INTRODUCTION

An alternative title to this book could have been *The Application of Classical Statistical Procedures to Econometrics* or something along these lines. What it purports to do is provide the reader with mathematical tools that facilitate the application of classical statistical procedures to the complicated statistical models that we are confronted with in econometrics. It then demonstrates how these procedures can be applied to a sequence of linear econometric models, each model being more complicated statistically than the previous one. The statistical procedures I have in mind are these centered around the likelihood function: procedures that involve the score vector, the information matrix, and the Cramer–Rao lower bound, together with maximum-likelihood estimation and classical test statistics.

Until recently, such procedures were little used by econometricians. The likelihood function in most econometric models is complicated, and the first-order conditions for maximizing this function usually give rise to a system of nonlinear equations that is not easily solved. As a result, econometricians developed their own class of estimators, instrumental variable estimators, that had the same asymptotic properties as those of maximum-likelihood estimators (MLEs) but were far more tractable mathematically [see Bowden and Turkington (1990)]. Nor did econometricians make much use of the prescribed classical statistical procedures for obtaining test statistics for the hypotheses of interest in econometric models; rather, test statistics were developed on an ad hoc basis.

All that changed in the last couple of decades, when there was renewed interest by econometricians in maximum-likelihood procedures and in developing Lagrangian multiplier test (LMT) statistics. One reason for this change was the advent of large, fast computers. A complicated system of nonlinear equations could now be solved so we would have in hand the maximum-likelihood estimates even though we had no algebraic expression for the underlying estimators. Another more recent explanation for this change in attitude is the advent of results on zero-one matrices and matrix calculus. Works by Graham (1981), Magnus (1988), Magnus and Neudecker (1988), and Lutkepohl (1996) have shown us the importance of zero-one matrices, their connection to matrix calculus, and the power of matrix calculus particularly with respect to applying classical statistical procedures.

In this introductory chapter, I have a brief and nonrigorous summary of the classical statistical procedures that are used extensively in the latter part of this book.

1.2. THE SCORE VECTOR, THE INFORMATION MATRIX, AND THE CRAMER–RAO LOWER BOUND

Let θ be a $k \times 1$ vector of unknown parameters associated with a statistical model and let $l(\theta)$ be the log-likelihood function that satisfies certain regularity conditions and is twice differentiable. Let $\partial l/\partial\theta$ denote the $k \times 1$ vector of partial derivatives of l. Then $\partial l/\partial\theta$ is called the **score vector**. Let $\partial^2 l/\partial\theta\partial\theta'$ denote the $k \times k$ Hessian matrix of $l(\theta)$. Then the (asymptotic) **information matrix** is defined as

$$I(\theta) = -\lim_{n\to\infty} \frac{1}{n} E(\partial^2 l/\partial\theta\partial\theta'),$$

where n denotes the sample size. Now the limit of the expectation need not be the same as the probability limit. However, for the models we consider in this book, based as they are on the multivariate normal distribution, the two concepts will be the same. As a result it is often more convenient to regard the information matrix as

$$I(\theta) = -p\lim \frac{1}{n}\partial^2 l/\partial\theta\partial\theta'.$$

The inverse of this matrix, $I^{-1}(\theta)$, is called the (asymptotic) **Cramer–Rao** lower bound. Let $\hat{\theta}$ be a consistent estimator of θ such that

$$\sqrt{n}(\hat{\theta} - \theta) \xrightarrow{d} N(0, V).$$

The matrix V is called the asymptotic covariance matrix of $\hat{\theta}$. Then V exceeds the Cramer–Rao lower bound $I^{-1}(\theta)$ in the sense that $V - I^{-1}(\theta)$ is a positive-semidefinite matrix. If $V = I^{-1}(\theta)$, then $\hat{\theta}$ is called a best asymptotically normally distributed estimator (which is shortened to BAN estimator).

1.3. MAXIMUM LIKELIHOOD ESTIMATORS AND TEST PROCEDURES

Classical statisticians prescribed a procedure for obtaining a BAN estimator, namely the maximum-likelihood procedure. Let $\oplus$ denote the parameter space. Then any value of θ that maximizes $l(\theta)$ over $\oplus$ is called a maximum-likelihood estimate, and the underlying estimator is called the MLE. The first-order conditions for this maximization are given by

$$\frac{\partial l(\theta)}{\partial \theta} = 0.$$

Let $\tilde{\theta}$ denote the MLE of θ. Then $\tilde{\theta}$ is consistent, and $\tilde{\theta}$ is the BAN estimator so

$$\sqrt{n}(\tilde{\theta} - \theta) \xrightarrow{d} N[0, I^{-1}(\theta)].$$

Let h be a $G \times 1$ vector whose elements are functions of the elements of θ. We denote this by $h(\theta)$. Suppose we are interested in developing test statistics for the null hypothesis

$$H_O : h(\theta) = 0$$

against the alternative

$$H_A : h(\theta) \neq 0.$$

Let $\tilde{\theta}$ denote the MLE of θ and $\bar{\theta}$ denote the constrained MLE of θ; that is, $\bar{\theta}$ is the MLE of θ we obtain after we impose H_O on our statistical model. Let $\partial h(\theta)/\partial \theta$ denote the $k \times G$ matrix whose (ij) element is $\partial h_j/\partial \theta_i$. Then classical statisticians prescribed three competing procedures for obtaining a test statistic for H_O. These are as follows.

LAGRANGIAN MULTIPLIER TEST STATISTIC

$$T_1 = \frac{1}{n}\frac{\partial l(\bar{\theta})'}{\partial \theta} I^{-1}(\bar{\theta}) \frac{\partial l(\bar{\theta})}{\partial \theta}.$$

Note that the LMT statistic uses the constrained MLE of θ. If H_O is true, $\bar{\theta}$ should be close to $\tilde{\theta}$ and as, by the first-order conditions, $\partial l(\tilde{\theta})/\partial \theta = 0$, the derivative $\partial l(\theta)/\partial \theta$ evaluated at $\bar{\theta}$ should also be close to the null vector. The test statistic is a measure of the distance $\partial l(\bar{\theta})/\partial \theta$ is from the null vector.

WALD TEST STATISTIC

$$T_2 = nh(\tilde{\theta})' \left[\frac{\partial h(\tilde{\theta})'}{\partial \theta} I^{-1}(\tilde{\theta}) \frac{\partial h(\tilde{\theta})}{\partial \theta} \right]^{-1} h(\tilde{\theta}).$$

Note that the Wald test statistic uses the (unconstrained) MLE of θ. Essentially it is based on the asymptotic distribution of $\sqrt{n}h(\tilde{\theta})$ under H_O, the statistic itself measuring the distance $h(\tilde{\theta})$ is from the null vector.

LIKELIHOOD RATIO TEST STATISTIC

$$T_3 = 2[l(\tilde{\theta}) - l(\bar{\theta})].$$

Note that the likelihood ratio test (LRT) statistic uses both the unconstrained MLE $\tilde{\theta}$ and the constrained MLE $\bar{\theta}$. If H_O is indeed true, it should not matter whether we impose it or not, so $l(\tilde{\theta})$ should be approximately the same as $l(\bar{\theta})$. The test statistic T_3 measures the difference between $l(\tilde{\theta})$ and $l(\bar{\theta})$.

All three test statistics are asymptotically equivalent in the sense that, under H_O, they all have the same limiting χ^2 distribution and under H_A, with local alternatives, they have the same limiting noncentral χ^2 distribution. Usually imposing the null hypothesis on our model leads to a simpler statistical model, and thus the constrained MLEs $\bar{\theta}$ are more obtainable than the $\tilde{\theta}$ MLEs. For this reason the LMT statistic is often the easiest statistic to form. Certainly it is the one that has been most widely used in econometrics.

1.4. NUISANCE PARAMETERS

Let us now partition θ into $\theta = (\alpha'\beta')'$, where α is a $k_1 \times 1$ vector of parameters of primary interest and β is a $k_2 \times 1$ vector of nuisance parameters, $k_1 + k_2 = k$. The terms used here do not imply that the parameters in β are unimportant to our statistical model. Rather, they indicate that the purpose of our analysis is to make statistical inference about the parameters in α instead of those in β.

In this situation, two approaches can be taken. First, we can derive the information matrix $I(\theta)$ and the Cramer–Rao lower bound $I^{-1}(\theta)$. Let

$$I(\theta) = \begin{bmatrix} I_{\alpha\alpha} & I_{\alpha\beta} \\ I_{\beta\alpha} & I_{\beta\beta} \end{bmatrix},$$

$$I^{-1}(\theta) = \begin{pmatrix} I^{\alpha\alpha} & I^{\alpha\beta} \\ I^{\beta\alpha} & I^{\beta\beta} \end{pmatrix}$$

be these matrices partitioned according to our partition of θ. As far as α is concerned we can now work with $I_{\alpha\alpha}$ and $I^{\alpha\alpha}$ in place of $I(\theta)$ and $I^{-1}(\theta)$, respectively. For example, $I^{\alpha\alpha}$ is the Cramer–Rao lower bound for the asymptotic covariance matrix of a consistent estimator of α. If $\tilde{\alpha}$ is the MLE of α, then

$$\sqrt{n}(\tilde{\alpha} - \alpha) \xrightarrow{d} N(0, I^{\alpha\alpha}),$$

and so on.

A particular null hypothesis that has particular relevance for us is

$$H_O : \alpha = 0$$

against

$$H_A : \alpha \neq 0.$$

Under this first approach, the classical test statistics for this null hypothesis would be the following test statistics.

LAGRANGIAN TEST STATISTIC

$$T_1 = \frac{1}{n}\frac{\partial l(\bar{\theta})'}{\partial \alpha} I^{\alpha\alpha}(\bar{\theta}) \frac{\partial l(\bar{\theta})}{\partial \alpha}.$$

WALD TEST STATISTIC

$$T_2 = n\tilde{\alpha}' I^{\alpha\alpha}(\tilde{\theta})^{-1}\tilde{\alpha}.$$

LIKELIHOOD RATIO TEST STATISTIC

$$T_3 = 2[l(\tilde{\theta}) - l(\bar{\theta})].$$

Under H_O all three test statistics would have a limiting χ^2 distribution with k_1 degrees of freedom, and the nature of the tests insists that we use the upper tail of this distribution to find the appropriate critical region.

The second approach is to work with the concentrated log-likelihood function. Here we undertake a stepwise maximization of the log-likelihood function. We first maximize $l(\theta)$ with respect to the nuisance parameters β to obtain $\bar{\beta} = \bar{\beta}(\alpha)$, say. The vector $\bar{\beta}$ is then placed back in the log-likelihood function to obtain

$$\bar{l}(\alpha) = l[\alpha, \bar{\beta}(\alpha)].$$

The function $\bar{l}(\alpha)$ is called the concentrated likelihood function. Our analysis can now be reworked with $\bar{l}(\alpha)$ in place of $l(\theta)$.

For example, let

$$\bar{I} = -p\lim \frac{1}{n}\frac{\partial \bar{l}}{\partial \alpha\, \partial \alpha'},$$

and let $\hat{\alpha}$ be any consistent estimator of α such that

$$\sqrt{n}(\hat{\alpha} - \alpha) \xrightarrow{d} N(0,\ V_\alpha).$$

Then $V_\alpha \geq \bar{I}^{-1}$ in the sense that their difference is a positive-semidefinite matrix. If $\tilde{\alpha}$ is the MLE of α, then $\tilde{\alpha}$ is obtained from

$$\frac{\partial \bar{l}}{\partial \alpha} = 0,$$

$$\sqrt{n}(\tilde{\alpha} - \alpha) \xrightarrow{d} N(0,\ \bar{I}^{-1}),$$

and so on. As far as test procedures go for the null hypothesis $H_O : h(\alpha) = 0$, under this second approach we rewrite the test statistics by using $\bar{l}$ and $\bar{I}$ in place of $l(\theta)$ and $I(\theta)$, respectively. In this book, I largely use the first approach as one of my expressed aims is to achieve the complete information matrix $I(\theta)$ for a sequence of econometric models.

1.5. DIFFERENTIATION AND ASYMPTOTICS

Before we leave this brief chapter, note that classical statistical procedures involve us in much differentiation. The score vector $\partial l/\partial\theta$, the Hessian matrix $\partial^2 l/\partial\theta\partial\theta'$, and $\partial h/\partial\theta$ all involve working out partial derivatives. It is at this stage that difficulties can arise in applying these procedures to econometric models. As hinted at in Section 1.2, the log-likelihood function $l(\theta)$ for most econometric models is a complicated function, and it is no trivial matter to obtain the derivatives required in our application. Usually it is too great a task for ordinary calculus. Although in some cases it can be done, [see, for example, Rothenberg and Leenders (1964)], what often happens when one attempts to do the differentiation by using ordinary calculus is that one is confronted with a hopeless mess. It is precisely this problem that has motivated the writing of this book. I hope that it will go some way toward alleviating it.

It is assumed that the reader is familiar with standard asymptotic theory. Every attempt has been made to make the rather dull but necessary asymptotic analysis in this book as readable as possible. Only the probability limits of the information matrices that are required in our statistical analysis are worked out in full. The probability limits themselves are assumed to exist – a more formal mathematical analysis would give a list of sufficient conditions needed to ensure this. Finally, as already noted, use is made of the shortcut notation

$$\sqrt{n}(\tilde{\beta} - \beta) \xrightarrow{d} N(0, V)$$

rather than the more formally correct notation

$$\sqrt{n}(\tilde{\beta} - \beta) \xrightarrow{d} x \sim N(0, V).$$

2 Elements of Matrix Algebra

2.1. INTRODUCTION

In this chapter, we consider matrix operators that are used throughout the book and special square matrices, namely triangular matrices and band matrices, that will crop up continually in our future work. From the elements of an $m \times n$ matrix, $A = (a_{ij})$ and a $p \times q$ matrix, $B = (b_{ij})$, the Kronecker product forms an $mp \times nq$ matrix. The vec operator forms a column vector out of a given matrix by stacking its columns one underneath the other. The devec operator forms a row vector out of a given matrix by stacking its rows one alongside the other. In like manner, a generalized vec operator forms a new matrix from a given matrix by stacking a certain number of its columns under each other and a generalized devec operator forms a new matrix by stacking a certain number of rows alongside each other. It is well known that the Kronecker product is intimately connected with the vec operator, but we shall see that this connection also holds for the devec and generalized operators as well. Finally we look at special square matrices with zeros above or below the main diagonal or whose nonzero elements form a band surrounded by zeros. The approach I have taken in this chapter, as indeed in several other chapters, is to list, without proof, well-known properties of the mathematical concept, in hand. If, however, I want to present a property in a different light or if I have something new to say about the concept, then I will give a proof.

2.2. KRONECKER PRODUCTS

Let $A = (a_{ij})$ be an $m \times n$ matrix and B a $p \times q$ matrix. The $mp \times nq$ matrix given by

$$\begin{bmatrix} a_{11}B & \dots & a_{1n}B \\ \vdots & & \vdots \\ a_{m1}B & \dots & a_{mn}B \end{bmatrix}$$

is called the **Kronecker product** of A and B, denoted by $A \otimes B$. The following useful properties concerning Kronecker products are well known:

$$A \otimes (B \otimes C) = (A \otimes B) \otimes C = A \otimes B \otimes C,$$

$$(A + B) \otimes (C + D) = A \otimes C + A \otimes D + B \otimes C + B \otimes D, \quad \text{if } A + B \text{ and } C + D \text{ exist,}$$

$$(A \otimes B)(C \otimes D) = AC \otimes BD, \text{ if } AC \text{ and } BD \text{ exist.}$$

The transpose of a Kronecker product is

$$(A \otimes B)' = A' \otimes B',$$

whereas the rank of a Kronecker product is

$$r(A \otimes B) = r(A)\, r(B).$$

If A is a square $n \times n$ matrix and B is a square $p \times p$ matrix, then the trace of the Kronecker product is

$$\text{tr}(A \otimes B) = \text{tr } A \text{ tr } B,$$

whereas the determinant of the Kronecker product is

$$|A \otimes B| = |A|^p |B|^n,$$

and if A and B are nonsingular, the inverse of the Kronecker product is

$$(A \otimes B)^{-1} = A^{-1} \otimes B^{-1}.$$

Other properties of Kronecker products, although perhaps less well known, are nevertheless useful and are used throughout this book. First note that, in general, Kronecker products do not obey the commutative law, so $A \otimes B \neq B \otimes A$. One exception to this rule is if a and b are two column vectors, not necessarily of the same order; then

$$a' \otimes b = b \otimes a' = ba'. \tag{2.1}$$

This exception allows us to write $A \otimes b$ in an interesting way, where A is an $m \times n$ matrix and b is a $p \times 1$ vector. Partitioning A into its rows, we write

$$A = \begin{pmatrix} a^{1'} \\ \vdots \\ a^{m'} \end{pmatrix},$$

where $a^{i'}$ is the ith row of A. Then clearly from our definition of Kronecker product

$$A \otimes b = \begin{pmatrix} a^{1'} \otimes b \\ \vdots \\ a^{m'} \otimes b \end{pmatrix} = \begin{pmatrix} b \otimes a^{1'} \\ \vdots \\ b \otimes a^{m'} \end{pmatrix}, \tag{2.2}$$

where we achieve the last equality by using Eq. (2.1).

Second, it is clear from the definition of the Kronecker product that if A is partitioned into submatrices, say

$$A = \begin{bmatrix} A_{11} & \cdots & A_{1K} \\ \vdots & & \vdots \\ A_{l1} & \cdots & A_{lK} \end{bmatrix}$$

then

$$A \otimes B = \begin{bmatrix} A_{11} \otimes B & \cdots & A_{1K} \otimes B \\ \vdots & & \vdots \\ A_{l1} \otimes B & \cdots & A_{lK} \otimes B \end{bmatrix}.$$

Suppose we now partition B into an arbitrary number of submatrices, say

$$B = \begin{bmatrix} B_{11} & \cdots & B_{1r} \\ \vdots & & \vdots \\ B_{s1} & \cdots & B_{sr} \end{bmatrix}.$$

Then, in general,

$$A \otimes B \neq \begin{bmatrix} A \otimes B_{11} & \dots & A \otimes B_{1r} \\ \vdots & & \vdots \\ A \otimes B_{s1} & \dots & A \otimes B_{sr} \end{bmatrix}.$$

One exception to this rule is given by the following theorem.

Theorem 2.1. Let a be an $m \times 1$ vector and B be a $p \times q$ matrix. Write $B = (B_1 \cdots B_r)$, where each submatrix of B has p rows. Then

$$a \otimes B = (a \otimes B_1 \cdots a \otimes B_r).$$

Proof of Theorem 2.1. Clearly

$$a \otimes B = \begin{pmatrix} a_1 B \\ \vdots \\ a_m B \end{pmatrix} = \begin{bmatrix} a_1(B_1 & \cdots & B_r) \\ & \vdots & \\ a_m(B_1 & \cdots & B_r) \end{bmatrix} = \begin{bmatrix} a_1 B_1 & \cdots & a_1 B_r \\ \vdots & & \vdots \\ a_m B_1 & \cdots & a_m B_r \end{bmatrix}$$
$$= (a \otimes B_1 \cdots a \otimes B_r). \qquad \square$$

Now consider A as an $m \times n$ matrix partitioned into its columns $A = (a_1 \cdots a_n)$ and a partitioned matrix $B = (B_1 \cdots B_r)$. Then, by using Theorem 2.1, it is clear that we can write

$$A \otimes B = (a_1 \otimes B_1 \cdots a_1 \otimes B_r \cdots a_n \otimes B_1 \cdots a_n \otimes B_r).$$

This property of Kronecker products allows us to write $A \otimes B$ in a useful way. Partitioning A and B into their columns, we write

$$A = (a_1 \cdots a_n), \quad B = (b_1 \cdots b_q).$$

Then

$$A \otimes B = (a_1 \otimes b_1 \cdots a_1 \otimes b_q \cdots a_n \otimes b_1 \cdots a_n \otimes b_q).$$

Third, note that if A and B are $m \times n$ and $p \times q$ matrices, respectively, and x is any column vector, then

$$A(I_n \otimes x') = (A \otimes 1)(I_n \otimes x') = A \otimes x',$$
$$(x \otimes I_p)B = (x \otimes I_p)(1 \otimes B) = x \otimes B.$$

This property, coupled with the Kronecker product of $A \otimes B$, where A is partitioned, affords us another useful way of writing $A \otimes B$. Partitioning A into its columns, we obtain

$$A \otimes B = (a_1 \otimes B \cdots a_n \otimes B) = [(a_1 \otimes I_p)B \cdots (a_n \otimes I_p)B].$$

Finally, note that for A $m \times n$, and B $p \times q$

$$A \otimes B = (A \otimes I_p)(I_n \otimes B) = (I_m \otimes B)(A \otimes I_q).$$

2.3. THE VEC AND THE DEVEC OPERATORS

2.3.1. Basic Definitions

Let A be an $m \times n$ matrix and a_j be its jth column. Then **vec** A is the $mn \times 1$ vector

$$\text{vec}\, A = \begin{bmatrix} a_1 \\ \vdots \\ a_n \end{bmatrix},$$

that is, the vec operator transforms A into a column vector by stacking the columns of A one underneath the other.

Let A be an $m \times n$ matrix and let $a^{i'}$ be the ith row of A. Then **devec** A is the $1 \times mn$ vector

$$\text{devec } A = (a^{1'} \cdots a^{m'}),$$

that is, the devec operator transforms A into a row vector by stacking the rows of A alongside each other.

Clearly the two operators are intimately connected. Writing $A = (a_1 \cdots a_n)$, we obtain

$$(\text{vec } A)' = (a_1' \cdots a_n') = \text{devec } A'. \tag{2.3}$$

Now let $A' = B$. Then

$$\text{vec } B' = (\text{devec } B)'. \tag{2.4}$$

These basic relationships mean that results for one of the operators can be readily obtained from results for the other operator.

2.3.2. Vec, Devec, and Kronecker Products

A basic connection between our operators and the Kronecker products can be derived from the property noted in Section 2.2 that, for any two column vectors a and b,

$$ab' = b' \otimes a = a \otimes b'.$$

From this property it is clear that the jth column of ab' is $b_j a$, where b_j is the jth element of b, so

$$\text{vec } ab' = \text{vec}(b' \otimes a) = b \otimes a. \tag{2.5}$$

Also, the ith row of ab' is $a_i b$, so

$$\text{devec } ab' = \text{devec}(a \otimes b') = a' \otimes b'.$$

More generally, if A, B, and C are three matrices such that the matrix product ABC is defined, then

$$\text{vec } ABC = (C' \otimes A) \text{ vec } B. \tag{2.6}$$

The corresponding result for the devec operator is

$$\begin{aligned} \text{devec } ABC &= [\text{vec}(C'B'A')]' = [(A \otimes C')\text{vec } B']' \\ &= (\text{vec } B')'(A' \otimes C) = \text{devec } B(A' \otimes C). \end{aligned} \tag{2.7}$$

Note that for A, an $m \times n$ matrix,

$$\text{vec } A = (I_n \otimes A)\text{vec } I_n = (A' \otimes I_m)\text{vec } I_m, \tag{2.8}$$

$$\text{devec } A = (\text{devec } I_n)\,(A' \otimes I_n) = (\text{devec } I_m)\,(I_m \otimes A). \tag{2.9}$$

Special cases of these results that we shall have occasion to refer to are those for a, an $m \times 1$ vector, and b, an $n \times 1$ vector:

$$a = \text{vec}\, a = (a' \otimes I_m)\text{vec}\, I_m,$$

$$b = \text{vec}\, b' = (I_n \otimes b')\text{vec}\, I_n,$$

$$b' = \text{devec}\, b' = (\text{devec}\, I_n)\,(b \otimes I_n),$$

$$a' = \text{devec}\, a = (\text{devec}\, I_m)\,(I_m \otimes a').$$

In future chapters, we often have to work with partitioned matrices. Suppose that A is an $m \times np$ matrix and partition A so that $A = (A_1 \cdots A_p)$, where each submatrix is $m \times n$. Then it is clear that

$$\text{vec}\, A = \begin{pmatrix} \text{vec}\, A_1 \\ \vdots \\ \text{vec}\, A_p \end{pmatrix}.$$

Suppose also that B is any $n \times q$ matrix and consider

$$A(I_p \otimes B) = (A_1 B \cdots A_p B).$$

If follows that

$$\text{vec}\, A(I_p \otimes B) = \begin{pmatrix} \text{vec}\, A_1 B \\ \vdots \\ \text{vec}\, A_p B \end{pmatrix} = \begin{pmatrix} I_q \otimes A_1 \\ \vdots \\ I_q \otimes A_p \end{pmatrix} \text{vec}\, B.$$

2.3.3. Vecs, Devecs, and Traces

Traces of matrix products can conveniently be expressed in terms of the vec and the devec operators. It is well known, for example, that

$$\text{tr}\, AB = (\text{vec}\, A')' \,\text{vec}\, B.$$

However, from Eq. (2.3) we can now write

$$\text{tr}\, AB = \text{devec}\, A \,\text{vec}\, B,$$

thus avoiding the awkward expression $(\text{vec}\, A')'$.

Similarly, we can obtain the many expressions for $\text{tr}\, ABC = \text{tr}\, BCA = \text{tr}\, CAB$, for example, by writing

$$\text{tr}\, ABC = \text{devec}\, A \,\text{vec}\, BC = \text{devec}\, AB \,\text{vec}\, C,$$

and then using equations (2.6) and (2.7).

2.3.4. Related Operators: Vech and $\bar{\nu}$

In taking the vec of a square matrix A, we form a column by using all the elements of A. The vech and the $\bar{\nu}$ operators form column vectors by using select elements of A.

Let A be an $n \times n$ matrix:

$$A = \begin{bmatrix} a_{11} & \cdots & a_{1n} \\ \vdots & & \vdots \\ a_{n1} & \cdots & a_{nn} \end{bmatrix}.$$

Then **vech A** is the $\frac{1}{2}n(n+1) \times 1$ vector

$$\text{vech } A = \begin{pmatrix} a_{11} \\ \vdots \\ a_{n1} \\ a_{22} \\ \vdots \\ a_{n2} \\ \vdots \\ a_{nn} \end{pmatrix},$$

that is, we form vech A by stacking the elements of A on and below the main diagonal, one underneath each other.

The vector $\bar{\nu}(A)$ is the $\frac{1}{2}n(n-1) \times 1$ vector given by

$$\bar{\nu}(A) = \begin{pmatrix} a_{21} \\ \vdots \\ a_{n1} \\ a_{32} \\ \vdots \\ a_{n2} \\ \vdots \\ a_{nn-1} \end{pmatrix},$$

that is, we form $\bar{\nu}(A)$ by stacking the elements of A below the main diagonal, one underneath the other.

If A is a symmetric matrix, that is, $A' = A$, then $a_{ij} = a_{ji}$ and the elements of A below the main diagonal are duplicated by the elements above the main diagonal. Often we wish to form a vector from A that consists of the essential elements of A without duplication. Clearly the vech operator allows us to do this.

An obvious application in statistics is that in which A is a covariance matrix. Then the unknown parameters associated with the covariance matrix are given by vech A. Suppose that now we wish to form a vector consisting of only the covariances of the covariance matrix but not the variances. Then such a vector is given by $\bar{v}(A)$.

Before we leave this section, note that for a square matrix A, not necessarily symmetric, vec A continues all the elements in vech A and in $\bar{v}(A)$ and more besides. It follows then that we could obtain vech A and $\bar{v}(A)$ by premultiplying vec A by a matrix whose elements are zeros or ones strategically placed. Such matrices are examples of the zero-one matrices called elimination matrices. Elimination matrices and other zero-one matrices are discussed in the next chapter.

2.4. GENERALIZED VEC AND DEVEC OPERATORS

In this section, we look at operators that are generalizations of the vec and the devec operators discussed in Section 2.3.

2.4.1. Generalized Vec Operator

Consider an $m \times p$ matrix partitioned into its columns $A = (a_1 \cdots a_p)$, where a_j is the jth column of A. Then $\text{vec}_1 A = \text{vec}\, A$, that is, $\text{vec}_1 A$ is the $mp \times 1$ vector given by

$$\text{vec}_1 A = \text{vec}\, A = \begin{pmatrix} a_1 \\ \vdots \\ a_p \end{pmatrix}.$$

Suppose now that A is an $m \times 2p$ matrix $A = (a_1 \cdots a_{2p})$. Then we define vec_2 as the $mp \times 2$ matrix given by

$$\text{vec}_2 A = \begin{bmatrix} a_1 & a_2 \\ a_3 & a_4 \\ & \vdots & \\ a_{2p-1} & a_{2p} \end{bmatrix},$$

that is, to form $\text{vec}_2 A$, we stack columns of A under each other, taking two at a time. More generally, if A is the $m \times np$ matrix $A = (a_1 \cdots a_{np})$ then $\textbf{vec}_{\boldsymbol{n}} \boldsymbol{A}$ is the $mp \times n$ matrix given by

$$\text{vec}_n A = \begin{bmatrix} a_1 & \dots & a_n \\ a_{n+1} & \dots & a_{2n} \\ \vdots & & \vdots \\ a_{n(p-1)} & \dots & a_{np} \end{bmatrix}.$$

Table 2.1. Vec Operations

K	**Vec Operators Performable on *A***																			
1	1																			
2	1	2																		
3	1		3																	
4	1	2		4																
5	1				5															
6	1	2	3			6														
7	1						7													
8	1	2		4				8												
9	1		3						9											
10	1	2			5					10										
11	1										11									
12	1	2	3	4		6						12								
13	1												13							
14	1	2					7							14						
15	1		3		5										15					
16	1	2		4				8								16				
17	1																17			
18	1	2	3			6			9									18		
19	1																		19	
20	1	2		4	5					10										20

For a given $m \times K$ matrix A, the number of generalized vec operations that can be performed on A clearly depends on the number of columns K of A. If K is a prime number, then only two generalized vec operators can be performed on A, $\text{vec}_1\, A = \text{vec}\, A$ and $\text{vec}_K\, A = A$. For K any other number, the number of generalized vec operations that can be performed on A is the number of divisors of K.

We then have the Table 2.1.[1]

2.4.2. Generalized Devec Operator

In applying a generalized vec operator, we form a matrix by stacking a certain number of columns of a given matrix underneath each other. In applying a generalized devec operator, we form a matrix by stacking a certain number of rows of a given matrix alongside each other. Consider a $p \times m$ matrix B that we partition into its rows $B = (b^1 \cdots b^p)'$, where $b^{j'}$ is the jth row of B. Then $\text{devec}_1\, B = \text{devec}\, B$ is the $1 \times mp$ vector given by

$$\text{devec}_1\, B = \text{devec}\, B = (b^{1'} \cdots b^{p'}).$$

[1] Number theorists assure me that it has not been possible as yet to derive a sequence for Table 2.1.

Suppose now that B is an $2p \times m$ matrix $B = (b^1 \cdots b^{2p})'$. Then we define $\text{devec}_2\, B$ as the $2 \times mp$ matrix given by

$$\text{devec}_2\, B = \begin{bmatrix} b^{1'} & b^{3'} & \cdots & b^{(2p-1)'} \\ b^{2'} & b^{4'} & \cdots & b^{2p'} \end{bmatrix},$$

that is, to form $\text{devec}_2\, B$, we stack rows of B alongside each other, taking two at a time. More generally, if B is an $np \times m$ matrix $B = (b^1 \cdots b^{np})'$, then **devec$_n$ B** is the $n \times mp$ matrix given by

$$\text{devec}_n\, B = \begin{bmatrix} b^{1'} & b^{n+1'} & \cdots & b^{n(p-1)'} \\ \vdots & \vdots & & \vdots \\ b^{n'} & b^{2n'} & \cdots & b^{np'} \end{bmatrix}.$$

Generalized devec operators performable on a given $K \times m$ matrix are given by a table similar to Table 2.1.

2.4.3. Vec$_n$ and Devec$_n$ Operators

2.4.3.1. Basic Relationship Between the Vec$_n$ and the Devec$_n$ Operators

Let A be an $m \times np$ matrix and write $A = (A_1 \cdots A_p)$, where each submatrix A_i is $m \times n$. Then

$$\text{vec}_n\, A = \begin{pmatrix} A_1 \\ \vdots \\ A_p \end{pmatrix},$$

so

$$(\text{vec}_n\, A)' = (A_1' \cdots A_p') = \text{devec}_n\, A'. \tag{2.10}$$

Now, letting $B = A'$, we have

$$(\text{devec}_n\, B)' = \text{vec}_n\, B'. \tag{2.11}$$

Again, these basic relationships mean that we have to derive theorems for only one of these operators. We can then readily obtain the corresponding results for the other operator by using Eq. (2.10) or Eq. (2.11).

2.4.3.2. Vec$_n$, Devec$_n$, and Kronecker Products

Let A and B be $p \times q$ and $m \times n$ matrices, respectively, and write $A = (a_1 \ldots a_q)$, where a_j is the jth columns of A. Then

$$A \otimes B = (a_1 \otimes B \cdots a_q \otimes B),$$

so

$$\operatorname{vec}_n(A \otimes B) = \begin{pmatrix} a_1 \otimes B \\ \vdots \\ a_q \otimes B \end{pmatrix} = \operatorname{vec} A \otimes B. \tag{2.12}$$

As a special case, $\operatorname{vec}_n(a' \otimes B) = a \otimes B$. Now write $A = (a^1 \cdots a^p)'$, where $a^{i'}$ is the ith row of A. Then

$$A \otimes B' = \begin{pmatrix} a^{1'} \otimes B' \\ \vdots \\ a^{p'} \otimes B' \end{pmatrix},$$

so

$$\operatorname{devec}_n(A \otimes B') = (a^{1'} \otimes B' \cdots a^{p'} \otimes B') = \operatorname{devec} A \otimes B' \tag{2.13}$$

As a special case, note that $\operatorname{devec}_n(a \otimes B') = a' \otimes B'$. Equations (2.12) and (2.13) mean that for complicated Kronecker products, where A is a product matrix for example, the results for vec_n and devec_n for these Kronecker products can again be obtained from known results of the vec operator.

2.4.4. Obvious Relationships between Generalized Vecs and Generalized Devecs for a Given Matrix

This section finishes with references to some obvious relationships between our operators for a given $T \times K$ matrix A. Let $\operatorname{vec}_j A$ refer to a generalized vec operator that is performable on A and let $\operatorname{devec}_i A$ refer to a generalized devec operator that is also performable on A. Then clearly the following relationships hold:

$\operatorname{Devec}(\operatorname{vec} A) = (\operatorname{vec} A)'$
$= \operatorname{devec} A'$.
$\operatorname{Devec}_T(\operatorname{vec}_j A) = A$.
$\operatorname{Devec}(\operatorname{vec}_j A) = 1 \times TK$ vector whose elements are obtained from a permutation of these of $(\operatorname{vec} A)'$.

$\operatorname{Vec}(\operatorname{devec} A) = \operatorname{vec} A'$
$= (\operatorname{devec} A)'$.
$\operatorname{Vec}_K(\operatorname{devec}_i A) = A$.
$\operatorname{Vec}_K(\operatorname{devec}_n A) = TK \times 1$ vector whose elements are obtained from permutation of those of $\operatorname{vec} A$.

2.4.5. Theorems about Generalized Vec and Devec Operators

In this subsection, we derive results concerning the generalized vec and devec operators that are important in the application of our concepts in future sections. These results are summarized in the following theorems.

Theorem 2.2. Let A, C, D, E, and α be $m \times np$, $r \times m$, $n \times s$, $p \times q$, and $p \times 1$ matrices, respectively. Then

1. $\text{vec}_n\, CA = (I_p \otimes C)\text{vec}_n\, A$ and $\text{devec}_n\, A'C' = \text{devec}_n\, A'(I_p \otimes C')$,
2. $A(\alpha \otimes I_n) = (\alpha' \otimes I_m)\,\text{vec}_n\, A$ and $(\alpha' \otimes I_n)A' = \text{devec}_n\, A'(\alpha \otimes I_m)$,
3. $\text{vec}_s[CA(I_p \otimes D)] = (I_p \otimes C)(\text{vec}_n\, A)D$ and $\text{devec}_s[(I_p \otimes D')A'C'] = D'(\text{devec}_n\, A')(I_p \otimes C')$,
4. $\text{vec}_s[A(E \otimes D)] = (I_q \otimes A)(\text{vec}\, E \otimes D)$ and $\text{devec}_s[(E' \otimes D')A'] = (\text{devec}\, E' \otimes D')(I_q \otimes A')$.

Proof of Theorem 2.2. We need to prove the results for only the generalized vec operator as we can readily obtain the equivalent results for the devec operator by using the basic relationship given by Eq. (2.10).

1. Partition A as $A = (A_1 \cdots A_p)$, where each submatrix A_j is $m \times n$; it follows that
$$\text{vec}_n\, CA = \begin{pmatrix} CA_1 \\ \vdots \\ CA_p \end{pmatrix} = (I_p \otimes C)\text{vec}_n\, A.$$
2. Writing $\alpha = (\alpha_1 \cdots \alpha_p)'$, we have
$$A(\alpha \otimes I_n) = (A_1 \cdots A_p)\begin{pmatrix} \alpha_1 I_n \\ \vdots \\ \alpha_p I_n \end{pmatrix} = \alpha_1 A_1 + \alpha_2 A_2 + \cdots + \alpha_p A_p.$$
However, $(\alpha' \otimes I_m)\,\text{vec}_n\, A = (\alpha_1 I_m \cdots \alpha_p I_m)\begin{pmatrix} A_1 \\ \vdots \\ A_p \end{pmatrix} = \alpha_1 A_1 + \alpha_2 A_2 + \cdots + \alpha_p A_p$.
3. Clearly $CA(I_p \otimes D) = (CA_1 D \cdots CA_p D)$ and, as each of these submatrices are $r \times s$,
$$\text{vec}_s[CA(I_p \otimes D)] = \begin{pmatrix} CA_1 D \\ \vdots \\ CA_p D \end{pmatrix} = (I_p \otimes C)(\text{vec}_n\, A)D.$$
4. From 1, we have
$$\text{vec}_s[A(E \otimes D)] = (I_q \otimes A)\text{vec}_s(E \otimes D) = (I_q \otimes A)(\text{vec}\, E \otimes D),$$
where we obtain the last equality by using Eq. (2.12). □

A special case that is of interest to us is that in which $s = n$ so D is a square $n \times n$ matrix. This case is summarized in the following corollary.

Corollary 2.1. For A, C, and E as prescribed in Theorem 2.1 and D $n \times n$,

$$\text{vec}_n[CA(I_p \otimes D)] = (I_p \otimes C)(\text{vec}_n A)D,$$
$$\text{devec}_n(I_p \otimes D')A'C' = D' \,\text{devec}_n A'(I_p \otimes C'),$$
$$\text{vec}_n[A(E \otimes D)] = (I_q \otimes A)(\text{vec}\, E \otimes D),$$
$$\text{devec}_n(E' \otimes D')A' = (\text{devec}\, E' \otimes D')(I_q \otimes A').$$

Often A is a square $np \times np$ matrix. For such a matrix, we have the following theorem.

Theorem 2.3. Let A be an $np \times np$ matrix so each submatrix is $np \times n$, and let D and α be as prescribed in Theorem 2.1. Then

$$\text{vec}_n[(D' \otimes \alpha')A] = (I_p \otimes D' \otimes \alpha')\text{vec}_n A,$$
$$\text{devec}_n[A'(D \otimes \alpha)] = \text{devec}_n A'(I_p \otimes D \otimes \alpha).$$

Proof of Theorem 2.3. We prove the result for the generalized vec operator. We write $A = (A_1 \cdots A_p)$, where each A_i is now $np \times n$. Then clearly

$$(D' \otimes \alpha')A = [(D' \otimes \alpha')A_1 \cdots (D' \otimes \alpha')A_p],$$

and, as each submatrix is $s \times n$,

$$\text{vec}_n(D' \otimes \alpha')A = \begin{bmatrix} (D' \otimes \alpha')A_1 \\ \vdots \\ (D' \otimes \alpha')A_p \end{bmatrix} = (I_p \otimes D' \otimes \alpha')\text{vec}_n A.$$

□

2.4.6. A More Convenient Notation

Generalized vec and devec operators arise naturally when we are working with partitioned $m \times np$ or $np \times m$ matrices, and it is convenient at this stage to introduce a separate notation for these operators that is more manageable. Let A be an $m \times np$ matrix and write

$$A = (A_1 \cdots A_p),$$

where each submatrix A_i is $m \times n$. Similarly let B be an $np \times m$ matrix and write

$$B = \begin{pmatrix} B_1 \\ \vdots \\ B_p \end{pmatrix},$$

where each submatrix B_i is $n \times m$. It is clear that the operators vec_n and devec_n are performable on A and B, respectively.

NOTATION. Let $A^{\tau} = \text{vec}_n A$ and $B^{\bar{\tau}} = \text{devec}_n B$. Our future work will involve the intensive use of this notation so it is convenient to list the results we have obtained so far in terms of this new notation.

2.4.6.1. Properties of the Operator τ

1. Let A and B be $p \times q$ and $m \times n$ matrices, respectively. Then from subsection 2.4.3.2. on vec_n, devec_n, and Kronecker products we have

   $$(A \otimes B)^{\tau} = \text{vec}\, A \otimes B.$$

   As a special case, let x and y be $q \times 1$ and $n \times 1$ vectors, respectively; then

   $$(x' \otimes y')^{\tau} = x \otimes y'.$$

2. From the basic relationship linking vec_n and devec_n given by Eq. (2.10) we have

   $$(A^{\tau})' = (A')^{\bar{\tau}}. \tag{2.14}$$

3. For A, C, E, and α as prescribed by Theorem 2.2 and for D an $n \times n$ matrix we have

   a. $(CA)^{\tau} = (I_p \otimes C)A^{\tau}$,
   b. $A(\alpha \otimes I_n) = (\alpha' \otimes I_n)A^{\tau}$,
   c. $[CA(I_p \otimes D)]^{\tau} = (I_p \otimes C)A^{\tau}D$,
   d. $[A(E \otimes D)]^{\tau} = (I_q \otimes A)\,(\text{vec}\, E \otimes D)$.

4. From the same theorem, if we set $D = x$, an $n \times 1$ vector, so that $s = 1$ we have

   e. $\text{vec}\, A(I_p \otimes x) = A^{\tau}x$,
   f. $\text{vec}[CA(I_p \otimes x)] = (I_p \otimes C)A^{\tau}x$.

5. If we set $D = x$, an $n \times 1$ vector, and $C = y'$, a $1 \times m$ vector, so that $s = 1$ and $r = 1$, we have

   g. $(y'A)^{\tau} = (I_p \otimes y')A^{\tau}$,
   h. $[y'A(I_p \otimes x)]^{\tau} = (I_p \otimes y')A^{\tau}x$.

2.4.6.2. Properties of the Operator $\bar{\tau}$

The following are the equivalent properties for the operator $\bar{\tau}$.

1. Let A and B be $p \times q$ and $m \times n$ matrices, respectively. Then

   $$(A' \otimes B')^{\bar{\tau}} = \text{devec}\, A' \otimes B',$$

   $$(x \otimes y)^{\bar{\tau}} = x' \otimes y.$$

2. $$(B^{\bar{\tau}})' = (B')^{\tau}. \tag{2.15}$$

3. Letting $B = A'$ and with A, C, E, and α as prescribed in Theorem 2.2, we have

   a. $(BC')^{\bar{\tau}} = B^{\bar{\tau}}(I_p \otimes C')$,
   b. $(\alpha' \otimes I_n)B = B^{\bar{\tau}}(\alpha \otimes I_n)$,
   c. $[(I_p \otimes D')BC']^{\bar{\tau}} = D'B^{\bar{\tau}}(I_p \otimes C')$,
   d. $[(E' \otimes D')B]^{\bar{\tau}} = (\text{devec } E' \otimes D')\,(I_q \otimes B)$.

4. For x, an $n \times 1$ vector,

   e. $\text{devec}(I_p \otimes x')B = x'B^{\bar{\tau}}$,
   f. $\text{devec}[(I_p \otimes x')BC'] = x'B^{\bar{\tau}}(I_p \otimes C')$.

5. If x and y are $n \times q$ and $m \times 1$ vectors, respectively,

   g. $(By)^{\bar{\tau}} = B^{\bar{\tau}}(I_p \otimes y)$,
   h. $[(I_p \otimes x')By]^{\bar{\tau}} = x'B^{\bar{\tau}}(I_p \otimes y)$.

2.4.6.3. Word of Warning on the Notation

As A is $m \times np$, the operator τ could be defined as

$$(A)^{\tau} = \text{vec}_n\, A$$

or

$$(A)^{\tau} = \text{vec}_p\, A,$$

and of course these two matrices are not the same. The convenience of presenting the operator as a superscript far outweighs this ambiguity. However, if in cases in which the possibility of confusion exists, we use the notation

$$A^{\tau_n} = \text{vec}_n\, A,$$
$$A^{\tau_p} = \text{vec}_p\, A.$$

A similar notation is used for devecs.

Given the extensive use we make of the operators τ and $\bar{\tau}$ it behooves us to distinguish them clearly from a similar operator, namely the transpose operator. Although the transpose operator is defined on any matrix and thus has more general applicability than the operators τ and $\bar{\tau}$, it can still be compared with these operators in the case in which A is an $m \times np$ matrix and B is an $np \times m$ matrix. This comparison is discussed in the next subsection.

2.4.7. The Operators τ, $\bar{\tau}$ and the Transpose Operator

Let A and B be $m \times np$ and $np \times m$ matrices, respectively, and write

$$A = (A_1 \cdots A_p),\ B = \begin{pmatrix} B_1 \\ \vdots \\ B_p \end{pmatrix},$$

where each submatrix A_j is $m \times n$ and each submatrix B_i is $n \times m$. Let $A^{\tau} = \text{vec}_n A$ and $B^{\bar{\tau}} = \text{devec}_n B$. Then the following properties highlight the differences between the generalized vec and devec operators and the transpose operator.

1. $A' = \begin{pmatrix} A_1' \\ \vdots \\ A_p' \end{pmatrix}, \quad A^{\tau} = \begin{pmatrix} A_1 \\ \vdots \\ A_p \end{pmatrix}, \quad \begin{matrix} B' = (B_1' \cdots B_p'), \\ B^{\bar{\tau}} = (B_1 \cdots B_p). \end{matrix}$

2. $A'A = \begin{pmatrix} A_1'A_1 & \cdots & A_1'A_p \\ \vdots & & \vdots \\ A_p'A_1 & \cdots & A_p'A_p \end{pmatrix}, \quad B'B = \sum_{i=1}^{p} B_i'B_i,$

   whereas for the case $m = n$ only

   $$A^{\tau}A = \begin{pmatrix} A_1^2 & \cdots & A_1A_p \\ \vdots & & \vdots \\ A_pA_1 & \cdots & A_p^2 \end{pmatrix}, \quad B^{\bar{\tau}}B = \sum_{i=1}^{p} B_i^2.$$

3. $AA' = \sum_{i=1}^{p} A_iA_i', \quad BB' = \begin{pmatrix} B_1B_1' & \cdots & B_1B_p' \\ \vdots & & \vdots \\ B_pB_1' & \cdots & B_pB_p' \end{pmatrix},$

   whereas for the case $m = n$ only

   $$AA^{\tau} = \sum_{i=1}^{p} A_i^2, \quad BB^{\bar{\tau}} = \begin{pmatrix} B_1^2 & \cdots & B_1B_p \\ \vdots & & \vdots \\ B_pB_1 & \cdots & B_p^2 \end{pmatrix}.$$

4. $(AB)' = B'A' = \sum_{i=1}^{p} B_i'A_i',$

   $$B^{\bar{\tau}}A^{\tau} = \sum_{i=1}^{p} B_iA_i'.$$

   For the case $m = n$,

   $$(AB)^{\tau} = AB = \sum_{i=1}^{p} A_iB_i = (AB)^{\bar{\tau}}.$$

5. If A is square and symmetric, $A' = A$. If A is square $n \times n$, $A^{\tau} = A^{\bar{\tau}} = A$.

6. $(A')' = A,\ (B')' = B$. For the case $m = n$,

   $(A^{\tau})^{\bar{\tau}} = A,\ (B^{\bar{\tau}})^{\tau} = B.$

7. $(A^{\tau})' = (A')^{\bar{\tau}} = (A_1' \cdots A_p') \quad (B^{\bar{\tau}})' = (B')^{\tau} = \begin{pmatrix} B_1' \\ \vdots \\ B_p' \end{pmatrix}.$

8. For x, an $n \times 1$ vector,

   $(x^{\bar{\tau}})' = x', (x')^{\tau} = x'.$

9. One final distinction can be drawn between the generalized vec and devec operators on the one hand and the transpose operator on the other. From the properties of the transpose operator and the Kronecker products,

   $[A(E \otimes D)]' = (E' \otimes D')A'.$

The corresponding results for the generalized vec and devec operators are given by the following theorem.

Theorem 2.4. Let $A,\ B,\ E$ and D be $m \times np,\ np \times m,\ p \times q$, and $n \times n$ matrices, respectively. Then

$$[A(E \otimes D)]^{\tau} = (E' \otimes I_n)A^{\tau} D,$$
$$[(E' \otimes D')B]^{\bar{\tau}} = D' B^{\bar{\tau}}(E \otimes I_n)$$

Proof of Theorem 2.4. From the properties of the operator τ,

$$[A(E \otimes D)]^{\tau} = (I_q \otimes A)\,(\text{vec } E \otimes D) = (I_q \otimes A)\,(\text{vec } E \otimes I_n)D.$$

Writing $E = (\varepsilon_1 \cdots \varepsilon_q)$, where ε_i is the ith column of E, we have

$$(I_q \otimes A)\,(\text{vec } E \otimes I_n) = \begin{bmatrix} A(\varepsilon_1 \otimes I_n) \\ \vdots \\ A(\varepsilon_q \otimes I_n) \end{bmatrix} = \begin{bmatrix} (\varepsilon_1' \otimes I_n)A^{\tau} \\ \vdots \\ (\varepsilon_q' \otimes I_n)A^{\tau} \end{bmatrix}$$
$$= (E' \otimes I_n)A^{\tau}.$$

We obtain the corresponding result for the devec operator by taking the transpose and by using Eq. (2.14) or Eq. (2.15). □

2.5. TRIANGULAR MATRICES AND BAND MATRICES

Special square matrices that crop up a lot in our future work are triangular matrices and band matrices. In this section, these matrices are defined and some theorems concerning triangular matrices that are important in our forthcoming analysis are proved.

A square matrix A, $n \times n$, is upper triangular if

$$A = \begin{bmatrix} a_{11} & a_{12} & \dots & a_{1n} \\ & a_{22} & \dots & a_{2n} \\ & O & \ddots & \vdots \\ & & & a_{nn} \end{bmatrix}$$

and lower triangular if

$$A = \begin{bmatrix} a_{11} & & & \\ a_{21} & a_{22} & O & \\ \vdots & & \ddots & \\ a_{n1} & \cdots & & a_{nn} \end{bmatrix}.$$

If in addition a_{ii} is 0 for $i = 1, \dots, n$, A is said to be strictly triangular. Working with triangular matrices is relatively easy as their mathematical properties are simple. For example, if A is upper (lower) triangular then A' is lower (upper) triangular. The determinant of a triangular matrix is the product of its main diagonal elements. The product of a finite number of upper (lower) triangular matrices is also upper (lower) triangular, and if one of the matrices in the product is strictly upper (lower) triangular the product itself is strictly upper (lower) triangular.

Two theorems that we will appeal to often in future chapters are the following.

Theorem 2.5. If A is lower (upper) triangular with ones as its main diagonal elements then A is nonsingular and A^{-1} is also lower (upper) triangular with ones as its main diagonal elements.

Proof of Theorem 2.5. Clearly A is nonsingular as $|A| = 1$. We prove that the main diagonal elements of A^{-1} are all ones by mathematical induction for the case in which A is lower triangular. Consider

$$A_2 = \begin{bmatrix} 1 & 0 \\ a & 1 \end{bmatrix},$$

where a is a constant. Then

$$A_2^{-1} = \begin{bmatrix} 1 & 0 \\ -a & 1 \end{bmatrix},$$

so it is clearly true for this case. Suppose it is true for A_n, an $n \times n$ matrix with the prescribed characteristics and consider

$$A_{n+1} = \begin{bmatrix} A_n & 0 \\ a' & 1 \end{bmatrix},$$

where a is an $n \times 1$ vector. Clearly

$$A_{n+1}^{-1} = \begin{bmatrix} A_n^{-1} & 0 \\ -a'A_n^{-1} & 1 \end{bmatrix},$$

so it is also true for an $(n+1) \times (n+1)$ matrix. We establish the proof for the lower triangular case by taking transposes. □

Theorem 2.6. Suppose A is an $nG \times nG$ matrix and let

$$A = \begin{bmatrix} A_{11} & \cdots & A_{1G} \\ \vdots & & \vdots \\ A_{G1} & \cdots & A_{GG} \end{bmatrix},$$

where each $n \times n$ matrix $A_{ii}, i = 1, \ldots, G$, is lower (upper) triangular with ones along its main diagonal and each $n \times n$ matrix $A_{ij}, i \neq j$, is strictly lower (upper) triangular. Suppose A is nonsingular and let

$$A^{-1} = \begin{bmatrix} A^{11} & \cdots & A^{1G} \\ \vdots & & \vdots \\ A^{G1} & \cdots & A^{GG} \end{bmatrix}.$$

Then each $n \times n$ matrix $A^{ii}, i = 1 \cdots G$, is also lower (upper) triangular with ones as its main diagonal elements and each A_{ij} is also strictly lower (upper) triangular.

Proof of Theorem 2.6. We use mathematical induction to established the result for the lower-triangular case. We then obtain the upper-triangular proof by taking transposes.

Consider A_2, a $2n \times 2n$ matrix, and let

$$A_2 = \begin{bmatrix} A_{11} & A_{12} \\ A_{21} & A_{22} \end{bmatrix},$$

where the submatrices are $n \times n$ with the characteristics prescribed by the theorem. Then as $|A_{11}| = 1$, A_{11} is nonsingular and lower triangular so $D = A_{22} - A_{21}A_{11}^{-1}A_{12}$ exists. Now $A_{21}A_{11}^{-1}A_{12}$ is the product of lower-triangular matrices and, as A_{21} is strictly lower triangular, this product is also strictly lower triangular. It follows then that D is lower triangular with ones as its main diagonal elements so $|D| = 1$ and D is nonsingular. Let

$$A_2^{-1} = \begin{bmatrix} A^{11} & A^{12} \\ A^{21} & A^{22} \end{bmatrix}.$$

Then

$$A^{11} = A_{11}^{-1} + A_{11}^{-1}A_{12}D^{-1}A_{21}A_{11}^{-1}, \quad A^{12} = -A_{11}^{-1}A_{12}D^{-1},$$
$$A^{21} = -D^{-1}A_{21}A_{11}^{-1}, \qquad A^{22} = D^{-1}.$$

Then, by using Theorem 2.5 and properties of products of triangular matrices, we clearly see that the submatrices A^{ij} have the required characteristics. Suppose now that it is true for A_p, an $np \times np$ matrix, and consider

$$B = \begin{bmatrix} A_p & B_{12} \\ B_{21} & A_{p+1p+1} \end{bmatrix},$$

where $B_{21} = (A_{p+11} \cdots A_{p+1p})$, $B_{12} = (A'_{1p+1} \cdots A'_{pp+1})'$ and all the submatrices A_{p+1i} and A_{ip+1}, $i = 1, \ldots, p$, are $n \times n$ and strictly lower triangular and A_{p+1p+1} is lower triangular with ones as its main diagonal elements. Let

$$A_p^{-1} = \begin{bmatrix} A^{11} & \cdots & A^{1p} \\ \vdots & & \vdots \\ A^{p1} & \cdots & A^{pp} \end{bmatrix},$$

where, by assumption, A_p^{-1} exists and each of the $n \times n$ submatrices A^{ij} has the desired characteristics. Consider

$$F = A_{p+1p+1} - B_{21} A_p^{-1} B_{12},$$

where $B_{21} A_p^{-1} B_{12} = \sum_i \sum_j A_{p+1i,} \; A^{ij} A_{p+1j}$ is the sum of products of lower-triangular matrices and each of these products is, in fact, strictly lower triangular. It follows that F is lower triangular with ones as its main diagonal elements so $|F| = 1$ and F is nonsingular. Let

$$B^{-1} = \begin{bmatrix} B^{11} & B^{12} \\ B^{21} & B^{22} \end{bmatrix}.$$

Then

$$\begin{aligned} B^{11} &= A_p^{-1} + A_p^{-1} B_{12} F^{-1} B_{21} A_p^{-1}, & B^{12} &= -A_p^{-1} B_{12} F^{-1} \\ B^{21} &= -F^{-1} B_{21} A_p^{-1}, & B^{22} &= F^{-1}. \end{aligned}$$

Expanding $B_{21} A_p^{-1}$ and $A_p^{-1} B_{12}$ as we did above and by using Theorem 2.5, we clearly see that the B^{ij}s have the required characteristics. □

In a triangular matrix, zeros appear on one side of the main diagonal whereas nonzero elements of the matrix appear on the other side of the main diagonal. In a band matrix, the nonzero elements appear in a band surrounded on both sides by zeros. More formally, a square $n \times n$ matrix $A = (a_{ij})$ is a band matrix with bandwidth $r + s + 1$ if $a_{ij} = 0$ for $i - j \geq s$ and for $j - i \geq r$, where

r and s are both less than n. That is,

$$A = \begin{bmatrix} a_{11} & \cdots & a_{1r} & 0 & 0 & & \cdots & & 0 \\ a_{21} & & & a_{2r+1} & 0 & & \cdots & & 0 \\ \vdots & & & & \ddots & & & & \vdots \\ a_{s1} & & & & & \ddots & & & \\ 0 & a_{s+12} & & & & & \ddots & & 0 \\ 0 & 0 & \ddots & & & & & \ddots & \\ \vdots & \vdots & & \ddots & & & & & a_{n-r+1n} \\ \vdots & \vdots & & & \ddots & & & & \vdots \\ 0 & 0 & \cdots & \cdots & 0 & a_{nn-s+1} & \cdots & \cdots & a_{nn} \end{bmatrix}.$$

In Subsection 3.7.4.3 of Chap. 3, we shall look at special types of band matrices that are linear combinations of a special zero-one matrix called a shifting matrix.

3 Zero-One Matrices

3.1. INTRODUCTION

A matrix whose elements are all either one or zero is, naturally enough, called a zero-one matrix. Probably the first zero-one matrix to appear in statistics and econometrics was a selection matrix. The columns of a selection matrix are made up of appropriately chosen columns from an identity matrix. When a given matrix A is postmultiplied by a selection matrix, the result is a matrix whose columns are selected columns from A. A related matrix is a permutation matrix whose columns are obtained from a permutation of the columns of an identity matrix. When a given matrix A is (premultiplied) postmultiplied by a permutation matrix, the resultant matrix is one whose (rows) columns we obtain by permutating the (rows) columns of A. Both selection matrices and permutation matrices are used through out this book.

Several zero-one matrices are associated with the vec, vech, and $\bar{v}$ operators discussed in Chap. 2. These are commutation matrices, elimination matrices, and duplication matrices. These matrices are important in our work as they arise naturally in matrix calculus. Other zero-one matrices that are important in this context are generalized vecs and devecs of commutation matrices.

A final zero-one matrix that is used throughout this book is what I call a shifting matrix. When a given matrix A is (premultiplied) postmultiplied by a shifting matrix, the (rows) columns of A are shifted across (down) a number of places and the spaces thus created are filled with zeros. Shifting matrices are useful, at least as far as asymptotic theory is concerned, in writing time-series processes in matrix notation. Their relationship to Toeplitz, circulant, and forward-shift matrices is explained.

Well-known results about our zero-one matrix are presented with references only, the proofs being reserved for results that I believe are new or that are presented in a different light than usual.

3.2. SELECTION MATRICES AND PERMUTATION MATRICES

Consider A, an $m \times n$ matrix, and write $A = (a_1 \cdots a_n)$, where a_i is the ith column of A. Suppose from A that we wish to form a new matrix B whose columns consist, say, of the first, fourth, and fifth columns of A. Let $\mathcal{S} = (e_1^n\ e_4^n\ e_5^n)$, where e_j^n is the jth column of the $n \times n$ identity matrix I_n. Then clearly

$$A\mathcal{S} = (a_1\ a_4\ a_5) = B.$$

The matrix $\mathcal{S}$, whose columns are made up of a selection of columns from an identity matrix, is called a **selection matrix**. Selection matrices have an obvious application in econometrics. The matrix A, for example, may represent the observations on all the endogenous variables in an econometric model, and the matrix B may represent the observations on the endogenous variables that appear on the right-hand side of a particular equation in the model. Often it is mathematically convenient for us to use selection matrices and write $B = A\mathcal{S}$.

This property generalizes to the case in which our matrices are partitioned matrices. Suppose A is an $m \times np$ matrix partitioned into p $m \times n$ matrices; that is, we write $A = (A_1 \cdots A_p)$, where each submatrix A_i is $m \times n$. Suppose we wish to form a new matrix B from A made up of A_1, A_4, and A_5. Then

$$B = (A_1\ A_4\ A_5) = A(\mathcal{S} \otimes I_n),$$

where $\mathcal{S} = (e_1^n\ e_4^n\ e_5^n)$, as in the beginning of this section.

A **permutation matrix** P is obtained from a permutation of the columns or rows of an identity matrix. The result is a matrix in which each row and each column of the matrix contains a single element, 1, and all the remaining elements are 0s. As the columns of an identity matrix form an orthonormal set of vectors it is quite clear that every permutation matrix is orthogonal, that is, $P' = P^{-1}$. When a given matrix A is premultiplied (postmultiplied) by a permutation matrix, the result is a matrix whose rows (columns) are obtained from a permutation of the rows (columns) of A.

3.3. THE COMMUTATION MATRIX AND GENERALIZED VECS AND DEVECS OF THE COMMUTATION MATRIX

3.3.1. The Commutation Matrix

Consider an $m \times n$ matrix A and write

$$A = (a_1 \cdots a_n) = \begin{pmatrix} a^{1'} \\ \vdots \\ a^{m'} \end{pmatrix},$$

where a_j is the jth column of A and $a^{i'}$ is the ith row of A. Then

$$\text{vec}\, A = \begin{pmatrix} a_1 \\ \vdots \\ a_n \end{pmatrix},$$

whereas

$$\text{vec}\, A' = \begin{pmatrix} a^1 \\ \vdots \\ a^m \end{pmatrix}.$$

Clearly both the vec A and the vec A' contain all the elements of A, although arranged in different orders. It follows that there exists an $mn \times mn$ permutation matrix K_{mn} that has the property

$$K_{mn}\, \text{vec}\, A = \text{vec}\, A'.$$

This matrix is called the **commutation matrix**. Under our notation K_{nm} is the commutation matrix associated with the $n \times m$ matrix. The two commutation matrices, K_{mn} and K_{nm}, are linked by

$$K_{nm} K_{mn}\, \text{vec}\, A = \text{vec}\, A,$$

so it follows that $K_{nm} = K_{mn}^{-1} = K'_{mn}$, where the last equality comes about because K_{mn} is a permutation matrix. Note also that

$$K_{1n} = K_{n1} = I_n.$$

Explicit expressions for the commutation matrix K_{mn} that are used extensively throughout this book are

$$K_{mn} = \begin{bmatrix} I_n \otimes e_1^{m'} \\ I_n \otimes e_2^{m'} \\ \vdots \\ I_n \otimes e_m^{m'} \end{bmatrix} = \left[I_m \otimes e_1^n \; I_m \otimes e_2^n \cdots I_m \otimes e_n^n \right],$$

where e_j^m is the jth column of the $m \times m$ identity matrix I_m and e_i^n is the ith column of the $n \times n$ identity matrix I_n. For example,

$$K_{23} = \left[\begin{array}{cc|cc|cc} 1 & 0 & 0 & 0 & 0 & 0 \\ 0 & 0 & 1 & 0 & 0 & 0 \\ 0 & 0 & 0 & 0 & 1 & 0 \\ \hline 0 & 1 & 0 & 0 & 0 & 0 \\ 0 & 0 & 0 & 1 & 0 & 0 \\ 0 & 0 & 0 & 0 & 0 & 1 \end{array}\right].$$

3.3.2. Commutation Matrices, Kronecker Products, and Vecs

An essential property of commutation matrices is that they allow us to interchange matrices in a Kronecker product. In particular, the following results are well known [see Neudecker and Magnus (1988), p. 47].

Let A be an $m \times n$ matrix, let B be a $p \times q$ matrix, and let b be a $p \times 1$ vector. Then

$$K_{pm}(A \otimes B) = (B \otimes A)K_{qn},$$

$$K_{pm}(A \otimes B)K_{nq} = B \otimes A,$$

$$K_{pm}(A \otimes b) = b \otimes A,$$

$$K_{mp}(b \otimes A) = A \otimes b.$$

Another interesting property of commutation matrices with respect to Kronecker products is not so well known. Consider A and B as above and partition B into its rows:

$$B = \begin{pmatrix} b^{1'} \\ \vdots \\ b^{p'} \end{pmatrix},$$

where $b^{i'}$ is the ith row of B. Then we saw in Section 2.2 of Chap. 2 that, in general,

$$A \otimes B = A \otimes \begin{pmatrix} b^{1'} \\ \vdots \\ b^{p'} \end{pmatrix} \neq \begin{pmatrix} A \otimes b^{1'} \\ \vdots \\ A \otimes b^{p'} \end{pmatrix}.$$

However, we have the following theorem for these matrices.

Theorem 3.1.

$$K_{pm}(A \otimes B) = \begin{pmatrix} A \otimes b^{1'} \\ \vdots \\ A \otimes b^{p'} \end{pmatrix}.$$

Proof of Theorem 3.1.

$$K_{pm}(A \otimes B) = \begin{pmatrix} I_m \otimes e_1^{p'} \\ \vdots \\ I_m \otimes e_p^{p'} \end{pmatrix} (A \otimes B)$$

$$= \begin{pmatrix} A \otimes e_1^{p'}B \\ \vdots \\ A \otimes e_p^{p'}B \end{pmatrix} = \begin{pmatrix} A \otimes b^{1'} \\ \vdots \\ A \otimes b^{p'} \end{pmatrix}.$$

□

Similarly, we partition B into its columns so that $B = (b_1 \cdots b_q)$, where b_j is the jth column of B. Then we saw in Section 2.2 of Chap. 2 that, in general,

$$A \otimes B = A \otimes (b_1 \cdots b_q) \neq (A \otimes b_1 \cdots A \otimes b_q).$$

However, we have the following result.

Theorem 3.2.

$$(A \otimes B)K_{nq} = (A \otimes b_1 \cdots A \otimes b_q).$$

Proof of Theorem 3.2.

$$\begin{aligned}(A \otimes B)K_{nq} &= (A \otimes B)\big(I_n \otimes e_1^q \cdots I_n \otimes e_q^q\big)\\ &= \big(A \otimes Be_1^q \cdots A \otimes Be_q^q\big)\\ &= (A \otimes b_1 \cdots A \otimes b_q).\end{aligned}$$

□

Related theorems are the following.

Theorem 3.3.

$$(K_{qm} \otimes I_p)(A \otimes \text{vec } B) = \begin{pmatrix} A \otimes b_1 \\ \vdots \\ A \otimes b_q \end{pmatrix}.$$

Proof of Theorem 3.3.

$$\begin{aligned}(K_{qm} \otimes I_p)(A \otimes \text{vec } B) &= \begin{bmatrix} I_m \otimes \big(e_1^{q'} \otimes I_p\big) \\ \vdots \\ I_m \otimes \big(e_q^{q'} \otimes I_p\big) \end{bmatrix}(A \otimes \text{vec } B)\\ &= \begin{bmatrix} A \otimes \big(e_1^{q'} \otimes I_p\big)\text{vec } B \\ \vdots \\ A \otimes \big(e_q^{q'} \otimes I_p\big)\text{vec } B \end{bmatrix} = \begin{pmatrix} A \otimes b_1 \\ \vdots \\ A \otimes b_q \end{pmatrix}.\end{aligned}$$

□

Theorem 3.4.

$$(I_n \otimes K_{pm})(\text{vec } A \otimes B) = \begin{pmatrix} B \otimes a_1 \\ \vdots \\ B \otimes a_n \end{pmatrix}.$$

Proof of Theorem 3.4.

$$(I_n \otimes K_{pm})(\text{vec } A \otimes B) = \begin{bmatrix} K_{pm} & & O \\ & \ddots & \\ O & & K_{pm} \end{bmatrix} \begin{pmatrix} a_1 \otimes B \\ \vdots \\ a_n \otimes B \end{pmatrix}$$

$$= \begin{bmatrix} K_{pm}(a_1 \otimes B) \\ \vdots \\ K_{pm}(a_n \otimes B) \end{bmatrix} = \begin{pmatrix} B \otimes a_1 \\ \vdots \\ B \otimes a_n \end{pmatrix}. \qquad \square$$

Using the fact that $K_{mn}^{-1} = K_{nm}$, we find that these theorems lead to the following corollaries:

$$A \otimes B = K_{mp} \begin{pmatrix} A \otimes b^{1'} \\ \vdots \\ A \otimes b^{p'} \end{pmatrix},$$

$$A \otimes B = (A \otimes b_1 \cdots A \otimes b_q)K_{qn},$$

$$(A \otimes \text{vec } B) = (K_{mq} \otimes I_p) \begin{pmatrix} A \otimes b_1 \\ \vdots \\ A \otimes b_q \end{pmatrix},$$

$$(\text{vec } A \otimes B) = (I_n \otimes K_{mp}) \begin{pmatrix} B \otimes a_1 \\ \vdots \\ B \otimes a_n \end{pmatrix}.$$

Several other similar results can be obtained; the analysis is left to the reader.

Theorems 3.3 and 3.4 allow us to convert the vec of a Kronecker product into the Kronecker product of vecs and vice versa. Consider an $m \times n$ matrix A and a $p \times q$ matrix B partitioned into their columns:

$$A = (a_1 \cdots a_n), \quad B = (b_1 \cdots b_q).$$

Then, as we saw in Section 2.2 of Chap. 2, we can write

$$A \otimes B = (a_1 \otimes b_1 \cdots a_1 \otimes b_q \cdots a_n \otimes b_1 \cdots a_n \otimes b_q),$$

so

$$\text{vec}(A \otimes B) = \begin{pmatrix} a_1 \otimes b_1 \\ \vdots \\ a_1 \otimes b_q \\ \vdots \\ a_n \otimes b_1 \\ \vdots \\ a_n \otimes b_q \end{pmatrix},$$

whereas

$$\text{vec}\, A \otimes \text{vec}\, B = \begin{bmatrix} a_1 \otimes \begin{pmatrix} b_1 \\ \vdots \\ b_q \end{pmatrix} \\ \vdots \\ a_n \otimes \begin{pmatrix} b_1 \\ \vdots \\ b_q \end{pmatrix} \end{bmatrix}.$$

Clearly both vectors have the same elements, although these elements are rearranged in moving from one vector to the other. Each vector must then be able to be obtained when the other is premultiplied by a suitable zero-one matrix. Applying Theorem 3.3 or Theorem 3.4 we have

$$\text{vec}(A \otimes B) = (I_n \otimes K_{qm} \otimes I_p)(\text{vec}\, A \otimes \text{vec}\, B), \tag{3.1}$$

$$(I_n \otimes K_{mq} \otimes I_p)\text{vec}(A \otimes B) = \text{vec}\, A \otimes \text{vec}\, B. \tag{3.2}$$

The same properties of the commutation matrix allow us to write $\text{vec}(A \otimes B)$ in terms of either vec A or vec B, as illustrated by the following theorem.

Theorem 3.5.

$$\text{vec}(A \otimes B) = \left[I_n \otimes \begin{pmatrix} I_m \otimes b_1 \\ \vdots \\ I_m \otimes b_q \end{pmatrix} \right] \text{vec}\, A,$$

$$\text{vec}(A \otimes B) = \left[\begin{pmatrix} I_q \otimes a_1 \\ \vdots \\ I_q \otimes a_n \end{pmatrix} \otimes I_p \right] \text{vec}\, B.$$

Proof of Theorem 3.5. By Eq. (3.1),

$$\begin{aligned}\text{vec}(A \otimes B) &= (I_n \otimes K_{qm} \otimes I_p)(\text{vec}\, A \otimes \text{vec}\, B) \\ &= (I_n \otimes K_{qm} \otimes I_p)\text{vec}[\text{vec}\, B(\text{vec}\, A)'],\end{aligned}$$

by Eq. 2.1. Now we can write

$$\begin{aligned}\text{vec}[\text{vec}\, B(\text{vec}\, A)'] &= [I_n \otimes (I_m \otimes \text{vec}\, B)]\, \text{vec}\, A \\ &= [(\text{vec}\, A \otimes I_q) \otimes I_p]\, \text{vec}\, B,\end{aligned}$$

so

$$\begin{aligned}\text{vec}(A \otimes B) &= \{I_n \otimes [(K_{qm} \otimes I_p)(I_m \otimes \text{vec}\, B)]\}\text{vec}\, A \\ &= \{[(I_n \otimes K_{qm})(\text{vec}\, A \otimes I_q)] \otimes I_p\}\text{vec}\, B.\end{aligned}$$

Applying Theorems 3.3 and 3.4 gives us the result. □

3.3.3. Generalized Vecs and Devecs of the Commutation Matrix

3.3.3.1. Explicit Expressions for $K_{mn}^{\bar{\tau}_n}$ and $K_{mn}^{\tau_m}$

Consider the commutation matrix K_{mn}, which we can write as

$$K_{mn} = \begin{bmatrix} I_n \otimes e_1^{m'} \\ \vdots \\ I_n \otimes e_m^{m'} \end{bmatrix} = \begin{bmatrix} I_m \otimes e_1^n \cdots I_m \otimes e_n^n \end{bmatrix}, \tag{3.3}$$

where e_j^n is the jth column of the $n \times n$ identity matrix I_n. It follows then that $K_{mn}^{\bar{\tau}_n}$ is the $n \times nm^2$ matrix given by

$$K_{mn}^{\bar{\tau}_n} = \begin{bmatrix} I_n \otimes e_1^{m'} \cdots I_n \otimes e_m^{m'} \end{bmatrix}, \tag{3.4}$$

and $K_{mn}^{\tau_m}$ is the $mn^2 \times m$ matrix given by

$$K_{mn}^{\tau_m} = \begin{bmatrix} I_m \otimes e_1^n \\ \vdots \\ I_m \otimes e_n^n \end{bmatrix}.$$

From Theorem 3.5, we see that for an $m \times n$ matrix A

$$\text{vec}(A \otimes I_G) = \left[I_n \otimes \begin{pmatrix} I_m \otimes e_1^G \\ \vdots \\ I_m \otimes e_G^G \end{pmatrix} \right] \text{vec}\, A. \tag{3.5}$$

If follows then that we can now write $\text{vec}(A \otimes I_G)$ in terms of generalized vecs as

$$\text{vec}(A \otimes I_G) = \left(I_n \otimes K_{mG}^{\tau_m}\right)\text{vec}\, A. \tag{3.6}$$

Note for the special case in which a is an $m \times 1$ vector, we have

$$\text{vec}(a \otimes I_G) = K^{\tau_m}_{mG} a.$$

In a similar fashion, we can write

$$\begin{aligned}\text{vec}(I_G \otimes A) &= \left[\begin{pmatrix} I_n \otimes e_1^{G'} \\ \vdots \\ I_n \otimes e_G^{G'} \end{pmatrix} \otimes I_m\right] \text{vec}\, A \\ &= \left(K^{\tau_n}_{nG} \otimes I_m\right)\text{vec}\, A, \qquad (3.7)\end{aligned}$$

and for the special case in which a is an $m \times 1$ vector we have

$$\text{vec}(I_G \otimes a) = (\text{vec}\, I_G \otimes I_m)a.$$

As we shall see in the next chapter, Eqs. (3.6) and (3.7) allow us to write the derivatives of $\text{vec}(A \otimes I_G)$ and $\text{vec}(I_G \otimes A)$ with respect to vec A in terms of generalized vecs and devecs of the commutation matrix.

3.3.3.2. Useful Properties of $K^{\tau_n}_{nG}$, $K^{\bar{\tau}_n}_{Gn}$

In deriving results for $K^{\tau_n}_{nG}$ and $K^{\bar{\tau}_n}_{Gn}$, it is often convenient to express these matrices in terms of the commutation matrix K_{Gn}. The following theorem does this.

Theorem 3.6.

$$K^{\tau_n}_{nG} = (K_{Gn} \otimes I_G)(I_n \otimes \text{vec}\, I_G) = (I_G \otimes K_{nG})(\text{vec}\, I_G \otimes I_n),$$
$$K^{\bar{\tau}_n}_{Gn} = [I_n \otimes (\text{vec}\, I_G)'](K_{nG} \otimes I_G) = [(\text{vec}\, I_G)' \otimes I_n](I_G \otimes K_{Gn}).$$

Proof of Theorem 3.6 Using Eq. (3.3), we can write

$$(K_{Gn} \otimes I_G)(I_n \otimes \text{vec}\, I_G) = \begin{bmatrix} I_n \otimes \left(e_1^{G'} \otimes I_G\right)(\text{vec}\, I_G) \\ \vdots \\ I_n \otimes \left(e_G^{G'} \otimes I_G\right)(\text{vec}\, I_G) \end{bmatrix}.$$

This clearly equals $K^{\tau_n}_{nG}$ as $(e_j^{G'} \otimes I_G)\text{vec}\, I_G = e_j^G$ for $j = 1 \cdots G$. Now

$$\begin{aligned}(I_G \otimes K_{nG})(\text{vec}\, I_G \otimes I_n) &= \begin{bmatrix} K_{nG}\left(e_1^G \otimes I_n\right) \\ \vdots \\ K_{nG}\left(e_G^G \otimes I_n\right) \end{bmatrix} \\ &= \begin{pmatrix} I_n \otimes e_1^{G'} \\ \vdots \\ I_n \otimes e_G^{G} \end{pmatrix} = K^{\tau_n}_{nG}.\end{aligned}$$

The equivalent results for $K^{\bar{\tau}_n}_{Gn}$ are readily obtained with $K^{\bar{\tau}_n}_{Gn} = (K^{\tau_n}_{nG})'$. □

Using Theorem 3.6 and known results about the commutation matrix, we can derive results for $K_{nG}^{\tau_n}$ and $K_{Gn}^{\bar{\tau}_n}$. For example, we know that for A, an $m \times n$ matrix, B, a $p \times q$ matrix, and b, a $p \times 1$ vector,

$$K_{pm}(A \otimes b) = b \otimes A,$$

$$K_{mp}(b \otimes A) = A \otimes b.$$

Using these results, Eqs. (2.7)–(2.9), and Theorem 3.6, we prove the following theorem.

Theorem 3.7. For A, B, and b, which are $m \times n$, $p \times q$, and $p \times 1$ matrices, respectively,

$$K_{mp}^{\bar{\tau}_p}(A \otimes b \otimes I_m) = b \otimes (\text{vec}\, A)',$$

$$K_{pm}^{\bar{\tau}_m}(b \otimes A \otimes I_p) = A \otimes b',$$

$$K_{mp}^{\bar{\tau}_p}(I_m \otimes b \otimes A) = \text{devec}\, A \otimes b,$$

$$K_{pm}^{\bar{\tau}_m}(I_p \otimes A \otimes b) = b' \otimes A.$$

Proof of Theorem 3.7.

$$\begin{aligned}
K_{mp}^{\bar{\tau}_p}(A \otimes b \otimes I_m) &= [I_p \otimes (\text{vec}\, I_m)'](b \otimes A \otimes I_m) \\
&= b \otimes (\text{vec}\, I_m)'(A \otimes I_m) \\
&= b \otimes (\text{vec}\, A)', \\
K_{pm}^{\bar{\tau}_m}(b \otimes A \otimes I_p) &= [I_m \otimes (\text{vec}\, I_p)'](A \otimes b \otimes I_p) \\
&= A \otimes (\text{vec}\, I_p)'(b \otimes I_p) \\
&= A \otimes b', \\
K_{mp}^{\bar{\tau}_p}(I_m \otimes b \otimes A) &= [(\text{vec}\, I_m)' \otimes I_p](I_m \otimes A \otimes b) \\
&= (\text{vec}\, I_m)'(I_m \otimes A) \otimes b \\
&= \text{devec}\, A \otimes b, \\
K_{pm}^{\bar{\tau}_m}(I_p \otimes A \otimes b) &= [(\text{vec}\, I_p)' \otimes I_m](I_p \otimes b \otimes A) \\
&= (\text{vec}\, I_p)'(I_p \otimes b) \otimes A \\
&= b' \otimes A.
\end{aligned}$$

□

We can obtain the equivalent results for the generalized vec of the commutation matrix $K_{mp}^{\tau_m}$ by taking appropriate transposes. However, such proofs are rather inefficient in that we can obtain the same results immediately, by using the properties of the generalized vec and devec operators discussed in Section 2.4 of Chap. 2.

For example, we have

$$K_{pm}(A \otimes b) = b \otimes A.$$

Taking the devec_m of both sides, we have

$$K_{pm}^{\bar{\tau}_m}(I_p \otimes A \otimes b) = b' \otimes A.$$

Similarly, taking the devec_p of both sides of $K_{mp}(b \otimes A) = A \otimes b$, we have

$$K_{mp}^{\bar{\tau}_p}(I_m \otimes b \otimes A) = \text{devec}\, A \otimes b.$$

In like manner, as $K_{pm}K_{mp} = I_{pm}$, taking the vec_m of both sides, we have

$$(I_p \otimes K_{pm})K_{mp}^{\tau_m} = (I_{pm})^{\tau_m}.$$

Further such proofs are left to the reader.

3.3.3.3. Other Theorems about K_{Gn}^{τ} and $K_{nG}^{\bar{\tau}}$

In subsequent chapters, we shall need to call on the following theorems involving $K_{nG}^{\bar{\tau}_G}$. (We can obtain the equivalent theorems for $K_{Gn}^{\tau_G}$ by taking appropriate transposes). For notational convenience for the rest of this section, we shall use $\bar{\tau}$ and τ to denote the devec_G and vec_G operators, respectively. Other generalized devec and vec operators shall be denoted by appropriate subscripts.

Theorem 3.8. Let a be an $n \times 1$ vector. Then

$$K_{nG}^{\bar{\tau}}(a \otimes I_{nG}) = (I_G \otimes a'),$$

$$K_{nG}^{\bar{\tau}}(I_{nG} \otimes a) = a' \otimes I_G.$$

Proof of Theorem 3.8. Let $a = (a_1 \cdots a_n)'$ and write

$$K_{nG}^{\bar{\tau}}(a \otimes I_{nG}) = \left(I_G \otimes e_1^{n'} \cdots I_G \otimes e_n^{n'}\right) \begin{bmatrix} a_1(I_G \otimes I_n) \\ \vdots \\ a_n(I_G \otimes I_n) \end{bmatrix}$$

$$= a_1\left(I_G \otimes e_1^{n'}\right) + \cdots + a_n\left(I_G \otimes e_n^{n'}\right)$$

$$= I_G \otimes a'.$$

Similarly, write

$$K_{nG}^{\bar{\tau}}(I_{nG} \otimes a) = \left(I_G \otimes e_1^{n'} \cdots I_G \otimes e_n^{n'}\right)[I_n \otimes (I_G \otimes a)]$$

$$= \left(I_G \otimes e_1^{n'} a \cdots I_G \otimes e_n^{n'} a\right)$$

$$= (I_G \otimes a_1 \cdots I_G \otimes a_n)$$

$$= (a_1 I_G \cdots a_n I_G)$$

$$= a' \otimes I_G.$$

□

Theorem 3.9. Let A be an $n \times p$ matrix. Then

$$(I_p \otimes K_{nG}^{\bar{\tau}})(\text{vec}\, A \otimes I_{nG}) = K_{pG}(I_G \otimes A'). \tag{3.8}$$

Proof of Theorem 3.9. Write $A = (a_1 \cdots a_p)$, where a_j is the $n \times 1$ jth column of A. Then we can write the left-hand side of Eq. (3.8) as

$$\begin{bmatrix} K_{nG}^{\bar{\tau}} & & O \\ & \ddots & \\ O & & K_{nG}^{\bar{\tau}} \end{bmatrix} \begin{pmatrix} a_1 \otimes I_{nG} \\ \vdots \\ a_p \otimes I_{nG} \end{pmatrix} = \begin{bmatrix} K_{nG}^{\bar{\tau}}(a_1 \otimes I_{nG}) \\ \vdots \\ K_{nG}^{\bar{\tau}}(a_p \otimes I_{nG}) \end{bmatrix}. \tag{3.9}$$

However, by using Theorem 3.7, we can write the right-hand side of Eq. (3.9) as $(I_G \otimes a_1 \cdots I_G \otimes a_p)'$, and, from the properties of the commutation matrix, this is equal to $K_{pG}(I_G \otimes A')$. □

Theorem 3.10. Let U be an $n \times G$ matrix and $u = \text{vec}\, U$. Then $K_{nG}^{\bar{\tau}}(I_n \otimes u) = U' = (u^{\bar{\tau}_n})'$.

Proof of Theorem 3.10. Clearly

$$K_{nG}^{\bar{\tau}}(I_n \otimes u) = \left(I_G \otimes e_1^{n'} \cdots I_G \otimes e_n^{n'}\right) \begin{bmatrix} u & & O \\ & \ddots & \\ O & & u \end{bmatrix}$$

$$= \left[\left(I_G \otimes e_1^{n'}\right)u \cdots \left(I_G \otimes e_n^{n'}\right)u\right].$$

Now write $u = (u_1' \cdots u_G')'$, where u_j is the jth column of U. Then

$$\left(I_G \otimes e_j^{n'}\right)u = \begin{pmatrix} e_j^{n'} u_1 \\ \vdots \\ e_j^{n'} u_G \end{pmatrix} = \begin{pmatrix} u_{j1} \\ \vdots \\ u_{jG} \end{pmatrix} = U_j'.$$

□

Theorem 3.11. Let u be an $nG \times 1$ vector. Then

$$K_{nG}^{\bar{\tau}}(u \times I_n) = u^{\bar{\tau}}.$$

Proof of Theorem 3.11. Write $u = (u_1' \cdots u_n')'$, where each vector u_i is $G \times 1$. Then

$$K_{nG}^{\bar{\tau}}(u \otimes I_n) = \left(I_G \otimes e_1^{n'} \cdots I_G \otimes e_n^{n'}\right) \begin{pmatrix} u_1 \otimes I_n \\ \vdots \\ u_n \otimes I_n \end{pmatrix}$$

$$= \left(u_1 \otimes e_1^{n'}\right) + \cdots + \left(u_n \otimes e_n^{n'}\right).$$

However, $u_j \otimes e_j^{n'} = u_j e_j^{n'} = (0 \cdots u_j \cdots 0)$,

so

$$K_{nG}^{\bar{\tau}}(u \otimes I_n) = (u_1 \cdots u_n) = u^{\bar{\tau}}. \qquad \square$$

Theorem 3.12.

$$\left(I_m \otimes K_{nG}^{\bar{\tau}}\right)K_{mn,nG} = K_{mG}\left(I_G \otimes K_{nm}^{\bar{\tau}_m}\right).$$

Proof of Theorem 3.12. We can write $K_{mn,nG} = [I_m \otimes (I_n \otimes e_1^{nG}) \cdots I_m \otimes (I_n \otimes e_{nG}^{nG})]$, so

$$\left(I_m \otimes K_{nG}^{\bar{\tau}}\right)K_{mn,nG} = \left[I_m \otimes K_{nG}^{\bar{\tau}}\left(I_n \otimes e_1^{nG}\right) \cdots I_m \otimes K_{nG}^{\bar{\tau}}\left(I_n \otimes e_{nG}^{nG}\right)\right]. \tag{3.10}$$

Now, by Theorem 3.10,

$$K_{nG}^{\bar{\tau}}\left(I_n \otimes e_1^{nG}\right) = \left[\left(e_1^{nG}\right)^{\bar{\tau}_n}\right]',$$

and, as $e_1^{nG} = e_1^G \otimes e_1^n$ from the properties of the generalized devec operator given in Section 2.4 of Chap. 2,

$$\left(e_1^{nG}\right)^{\bar{\tau}_n} = e_1^{G'} \otimes e_1^n,$$

so

$$K_{nG}^{\bar{\tau}}\left(I_n \otimes e_1^{nG}\right) = e_1^G \otimes e_1^{n'} = e_1^G e_1^{n'}.$$

The first n matrices on the right-hand side of Eq. (3.10) can then be written as

$$\begin{aligned} I_m \otimes e_1^G e_1^{n'} \cdots I_m \otimes e_1^G e_n^{n'} &= \left(I_m \otimes e_1^G\right)\left(I_m \otimes e_1^{n'} \cdots I_m \otimes e_n^{n'}\right) \\ &= \left(I_m \otimes e_1^G\right)\left(K_{nm}^{\bar{\tau}_m}\right). \end{aligned}$$

It follows then that the left-hand side of Eq. (3.10) can be written as

$$\left[\left(I_m \otimes e_1^G\right)K_{nm}^{\bar{\tau}_m} \cdots \left(I_m \otimes e_G^G\right)K_{nm}^{\bar{\tau}_m}\right] = K_{mG}\left(I_G \otimes K_{nm}^{\bar{\tau}_m}\right). \qquad \square$$

Theorem 3.13. Let b and d be $n \times 1$ vectors and let c be a $G \times 1$ vector. Then

$$K_{nG}^{\bar{\tau}}(b \otimes c \otimes d) = d'bc.$$

Proof of Theorem 3.13.

$$\begin{aligned} K_{nG}^{\bar{\tau}}(b \otimes c \otimes d) &= \left(I_G \otimes e_1^{n'} \cdots I_G \otimes e_n^{n'}\right)\begin{bmatrix} b_1(c \otimes d) \\ \vdots \\ b_n(c \otimes d) \end{bmatrix} \\ &= b_1(c \otimes d_1) + \cdots + b_n(c \otimes d_n) \\ &= (b_1 d_1 + \cdots + b_n d_n)c. \end{aligned} \qquad \square$$

Theorem 3.14. Let b be an $n \times 1$ vector and let A be a $Gn \times p$ matrix. Then

$$K_{nG}^{\bar{\tau}}(b \otimes A) = (I_G \otimes b')A.$$

Proof of Theorem 3.14.

$$K_{nG}^{\bar{\tau}}(b \otimes A) = \left(I_G \otimes e_1^{n'} \cdots I_G \otimes e_n^{n'}\right)\begin{pmatrix} b_1 A \\ \vdots \\ b_n A \end{pmatrix}$$
$$= b_1\left(I_G \otimes e_1^{n'}\right)A + \cdots + b_n\left(I_G \otimes e_n^{n'}\right)A.$$

Let $A = (A_1' \cdots A_G')'$, where each submatrix A_i is $n \times p$. Then

$$\left(I_G \otimes e_1^{n'}\right)A = \left(A_1' e_1^n \cdots A_G' e_1^n\right)',$$

so

$$K_{nG}^{\bar{\tau}}(b \otimes A) = b_1\left(A_1' e_1^n \cdots A_G' e_1^n\right)' + \cdots + b_n\left(A_1' e_n^n \cdots A_G' e_n^n\right)'.$$

Consider the first submatrix,

$$b_1 e_1^{n'} A_1 + \cdots + b_n e_n^{n'} A_1 = b' A_1,$$

so we can write

$$K_{nG}^{\bar{\tau}}(b \otimes A) = \left(A_1' b \cdots A_G' b\right)' = (I_G \otimes b')A. \qquad \square$$

3.3.3.4. $K_{p,np}$ versus $K_{np}^{\tau_n}$

Note that both $K_{p,np}$ and $K_{np}^{\tau_n}$ have np^2 columns, and it is of some interest what happens to a Kronecker product with np^2 rows when it is postmultiplied by these matrices. Let A be an $m \times p$ matrix and let B be an $r \times np$ matrix; then $A \otimes B$ is such a Kronecker product. From Theorem 3.2,

$$(A \otimes B)K_{p,np} = (A \otimes b_1 \cdots A \otimes b_{np}), \tag{3.11}$$

where b_i is the ith column of B. The equivalent result for $K_{np}^{\tau_n}$ is given by the following theorem.

Theorem 3.15. Let A be an $m \times p$ matrix and let B be an $r \times np$ matrix. Then

$$(A \otimes B)K_{np}^{\tau_n} = \begin{bmatrix} B(I_n \otimes a^1) \\ \vdots \\ B(I_n \otimes a^m) \end{bmatrix}, \tag{3.12}$$

where $a^{i'}$ is the ith row of A.

Proof of Theorem 3.15.

$$(A \otimes B)K_{np}^{\tau_n} = \begin{bmatrix} (a^{1'} \otimes B)K_{np}^{\tau_n} \\ \vdots \\ (a^{m'} \otimes B)K_{np}^{\tau_n} \end{bmatrix}.$$

However, from Theorem 3.14, $(a^{1'} \otimes B)K_{np}^{\tau_n} = B(I_n \otimes a^1)$. □

Taking the transposes of Eqs. (3.11) and (3.12), we find that if C and D are $p \times m$ and $np \times r$ matrices, respectively,

$$K_{np,p}(C \otimes D) = \begin{pmatrix} C \otimes d^{1'} \\ \vdots \\ C \otimes d^{np'} \end{pmatrix}, \tag{3.13}$$

whereas

$$K_{pn}^{\bar{\tau}_n}(C \otimes D) = [(I_n \otimes c_1')D \cdots (I_n \otimes c_m')D], \tag{3.14}$$

where $d^{i'}$ is the ith row of D and c_j is the jth column of C.

3.3.4. The Matrix N_n

Associated with the commutation matrix K_{nn} is the $n^2 \times n^2$ matrix N_n, which is defined by

$$N_n = \frac{1}{2}(I_{n^2} + K_{nn}).$$

For a square $n \times n$ matrix A,

$$N_n \operatorname{vec} A = \operatorname{vec}\frac{1}{2}(A + A').$$

From the properties of the commutation matrix, it is clear that N_n is symmetric idempotent, that is, $N_n' = N_n = N_n^2$. Other properties of N_n that can easily be derived from the properties of K_{nn}, in which A and B are $n \times n$ matrices and b is an $n \times 1$ vector, are

1. $N_n K_{nn} = N_n = K_{nn} N_n$,
2. $N_n(A \otimes B)N_n = N_n(B \otimes A)N_n$,

3. $N_n(A \otimes B + B \otimes A)N_n = N_n(A \otimes B + B \otimes A)$
$= (A \otimes B + B \otimes A)N_n = 2N_n(A \otimes B)N_n,$
4. $N_n(A \otimes A)N_n = N_n(A \otimes A) = (A \otimes A)N_n,$
5. $N_n(A \otimes b) = N_n(b \otimes A) = \frac{1}{2}(A \otimes b + b \otimes A).$

In subsequent chapters, it is often convenient to drop the subscripts from K_{nn} and N_n. Thus, we often use the symbol K for K_{nn} and N for N_n, in which the order for these matrices is clear. In like fashion, we drop the subscripts from elimination matrices and duplication matrices, which are discussed in Sections 3.4 and 3.5.

3.4. ELIMINATION MATRICES $L, \bar{L}$

It was noted in Section 2.3 of Chap. 2 that if A is an $n \times n$ matrix, then vec A contains all the elements in vech A and in $\bar{v}(A)$ and more besides. It follows that there exists zero-one matrices L and $\bar{L}$ whose orders are $\frac{1}{2}n(n+1) \times n^2$ and $\frac{1}{2}n(n-1) \times n^2$, respectively, such that

$$L \operatorname{vec} A = \operatorname{vech} A,$$

$$\bar{L} \operatorname{vec} A = \bar{v}(A).$$

These matrices are called **elimination matrices**. For example, for a 3×3 matrix A,

$$L_3 = \left[\begin{array}{ccc|ccc|ccc} 1 & 0 & 0 & 0 & 0 & 0 & 0 & 0 & 0 \\ 0 & 1 & 0 & 0 & 0 & 0 & 0 & 0 & 0 \\ 0 & 0 & 1 & 0 & 0 & 0 & 0 & 0 & 0 \\ \hline 0 & 0 & 0 & 0 & 1 & 0 & 0 & 0 & 0 \\ 0 & 0 & 0 & 0 & 0 & 1 & 0 & 0 & 0 \\ \hline 0 & 0 & 0 & 0 & 0 & 0 & 0 & 0 & 1 \end{array}\right],$$

$$\bar{L}_3 = \left[\begin{array}{ccc|ccc|ccc} 0 & 1 & 0 & 0 & 0 & 0 & 0 & 0 & 0 \\ 0 & 0 & 1 & 0 & 0 & 0 & 0 & 0 & 0 \\ 0 & 0 & 0 & 0 & 0 & 1 & 0 & 0 & 0 \end{array}\right].$$

3.5. DUPLICATION MATRICES $D, \bar{L}'$

In Chap. 2 it was also noted that if an $n \times n$ matrix A is symmetric, then vech A contains all the essential elements of A, with some of these elements duplicated in vec A. It follows therefore that there exists an $n^2 \times \frac{1}{2}n(n+1)$ zero-one matrix D such that

$$D \operatorname{vech} A = \operatorname{vec} A.$$

For example, for a 3 × 3 symmetric matrix,

$$D_3 = \left[\begin{array}{ccc|cc|c} 1 & 0 & 0 & 0 & 0 & 0 \\ 0 & 1 & 0 & 0 & 0 & 0 \\ 0 & 0 & 1 & 0 & 0 & 0 \\ \hline 0 & 1 & 0 & 0 & 0 & 0 \\ 0 & 0 & 0 & 1 & 0 & 0 \\ 0 & 0 & 0 & 0 & 1 & 0 \\ \hline 0 & 0 & 1 & 0 & 0 & 0 \\ 0 & 0 & 0 & 0 & 1 & 0 \\ 0 & 0 & 0 & 0 & 0 & 1 \end{array}\right].$$

Similarly, if A is strictly lower triangular then $\bar{v}(A)$ contains all the essential nonzero elements of A. Hence there exists an $n^2 \times \frac{1}{2}n(n-1)$ zero-one matrix, $\bar{L}'$ as it turns out, such that

$$\bar{L}'\bar{v}(A) = \text{vec}\, A.$$

The matrices D and $\bar{L}'$ are called **duplication matrices.**

3.6. RESULTS CONCERNING ZERO-ONE MATRICES ASSOCIATED WITH AN $n \times n$ MATRIX

The following results are well known and may be found in Magnus (1988).

1. $KD = D = ND$, $LD = I$.
2. $L'L = I$.
3. $DLN = N$.
4. $D'D = (LNL)^{-1} = 2I - LKL'$.
5. $D = NL(LNL)^{-1} = 2NL' - L'LKL'$.
6. $DD' = 2N - L'LKL'L$.
7. $\bar{L}\bar{L}' = I$.
8. $\bar{L}KL' = O$.
9. The generalized inverse of D is $D^+ = LN$.
10. $D^+(A \otimes B)D = D^+(B \otimes A)D$.
11. For a nonsingular matrix A, $[D'(A \otimes A)D]^{-1} = LN(A^{-1} \otimes A^{-1})NL'$.
12. Let $A = \{a_{ij}\}$ be an $n \times n$ matrix. Then $\bar{L}'\bar{L}$ vec A = vec $\bar{A}$, where $\bar{A}$ is the strict lower-triangular matrix given by

$$\bar{A} = \begin{bmatrix} 0 & 0 & \cdots & 0 & 0 \\ a_{21} & a_{32} & \cdots & 0 & 0 \\ \vdots & \vdots & & \vdots & \vdots \\ a_{n1} & a_{n2} & \cdots & a_{nn-1} & 0 \end{bmatrix}.$$

One further result that is useful to us is given by the following theorem.

Theorem 3.16. Suppose A is an $n \times n$ diagonal matrix with diagonal elements $a_{11},\ a_{22} \cdots a_{nn}$. Then $D'(A \otimes A)D$ is also a diagonal matrix given by

$$D'(A \otimes A)D = \begin{bmatrix} a_{11}^2 & & & & & & & & O \\ & 2a_{11}a_{22} & & & & & & & \\ & & \ddots & & & & & & \\ & & & 2a_{11}a_{nn} & & & & & \\ & & & & a_{22}^2 & & & & \\ & & & & & \ddots & & & \\ & O & & & & & 2a_{22}a_{nn} & & \\ & & & & & & & \ddots & \\ & & & & & & & & a_{nn}^2 \end{bmatrix}.$$

Proof of Theorem 3.16. From Theorem 4.9 of Magnus (1988), $D^+(A \otimes A)D$ is a diagonal matrix with diagonal elements $a_{ii}a_{jj}$ for $1 \leq j \leq i \leq n$. Now $D'(A \otimes A)D = D'DD^+(A \otimes A)D$, but Magnus (1988) in Theorem 4.4 shows that we can write $D'D = 2I_{\frac{1}{2}n(n+1)} - \sum_{i=1}^{n} u_{ii}u_{ii}'$, where u_{ii} is a unit vector of the order of $\frac{1}{2}n(n+1) \times 1$, with one in the $(i-1)n + \frac{2}{3}i - \frac{1}{2}i^2$ position and zeros elsewhere. However, it is easily seen that

$$\sum_{i=1}^{n} u_{ii}u_{ii}' D^+(A \otimes A)D = \begin{bmatrix} a_{11}^2 & & & & & & & O \\ & 0 & & & & & & \\ & & \ddots & & & & & \\ & & & 0 & & & & \\ & & & & a_{22}^2 & & & \\ & & & & & \ddots & & \\ & O & & & & & 0 & \\ & & & & & & \ddots & \\ & & & & & & & a_{nn}^2 \end{bmatrix}. \qquad \square$$

Note that as $[D'(A \otimes A)D]^{-1} = LN(A^{-1} \otimes A^{-1})LN$ for nonsingular A, it follows that

$$LN(A^{-1} \otimes A^{-1})LN$$

$$= \begin{bmatrix} a_{11}^{-1} & & & & & & & & & & \\ & \frac{1}{2}a_{11}^{-1}a_{22}^{-1} & & & & & & & & O & \\ & & \ddots & & & & & & & & \\ & & & \frac{1}{2}a_{11}^{-1}a_{nn}^{-1} & & & & & & & \\ & & & & a_{22}^{-1} & & & & & & \\ & & & & & \frac{1}{2}a_{22}^{-1}a_{33}^{-1} & & & & & \\ & & & & & & \ddots & & & & \\ & & & O & & & & \frac{1}{2}a_{22}^{-1}a_{nn}^{-1} & & & \\ & & & & & & & & \ddots & & \\ & & & & & & & & & & a_{nn}^{-1} \end{bmatrix}$$

for a diagonal matrix A.

3.7. SHIFTING MATRICES

3.7.1. Introduction

In this section, a zero-one matrix is introduced that will be useful to us in a future analysis of time-series models. When a time-series process is written in matrix notation, shifting matrices, at least as far as asymptotic theory is concerned, play the same role as that of the lag operators that appear when we write the process for a particular time period. However, specifying the process in matrix notation using these zero-one matrices greatly facilitates the use of matrix calculus and hence the application of classical statistical procedures to the model.

3.7.2. Definition and Basic Operations

Consider the $n \times n$ matrix

$$S_1 = \begin{bmatrix} 0 & & & & \\ 1 & \ddots & & O & \\ & \ddots & \ddots & & \\ & O & \ddots & \ddots & \\ & & & 1 & 0 \end{bmatrix} = \begin{bmatrix} 0' & 0 \\ I_{n-1} & 0 \end{bmatrix}.$$

Clearly S_1 is a strictly lower-triangular zero-one matrix. It is called a **shifting matrix** as when a given matrix is premultiplied or postmultiplied by S_1, the elements of that matrix are shifted one space and zeros are placed in the spaces thus created. For example, let $A = \{a_{ij}\}$ and $B = \{b_{ij}\}$ be $n \times m$ and $m \times n$

matrices, respectively. Then

$$S_1 A = \begin{bmatrix} 0 & \cdots & 0 \\ a_{11} & \cdots & a_{1m} \\ \vdots & & \vdots \\ a_{n-11} & \cdots & a_{n-1} \end{bmatrix},$$

that is, in forming $S_1 A$ we shift the rows of A down one space and replace the first row of A with the null row vector. Similarly

$$BS_1 = \begin{bmatrix} b_{12} & \cdots & b_{1n} & 0 \\ \vdots & & \vdots & \vdots \\ b_{m2} & \cdots & b_{mn} & 0 \end{bmatrix},$$

that is, in forming BS_1 we shift the columns of B to the left one place and replace the last column of B with the null column vector. Notice that for a, an $n \times 1$ vector,

$$S_1 a = \begin{pmatrix} 0 \\ a_1 \\ \vdots \\ a_{n-1} \end{pmatrix}, \qquad a' S_1 = (a_2 \cdots a_n 0).$$

From S_1, other shifting matrices can be formed that will also shift the elements of a given matrix one space. Clearly

$$S_1' A = \begin{bmatrix} a_{21} & \cdots & a_{2m} \\ \vdots & & \vdots \\ a_{n1} & \cdots & a_{nm} \\ 0 & \cdots & 0 \end{bmatrix}$$

shift the rows of A up one and replaces the last row of A with the null row vector and

$$BS_1' = \begin{bmatrix} 0 & b_{11} & \cdots & b_{1n-1} \\ \vdots & \vdots & & \vdots \\ 0 & b_{m1} & \cdots & b_{mn-1} \end{bmatrix}$$

shifts the colums of B to the right one and replaces the first column of B with the null vector.

Suppose now that we want to replace the first or the last row (column) of a matrix with a null vector while leaving the other elements of the matrix the same. We can achieve this too by using the shifting matrix S_1. Clearly

$$S_1 S_1' A = \begin{bmatrix} 0 & \cdots & 0 \\ a_{21} & \cdots & a_{2m} \\ \vdots & & \vdots \\ a_{n1} & \cdots & a_{nm} \end{bmatrix}, \quad B S_1 S_1' = \begin{bmatrix} 0 & b_{12} & \cdots & b_{1n} \\ \vdots & \vdots & & \vdots \\ 0 & b_{m2} & \cdots & b_{mn} \end{bmatrix},$$

$$S_1' S_1 A = \begin{bmatrix} a_{11} & \cdots & a_{1m} \\ \vdots & & \vdots \\ a_{n-11} & \cdots & a_{n-1m} \\ 0 & \cdots & 0 \end{bmatrix}, \quad B S_1' S_1 = \begin{bmatrix} b_{11} & \cdots & b_{1n-1} & 0 \\ \vdots & & \vdots & \vdots \\ b_{m1} & \cdots & b_{mn-1} & 0 \end{bmatrix}.$$

Alternatively, we can use S_1 to leave the first or the last row (column) of a matrix unaltered while multiplying all other elements of the matrix by a given constant, k, say. For example, if I_n is the $n \times n$ identity matrix, then

$$[I_n + (k-1)S_1 S_1']A = \begin{bmatrix} a_{11} & \cdots & a_{1m} \\ ka_{21} & \cdots & ka_{2m} \\ \vdots & & \vdots \\ ka_{n1} & \cdots & ka_{nm} \end{bmatrix}.$$

The other cases are left to the reader.

3.7.3. Shifting Matrices Associated with an $n \times n$ Matrix

When a given matrix is premultiplied (postmultiplied) by the shifting matrix S_1 or S_1', the rows (columns) of that matrix are shifted one space. Other shifting matrices can similarly be defined that will shift the elements of a given matrix any number of spaces. In fact, a given $n \times n$ matrix has n shifting matrices associated with it[1]:

$$I_n = \begin{bmatrix} 1 & & O \\ & \ddots & \\ O & & 1 \end{bmatrix}$$

shifts elements zero spaces;

$$S_1 = \begin{bmatrix} 0 & & & & \\ 1 & \ddots & & & O \\ & \ddots & \ddots & & \\ & & \ddots & \ddots & \\ & O & & 1 & 0 \end{bmatrix}$$

[1] We do not consider shifting matrices that convert the matrix into the null matrix.

shifts elements one space. Zeros go in the spaces created;

$$S_2 = \begin{bmatrix} 0 & & & & \\ 0 & \ddots & & & O \\ 1 & \ddots & \ddots & & \\ & \ddots & \ddots & \ddots & \\ O & & 1 & 0 & 0 \end{bmatrix}$$

shifts elements two spaces. Zeros go in the spaces created;

$$\begin{matrix} \vdots & & \vdots \\ \vdots & & \vdots \\ \vdots & & \vdots \\ \vdots & & \vdots \end{matrix}$$

$$S_{n-1} = \begin{bmatrix} 0 & & & \\ & \ddots & & O \\ O & & \ddots & \\ 1 & 0 \cdots & & 0 \end{bmatrix}$$

shifts elements $n-1$ spaces. Zeros go in the spaces created.

Suppose we denote the *j*th column of the $n \times n$ identity matrix by e_j. Then clearly

$$S_j = \sum_{i=j+1}^{n} e_i e'_{i-1},$$

$$S_j e_i = e_{i+j}, \quad i + j \leq n,$$

$$S_j e_i = 0, \quad i + j > n.$$

Moreover,

$$S_j = S_1^j, \quad j = 0, 1, \ldots, n-1,$$

provided we take $S_1^o = I_n$.

A similar analysis as that conducted for S_1 can now be made for S_j. For example, $S_j S'_j$ when premultiplied (postmultiplied) by a given matrix, replaces the first j rows (columns) of that matrix with zeros while leaving the other elements unaltered.

If A is an $n \times n$ matrix, then $S'_i A S_j$ is the matrix formed when we move the elements of A up i rows and across to the left j columns, filling the spaces thus created with zeros. Similarly $S_i A S'_j$ is the matrix formed when we move the elements of A down i rows and across to the right j columns, filling the spaces thus created with zeros.

3.7.4. Some Properties of Shifting Matrices

3.7.4.1. Obvious Properties

It is clear that all shifting matrices other than the identity matrix have the following properties:

1. They are all singular. In fact, $r(S_j) = n - j$.
2. They all are nilpotent. For example, $S_1^n = O$.
3. $S_i S_j = S_{i+j}, \quad i + j < n,$
   $= O, \quad i + j \geq n.$

The last property can be used to obtain inverses of matrices involving shifting matrices. An example is the following theorem.

Theorem 3.17. Let R be an $m \times m$ matrix, and consider the $mn \times mn$ matrix given by

$$M(r) = I_{nm} + (R \otimes S_1).$$

Then

$$M(r)^{-1} = I_{nm} - R \otimes S_1 + R^2 \otimes S_2 + \cdots + (-1)^{n-1}(R^{n-1} \otimes S_{n-1}).$$

Proof of Theorem 3.17. Let $A = I_{nm} - R \otimes S_1 + R^2 \otimes S_2 + \cdots + (-1)^{n-1} \times (R^{n-1} \otimes S_{n-1})$, and consider

$$\begin{aligned} M(r)A &= A + R \otimes S_1 - R^2 \otimes S_2 + \cdots + (-1)^{n-2}(R^{n-1} \otimes S_{n-1}) \\ &\quad + (-1)^{n-1}(R^n \otimes S_n) \\ &= I_{nm}, \end{aligned}$$

as S_n is the null matrix. Hence, by the uniqueness of the inverse, $A = M(r)^{-1}$. □

Matrices like $M(r)$ crop up in the application of shifting matrices to time-series models. Also, in this application we will need to consider how shifting matrices interact with triangular matrices. This topic is taken up in the next subsection.

3.7.4.2. Shifting Matrices and Triangular Matrices

Suppose A is the upper-triangular matrix

$$A = \begin{bmatrix} a_{11} & a_{12} & \cdots & a_{1n} \\ 0 & a_{22} & \cdots & a_{2n} \\ \vdots & \vdots & & \vdots \\ 0 & 0 & \cdots & a_{nn} \end{bmatrix}.$$

Then

$$S'_j A = \begin{bmatrix} 0 & \cdots & 0 & & a_{j+1\,j+1} & \cdots & a_{j+1\,n} \\ & \ddots & & \ddots & \ddots & & \vdots \\ & & \ddots & & \ddots & \ddots & \vdots \\ & & & \ddots & & \ddots & a_{nn} \\ & O & & & \ddots & & 0 \\ & & & & & \ddots & \vdots \\ & & & & & & 0 \end{bmatrix},$$

that is, $S'_j A$ is strictly upper triangular with zeros in the $j-1$ diagonals above the main diagonal. The matrix AS'_j has a like configuration, with

$$AS'_j = \begin{bmatrix} 0 & \cdots & 0 & a_{11} & \cdots & a_{1\,n-j} \\ & \ddots & & \ddots & \ddots & \vdots \\ O & & \ddots & & \ddots & a_{n-j\,n-j} \\ & & & 0 & \cdots & 0 \end{bmatrix}.$$

Similarly, if B is lower triangular, then

$$S_j B = \begin{bmatrix} 0 & & & & & & & \\ \vdots & \ddots & & & & & & \\ 0 & & \ddots & & & O & & \\ & \ddots & & \ddots & & & & \\ b_{11} & & \ddots & & \ddots & & & \\ \vdots & \ddots & & \ddots & & \ddots & & \\ & & \ddots & & \ddots & & \ddots & \\ b_{n-j\,1} & \cdots & \cdots & b_{n-j\,n-j} & & 0 & \cdots & 0 \end{bmatrix},$$

$$BS_j = \begin{bmatrix} 0 & & & & & \\ \vdots & \ddots & & & O & \\ 0 & & \ddots & & & \\ b_{jj} & \ddots & & 0 & \cdots & 0 \\ \vdots & \ddots & \ddots & \vdots & & \vdots \\ b_{n-j\,j} & \cdots & b_{nn} & 0 & \cdots & 0 \end{bmatrix}.$$

3.7.4.3. Shifting Matrices and Toeplitz Matrices

Shifting matrices form the building blocks for **Toeplitz matrices**. An $n \times n$ matrix A is Toeplitz if it takes the form

$$A = \begin{bmatrix} a_1 & a_2 & a_3 & \cdots & a_n \\ b_1 & a_1 & a_2 & & \vdots \\ \vdots & \ddots & \ddots & \ddots & \vdots \\ \vdots & & \ddots & \ddots & a_2 \\ b_{n-1} & \cdots & & b_1 & a_1 \end{bmatrix},$$

that is, the matrix takes on a constant along all its diagonals running from upper left to lower right. It is easily seen that A is Toeplitz if and only if it can be written as

$$\begin{aligned} A &= \sum_{i=1}^{n-1} b_i S_i + \sum_{i=1}^{n} a_i S'_{i-1} \\ &= \sum_{i=1}^{n-1} b_i S_1^i + \sum_{i=1}^{n} a_i S_1^{i-1'}, \end{aligned}$$

where $S_0 = S_1^0 = I_n$. Two special sorts of Toeplitz matrices which we will come across a lot in future are

$$A = I_n + a_1 S_1 + \cdots + a_p S_p$$

$$= \begin{bmatrix} 1 & & & \\ & \ddots & & O \\ & & \ddots & \\ O & & \ddots & \\ & & & 1 \end{bmatrix} + \begin{bmatrix} 0 & & & O \\ a_1 & \ddots & & \\ & \ddots & \ddots & \\ & & \ddots & \ddots \\ O & & a_1 & 0 \end{bmatrix}$$

$$+ \cdots + \begin{bmatrix} 0 & & O & \\ \vdots & \ddots & & \\ a_p & & \ddots & \\ & \ddots & & \ddots \\ O & & a_p \cdots & 0 \end{bmatrix} = \begin{bmatrix} 1 & & & & \\ a_1 & \ddots & & & O \\ \vdots & \ddots & \ddots & & \\ a_p & & \ddots & \ddots & \\ & \ddots & & \ddots & \ddots \\ O & & a_p & \cdots \; a_1 & 1 \end{bmatrix},$$

$$B = b_1S_1 + \cdots + b_pS_p = \begin{bmatrix} 0 & & & & & \\ b_1 & \ddots & & O & & \\ \vdots & \ddots & \ddots & & & \\ b_p & & \ddots & \ddots & & \\ & \ddots & & \ddots & \ddots & \\ O & & b_p & \cdots & b_1 & 0 \end{bmatrix}.$$

Both these matrices are Toeplitz matrices that are lower triangular and band. As we shall be working with such matrices quite a lot in future chapters we finish off this section by looking at some of their useful properties as presented in the following theorems:

Theorem 3.18. Let A and B be the $n \times n$ matrices given by

$$A = I_n + a_1S_1 + \cdots + a_pS_p,$$
$$B = b_1S_1 + \cdots + b_pS_p.$$

Then

$$AB = BA = b_1S_1 + c_2S_2 + \cdots + c_{2p}S_{2p}$$
$$= \begin{bmatrix} 0 & & & & & & & \\ b_1 & \ddots & & & & & & \\ c_2 & \ddots & \ddots & & & O & & \\ \vdots & \ddots & \ddots & \ddots & & & & \\ c_{2p} & & \ddots & \ddots & \ddots & & & \\ & \ddots & & \ddots & \ddots & \ddots & & \\ & O & \ddots & & \ddots & \ddots & \ddots & \\ & & & c_{2p} & \cdots & c_2 & b_1 & 0 \end{bmatrix},$$

provided that $2p < n$, where $c_2 \cdots c_{2p}$ are formed from the as and the bs. If $n < 2p$, then

$$AB = BA = b_1S_1 + c_2S_2 + \cdots + c_{n-1}S_{n-1}.$$

Proof of Theorem 3.18.

$$AB = (I_n + a_1S_1 + \cdots + a_pS_p)(b_1S_1 + \cdots + b_pS_p).$$

Using the property of shifting matrices that

$$\begin{aligned} S_i S_j &= S_{i+j}, \quad i+j<n, \\ &= O, \quad i+j \geq n, \end{aligned}$$

we can write the product AB as

$$\begin{aligned} AB = b_1S_1 + b_2S_2 + \cdots + b_pS_p & \\ + a_1b_1S_2 + \cdots + a_1b_{p-1}S_p + a_1b_pS_{p+1} & \\ \ddots \qquad \qquad \ddots & \\ + a_{p-1}b_1S_p + \cdots + a_{p-1}b_pS_{2p-1} & \\ + a_pb_1S_{p+1} + \cdots + a_pb_pS_{2p}, & \end{aligned}$$

with the understanding that some of these shifting matrices will be the null matrix if $2p > n$. Collecting shifting matrices of the same order gives the result. Moreover, writing the product BA in the same manner shows that $AB = BA$. □

Theorem 3.19. Let A be the $n \times n$ matrix

$$A = I_n + a_1S_1 + \cdots + a_pS_p.$$

Then

$$A^{-1} = I_n + c_1S_1 + \cdots + c_{n-1}S_{n-1}$$
$$= \begin{bmatrix} 1 & & & & \\ c_1 & \ddots & & O & \\ \vdots & \ddots & \ddots & & \\ c_{n-2} & & \ddots & \ddots & \\ c_{n-1} & c_{n-2} & \cdots & c_1 & 1 \end{bmatrix}$$

where the c_js are products of the a_is.

Proof of Theorem 3.19. This proof is similar to that of Theorem 2.5 of Section 2.5 of Chap. 2. □

Theorem 19 gives us the form of the inverse A^{-1}, and this is all we really need. However, if we like, we can go further often and actually specify the elements c_js of the inverse as shown by the following theorem

Theorem 3.20.[2] Let A and A^{-1} be the matrices specified in Theorem 3.19.

[2] I am grateful to Shiqing Ling for providing me with this theorem and proof.

Then

$$c_j = (-1)^j A_{jj}, \quad j = 1, \ldots, n-1,$$

where the A_{jj}s are the leading principal minors of the $(n-1) \times (n-1)$ matrix

$$\begin{bmatrix} a_1 & 1 & 0 & \cdots & \cdots & 0 \\ a_2 & a_1 & 1 & \cdots & \cdots & 0 \\ \vdots & \ddots & \ddots & \ddots & & \vdots \\ a_p & & \ddots & \ddots & \ddots & \vdots \\ & \ddots & & \ddots & \ddots & 1 \\ O & & a_p & \cdots & a_2 & a_1 \end{bmatrix}.$$

Proof of Theorem 3.20. As A is lower triangular with ones as its main diagonal elements, by Theorem 2.5 of Section 2.5 of Chap. 2, A^{-1} is also lower triangular with ones as its main diagonal elements. Hence, in forming the inverse A^{-1}, we need consider only the cofactors c_{ij} for $j > i$, $i, j = 1, \ldots, n-1$. Interchanging rows and columns if necessary, we see that

$$c_{ii+k} = (-1)^{2i+k} \left| \begin{array}{cccc|c} a_1 & 1 & & O & \\ a_2 & \ddots & \ddots & & O \\ \vdots & \ddots & \ddots & 1 & \\ a_k & \cdots & a_2 & a_1 & \\ \hline & & B & & I_{n-k} \end{array} \right|$$

for a suitable submatrix B of A. However,

$$\begin{vmatrix} C & O \\ D & E \end{vmatrix} = \begin{vmatrix} C & F \\ O & E \end{vmatrix} = |C||E|$$

for square matrices C and E, so

$$c_{ii+k} = (-1)^k A_{kk}.$$

Moreover, as A is triangular with ones as its main diagonal elements, $|A| = 1$, and c_{ii+k} is the $(i+k, i)$ element of A^{-1}. □

With this theorem in hand, we can prove the following theorem.

Theorem 3.21. Suppose A is an $nG \times nG$ matrix and write

$$A = \begin{bmatrix} A_{11} & \cdots & A_{1G} \\ \vdots & & \vdots \\ A_{G1} & \cdots & A_{GG} \end{bmatrix}$$

where each submatrix A_{ij} is $n \times n$ and each A_{ii} is of the form

$$I_n + a_1 S_1 + \cdots + a_p S_p = \begin{bmatrix} 1 & & & & & O \\ a_1 & \ddots & & & & \\ \vdots & \ddots & \ddots & & & \\ a_p & & \ddots & \ddots & & \\ & \ddots & & \ddots & \ddots & \\ O & & a_p & \cdots & a_1 & 1 \end{bmatrix}$$

for $i = 1 \cdots G$, whereas each A_{ij}, for $i \neq j$, is of the form

$$b_1 S_1 + \cdots + b_p S_p = \begin{bmatrix} 0 & & & & & O \\ b_1 & \ddots & & & & \\ \vdots & \ddots & \ddots & & & \\ b_p & & \ddots & \ddots & & \\ & \ddots & & \ddots & \ddots & \\ O & & b_p & \cdots & b_1 & 0 \end{bmatrix}.$$

Suppose A is nonsingular and let

$$A^{-1} = \begin{bmatrix} A^{11} & \cdots & A^{1G} \\ \vdots & & \vdots \\ A^{G1} & \cdots & A^{GG} \end{bmatrix}.$$

Then each $n \times n$ matrix A^{ii} is of the form

$$A^{ii} = I_n + c_1 S_1 + \cdots + c_{n-1} S_{n-1} = \begin{bmatrix} 1 & & & & O \\ c_1 & \ddots & & & \\ \vdots & \ddots & \ddots & & \\ c_{n-2} & & \ddots & \ddots & \\ c_{n-1} & c_{n-2} & \cdots & c_1 & 1 \end{bmatrix},$$

whereas each A^{ij}, $i \neq j$, is of the form

$$A^{ij} = d_1 S_1 + \cdots + d_{n-1} S_{n-1} = \begin{bmatrix} 0 & & & & O \\ d_1 & \ddots & & & \\ \vdots & \ddots & \ddots & & \\ d_{n-2} & & \ddots & \ddots & \\ d_{n-1} & d_{n-2} & \cdots & d_1 & 0 \end{bmatrix}$$

where the c_is and d_js are products of the elements of A.

Proof of Theorem 3.21. This proof is, similar to that of Theorem 2.6 of Section 2.5 of Chap. 2. □

We finish this discussion by showing that the $nG \times nG$ matrix A specified in Theorem 3.21 can be written as

$$A = I_{nG} + (R \otimes I_n)C,$$

where R is a $G \times Gp$ matrix and C is the $Gpn \times Gn$ matrix given by

$$C = \begin{bmatrix} I_G \otimes S_1 \\ \vdots \\ I_G \otimes S_p \end{bmatrix}.$$

To do this, we let $N(r) = (R \otimes I_n)C$ and write $R = (R_1 \cdots R_p)$, where each submatrix R_i is $G \times G$ so

$$N(r) = (R_1 \otimes S_1) + \cdots + (R_p \otimes S_p).$$

Now, letting

$$R_l = \{r^l_{ij}\}$$

for $l = 1 \cdots p$, we have

$$N(r) = \begin{bmatrix} r^1_{11}S_1 & \cdots & r^1_{1G}S_1 \\ \vdots & & \vdots \\ r^1_{G1}S_1 & \cdots & r^1_{GG}S_1 \end{bmatrix} + \cdots + \begin{bmatrix} r^p_{11}S_p & \cdots & r^p_{1G}S_p \\ \vdots & & \vdots \\ r^p_{G1}S_p & \cdots & r^p_{GG}S_p \end{bmatrix},$$

so if we write

$$N(r) = \begin{bmatrix} N_{11} & \cdots & N_{1G} \\ \vdots & & \vdots \\ N_{G1} & \cdots & N_{GG} \end{bmatrix}$$

then

$$\begin{aligned} N_{ij} &= r^1_{ij}S_1 + r^2_{ij}S_2 + \cdots + r^p_{ij}S_p \\ &= \begin{bmatrix} 0 & & & & & \\ r^1_{ij} & \ddots & & & O & \\ \vdots & \ddots & \ddots & & & \\ r^p_{ij} & & \ddots & \ddots & & \\ & \ddots & & \ddots & \ddots & \\ O & & r^p_{ij} & \cdots & r^1_{ij} & 0 \end{bmatrix}. \end{aligned}$$

As under this notation

$$A = \begin{bmatrix} I_n & & O \\ & \ddots & \\ O & & I_n \end{bmatrix} + \begin{bmatrix} N_{11} & \cdots & N_{1G} \\ \vdots & & \vdots \\ N_{G1} & \cdots & N_{GG} \end{bmatrix},$$

we see that $A = I_{nG} + (R \otimes I_n)C$ meets the specifications of Theorem 3.21. Finally, it follows that A^{-1} can be written as

$$A^{-1} = I_{nG} + (\bar{R} \otimes I_n)\bar{C},$$

say, where $\bar{R}$ is a $G \times G(n-1)$ matrix whose elements are formed from those of A and $\bar{C}$ is the $Gn(n-1) \times Gn$ matrix given by

$$\bar{C} = \begin{bmatrix} I_G \otimes S_1 \\ \vdots \\ I_G \otimes S_{n-1} \end{bmatrix}.$$

3.7.4.4. Shifting Matrices and Circulant Matrices

Circulant matrices form a subset of the set of Toeplitz matrices. A **circulant matrix** of the order of n is an $n \times n$ matrix of the form

$$C = \text{circ}(c_1, c_2, \ldots, c_n) = \begin{bmatrix} c_1 & c_2 & \cdots & c_n \\ c_n & c_1 & \cdots & c_{n-1} \\ \vdots & \vdots & & \vdots \\ c_2 & c_3 & \cdots & c_n \, c_1 \end{bmatrix},$$

that is, the elements of each row of the circulant matrix C are identical to those of the previous row but moved to the right one position and wrapped around. Unlike most other matrices, circulant matrices commute under multiplication. If C and D are $n \times n$ circulant matrices then so is their product CD. If C is circulant then so is C', and if C is circulant and nonsingular then so is C^{-1}. Any linear function of circulant matrices of the same order is circulant. Finally, any circulant matrix is symmetric about its main counterdiagonal.

A zero-one matrix that is circulant is the **forward-shift matrix**, which is defined as

$$\Pi_1 = \text{circ}(0, 1, 0, \cdots, 0) = \begin{bmatrix} 0 & 1 & & 0 \\ 0 & \ddots & \ddots & \\ & & \ddots & 1 \\ 1 & 0 & \cdots & 0 \end{bmatrix}.$$

Note that the forward-shift matrix is also a permutation matrix so $\Pi_1' = \Pi_1^{-1}$, and this inverse is also circulant.

Suppose now $A = \{a_{ij}\}$ is an $n \times m$ matrix. Then

$$\Pi_1 A = \begin{bmatrix} a_{21} & \cdots & a_{2m} \\ \vdots & & \vdots \\ a_{n1} & \cdots & a_{nm} \\ a_{11} & \cdots & a_{1m} \end{bmatrix},$$

that is, when a matrix A is premultiplied by the forward-shift matrix, the rows of A are shifted up one place and wrapped around. It operates similarly to the shifting matrix S_1', the difference in the two operations being this: When A is premultiplied by S_1', the rows of A are pushed up one and zeros are placed in the last row of A. When A is premultiplied by Π_1, the rows of A are pushed up one and wrapped around.

As with shifting matrices, we can define a series of forward-shift matrices as

$$\Pi_j = \text{circ}\left(0, \ldots, 0, \underset{j+1}{1}, \ldots, 0\right), \quad j = 0, \ldots, n-1.$$

Then, when A is premultiplied by Π_j, the rows of A are pushed up j places and wrapped around. Like shifting matrices,

$$\Pi_j = \Pi_1^j, \quad j = 0, \ldots, n-1.$$

However, unlike shifting matrices, these forward-shift matrices are permutation matrices and are therefore orthogonal. To use this property, we write

$$\Pi^n = \text{circ}(1, 0, \ldots, 0) = \Pi^j \Pi^{n-1} = I_n = \Pi^0, \text{ for } j = 0, \ldots, n.$$

It follows then that

$$\Pi^{n-j} = (\Pi^j)^{-1} = \Pi^{j'}, \quad j = 0, \ldots, n.$$

The matrices $\Pi^{j'}$ behave in much the same way as the shifting matrices S^j except with wrapping around.

Forward-shift matrices are, in fact, the sum of shifting matrices as

$$\Pi^j = S_j' + S_{n-j}, \quad j = 0, \ldots, n-1.$$

We can write any $n \times n$ circulant matrix $C = \text{circ}(c_1, c_2, \ldots, c_n)$ first as a linear combination of forward-shift matrices and by using this property as a linear combination of shifting matrices:

$$\begin{aligned} C &= c_1 I_n + c_2 \Pi_1 + \cdots + c_n \Pi^{n-1} \\ &= c_1 I_n + c_2(S_1' + S_{n-1}) + \cdots + c_n(S_{n-1}' + S_1) \\ &= c_1 I_n + c_2 S_1' + \cdots + c_n S_{n-1}' \\ &\quad + c_n S_1 + \cdots + c_2 S_{n-1}. \end{aligned}$$

A good reference for both Toeplitz and circulant matrices is Davis (1979).

3.7.4.5. Traces and Shifting Matrices

In the application of shifting matrices to time-series models, we often have occasion to consider tr $S_i' A S_j$, where A is an $n \times n$ matrix. First, we consider tr $S_i' A S_i$. To obtain $S_i' A S_i$ we imagine shifting the lower right-hand corner of A up the main diagonal i places. It follows then that

$$\begin{aligned}\operatorname{tr} S_i' A S_i &= \operatorname{tr} A - a_{11} - a_{22} - \cdots - a_{ii} \\ &= \operatorname{tr} A - \operatorname{tr} S_{n-i}' A S_{n-i}, \quad i = 1, \ldots, n-1.\end{aligned}$$

Now we consider tr $S_i' A S_j$. If $j > i$, then we are shifting the elements of A across more spaces than we are raising them. It follows then that tr $S_i' A S_j$ is the sum of the elements of the $j-1$ diagonal above the main diagonal minus the first i elements of this diagonal.

If, however, $j < i$, then we are shifting the elements of A up further than we are moving them across. It follows then that tr $S_i' A S_j$ is the sum of the elements of the $i-1$ diagonal below the main diagonal minus the first j elements of this diagonal.

3.7.4.6. Shifting Matrices and Partitioned Matrices

Consider an $np \times r$ matrix A that we partition into p matrices:

$$A = \begin{pmatrix} A_1 \\ \vdots \\ A_p \end{pmatrix},$$

where each submatrix A_i is $n \times r$. Suppose we wish to shift the partitioned matrices down one and replace the spaces thus created with zeros; that is, we wish to form

$$C = \begin{pmatrix} O \\ A_1 \\ \vdots \\ A_{p-1} \end{pmatrix}.$$

Then it is easily seen that

$$C = (S_1 \otimes I_n) A.$$

In like manner,

$$\begin{pmatrix} A_2 \\ \vdots \\ A_p \\ O \end{pmatrix} = (S_1' \otimes I_n) A.$$

Similar results hold for an $r \times np$ matrix B that we partition into p matrices:

$$B = (B_1 \cdots B_p),$$

where each submatrix B_i is $r \times n$. Suppose we wish to move the partitioned matrices to the right one and replace the spaces thus created with zeros; that is, we wish to consider

$$D = (O B_1 \cdots B_{p-1}).$$

Again, it is easily seen that

$$D = B(S_1' \otimes I_n).$$

In like manner,

$$(B_2 \cdots B_p O) = B(S_1 \otimes I_n).$$

3.7.5. Some Theorems About Shifting Matrices

In this subsection we prove some theorems about shifting matrices that are important for the work in Chap. 5. These theorems involve the n shifting matrices $I_n\ S_1\ S_2 \cdots S_{n-1}$. Let $\bar{S}$ be the $n \times n^2$ matrix given by

$$\bar{S} = (I_n\ S_1\ S_2 \cdots S_{n-1})$$

and let $\bar{S^\tau}$ be the $n^2 \times n$ matrix given by

$$\bar{S^\tau} = \begin{pmatrix} I_n \\ S_1 \\ S_2 \\ \vdots \\ S_{n-1} \end{pmatrix},$$

that is, $\bar{S^\tau}$ is $\text{vec}_n\, \bar{S}$. Then we have the following theorems concerning $\bar{S}$ and $\bar{S^\tau}$.

Theorem 3.22. Let x be an $n \times 1$ vector. Then

$$\bar{S}(x \otimes I_n) = \bar{S}(I_n \otimes x) = (x' \otimes I_n)\bar{S}^\tau.$$

Proof of Theorem 3.22. Consider

$$\begin{aligned} \bar{S}(I_n \otimes x) &= (x\ S_1 x \cdots S_{n-1} x) \\ &= \begin{bmatrix} x_1 & 0 & \cdots & 0 \\ x_2 & x_1 & \cdots & 0 \\ \vdots & \vdots & & \vdots \\ x_n & x_{n-1} & \cdots & x_1 \end{bmatrix}. \end{aligned}$$

Now

$$\bar{S}(x \otimes I_n) = x_1 I_n + x_2 S_1 + \cdots + x_n S_{n-1}$$

$$= \begin{bmatrix} x_1 & & O \\ & \ddots & \\ O & & x_1 \end{bmatrix} + \begin{bmatrix} 0 & \cdots & & 0 \\ x_2 & 0 & & 0 \\ & \ddots & \ddots & \vdots \\ O & & x_2 & 0 \end{bmatrix} + \cdots + \begin{bmatrix} 0 & 0 & \cdots & 0 \\ \vdots & \vdots & & \vdots \\ 0 & 0 & \cdots & 0 \\ x_n & 0 & \cdots & 0 \end{bmatrix}$$

$$= \bar{S}(I_n \otimes x).$$

Similarly, $(x' \otimes I_n)\bar{S}^\tau = \bar{S}(I_n \otimes x)$. □

Theorem 3.23. $(I_n \otimes x')\bar{S}^\tau$ is symmetric.

Proof of Theorem 3.23. This is obvious, as

$$(I_n \otimes x')\bar{S}^\tau = \begin{bmatrix} x_1 & x_2 & & \cdots & x_n \\ x_2 & x_3 & \cdots & x_n & 0 \\ \vdots & & \cdot^{\cdot^{\cdot}} & & \\ x_n & & & O & \end{bmatrix}$$ □

Theorem 3.24. Let S be an $n \times np$ matrix made up of a selection of any p shifting matrices so

$$S = \bar{S}(\mathcal{S} \otimes I_n),$$

where $\mathcal{S}$ is an $n \times p$ selection matrix whose columns are the appropriate columns of I_n. Then, for α, a $p \times 1$ vector, and x, an $n \times 1$ vector,

1. $S(\alpha \otimes I_n) = \bar{S}(\mathcal{S}\alpha \otimes I_n) = \bar{S}(I_n \otimes \mathcal{S}\alpha) = (\alpha'\mathcal{S}' \otimes I_n)\bar{S}^\tau$,
2. $S(I_p \otimes x) = (x' \otimes I_n)\bar{S}^\tau \mathcal{S}$,
3. $(I_p \otimes x')S^\tau = \mathcal{S}'\bar{S}^{\tau'}(I_n \otimes x)$.

Proof of Theorem 3.24.

1. Clearly,

$$S(\alpha \otimes I_n) = \bar{S}(\mathcal{S} \otimes I_n)(\alpha \otimes I_n) = \bar{S}(\mathcal{S}\alpha \otimes I_n).$$

The result follows from the application of Theorem 3.22.
2. $S(I_p \otimes x) = \bar{S}(\mathcal{S} \otimes x) = \bar{S}(I_n \otimes x)\mathcal{S}$. The result follows from Theorem 3.22.
3. Consider

$$(I_p \otimes x')S^\tau = (I_p \otimes x')[\bar{S}(\mathcal{S} \otimes I_n)]^\tau = (I_p \otimes x')(\mathcal{S}' \otimes I_n)\bar{S}^\tau$$

by Theorem 2.4 of Chap. 2. However, clearly this is $\mathcal{S}'(I_n \otimes x')\bar{S}^\tau$; the result follows from Theorem 3.23. □

It is illuminating to consider the types of matrices presenting themselves in Theorem 3.24. Two important cases need to be considered.

1. $S = (S_1 S_2 \cdots S_p)$:
   Here $\mathcal{S} = (e_2 \cdots e_{p+1})$, where e_j is the jth column of I_n, and

$$S(\alpha \otimes I_n) = \begin{bmatrix} 0 & \cdots & \cdots & 0 \\ \alpha_1 & & & \vdots \\ \vdots & \ddots & & \vdots \\ \alpha_p & & \ddots & 0 \\ & \ddots & & \alpha_1 \\ & & \ddots & \vdots \\ O & & & \alpha_p \end{bmatrix},$$

$$S(I_p \otimes x) = \begin{bmatrix} 0 & 0 & \cdots & 0 \\ x_1 & 0 & & \vdots \\ x_2 & x_1 & \ddots & \vdots \\ \vdots & x_2 & \ddots & 0 \\ \vdots & \vdots & \ddots & x_1 \\ \vdots & \vdots & & x_2 \\ \vdots & \vdots & & \vdots \\ x_{n-1} & x_{n-2} & \cdots & x_{n-p} \end{bmatrix},$$

$$(I_p \otimes x')S^\tau = \begin{bmatrix} x_2 & \cdots & \cdots & \cdots & x_n & 0 \\ x_3 & \cdots & \cdots & x_n & 0 & 0 \\ \vdots & & \cdot^{\cdot^{\cdot}} & \cdot^{\cdot^{\cdot}} & & \vdots \\ x_{n-p-1} & \cdots & x_n & 0 & \cdots & 0 \end{bmatrix}.$$

2. $S = (S_{n-1} \cdots S_1 I_n)$:
   Here $\mathcal{S} = (e_n e_{n-1} \cdots e_1)$, and

$$S(\alpha \otimes I_n) = \begin{bmatrix} \alpha_n & & O & \\ \alpha_{n-1} & \ddots & & \\ \vdots & \ddots & \ddots & \\ \alpha_1 & \cdots & \alpha_{n-1} & \alpha_n \end{bmatrix},$$

$$S(I_n \otimes x) = \begin{bmatrix} & & & x_1 \\ & O & \cdot^{\cdot^{\cdot}} & \vdots \\ & \cdot^{\cdot^{\cdot}} & & \vdots \\ x_1 & x_2 & \cdots & x_n \end{bmatrix},$$

which is symmetrical, and

$$(I_n \otimes x')S^{\tau} = \begin{bmatrix} x_n & & O & \\ \vdots & \ddots & & \\ \vdots & & \ddots & \\ x_1 & \cdots & \cdots & x_n \end{bmatrix}.$$

3.7.6. Shifting Matrices and Time-Series Processes

An obvious application of shifting matrices is in time-series analysis. In writing a time series process in matrix notation, shifting matrices, at least as far as our asymptotic theory is concerned, play the same role as that of lag operators when we write the process for a particular time period t. Consider an autoregressive process of the order [3] of 1, $u_t + \alpha_1 u_{t-1} = \varepsilon_t$, $t = 1, \ldots, 0$, and the ε_t are assumed to be i.i.d random variables. Using the lag operator l_1, where $l_1 u_t = u_{t-1}$, we can write the process at time t as $(1 + \alpha_1 l_1)u_t = \varepsilon_t$.

In matrix notation, we write this process as

$$u + \alpha_1 u_{-1} = \varepsilon,$$

[3] The correspondence between lag operators and shifting matrices can be used to derive results for shifting matrices. For example, for $-1 < \alpha_1 < 1$, we know we can convert the moving-average process of the order of 1 to an autoregressive process by using the expansion

$$(1 + \alpha_1 l_1)^{-1} u_t = \left(1 - \alpha_1 l_1 + \alpha_1^2 l_1^2 \cdots\right) u_t,$$

where $l^j u_t = u_{t-j}$. It follows that

$$(I_n + \alpha_1 S_1)^{-1} = I_n - \alpha_1 S_1 + \alpha_1^2 S_1^2 + \cdots$$

However, we know that

$$S_i S_j = S_{i+j}, \quad \text{if } i + j < n,$$
$$S_i S_j = O, \quad \text{if } i + j \geq n,$$

so

$$(I_n + \alpha_1 S_1)^{-1} = I_n - \alpha_1 S_1 + \alpha_1^2 S_2 \cdots + (-1)^{n-1} \alpha_1^{n-1} S_{n-1}.$$

This is just a special example of Theorem 3.17.

where

$$u = \begin{pmatrix} u_1 \\ \vdots \\ \vdots \\ u_n \end{pmatrix}, \quad u_{-1} = \begin{pmatrix} u_0 \\ u_1 \\ \vdots \\ u_{n-1} \end{pmatrix}, \quad \varepsilon = \begin{pmatrix} \varepsilon_1 \\ \vdots \\ \vdots \\ \varepsilon_n \end{pmatrix}.$$

As far as asymptotic theory is concerned, all presample values may be replaced with zeros without affecting our asymptotic results. If we do this, then

$$u_{-1} = \begin{pmatrix} 0 \\ u_1 \\ \vdots \\ u_{n-1} \end{pmatrix} = S_1 u,$$

and we can write the autoregressive process in matrix notation as

$$(I_n + \alpha_1 S_1)u = \varepsilon.$$

In like manner, consider an autoregressive process of the order of p:

$$u_t + \alpha_1 u_{t-1} + \cdots + \alpha_p u_{t-p} = \varepsilon_t, t = 1, \cdots, n, \tag{3.15}$$

and $p < n$. In matrix notation, we write the process as

$$u + \alpha_1 u_{-1} + \cdots + \alpha_p u_{-p} = \varepsilon,$$

where

$$u_{-j} = \begin{pmatrix} u_{-j+1} \\ \vdots \\ u_0 \\ u_1 \\ \vdots \\ u_{n-j} \end{pmatrix}.$$

Again, replacing presample values with zeros, we have

$$u_{-j} = \begin{pmatrix} 0 \\ \vdots \\ 0 \\ u_1 \\ \vdots \\ u_{n-j} \end{pmatrix} = S_j u,$$

and we can write the autoregressive process as

$$u + \alpha_1 S_1 u + \cdots + \alpha_p S_p u = \varepsilon,$$

or

$$u + U_p \alpha = \varepsilon,$$

where

$$U_p = (S_1 u \cdots S_p u) = S(I_p \otimes u), \tag{3.16}$$

and S is the $n \times np$ matrix $S = (S_1 \cdots S_p)$.

4 Matrix Calculus

4.1. INTRODUCTION

The advent of matrix calculus, as mentioned in Chap. 2, has greatly facilitated the complicated differentiation required in applying classical statistic techniques to econometric models. In this chapter, we develop the matrix calculus results that are needed in the applications examined in future chapters.

Two things should be noted about the approach taken in this chapter. First, the method used in deriving proofs for our matrix calculus results is different from that used by Magnus and Neudecker. In their book, *Matrix Differential Calculus*, these authors derive their proofs by first taking differentials. Although this approach has mathematical elegance, it is not really necessary. After all, in ordinary calculus we do not usually derive results for derivatives by first appealing to differentials but by referring to a few general rules of differentiation such as the chain rule and the product rule. This is the approach taken in this chapter. We will obtain our matrix calculus results on the whole by appealing to a few general rules, which are the generalizations of the chain rule and the product rule of univariate calculus.

Second, consider an $m \times n$ matrix Y whose elements y_{ij} are differentiable functions of the elements x_{kl} of a $p \times q$ matrix X. Then we have $mnpq$ partial derivatives we can consider:

$$\frac{\partial y_{ij}}{\partial x_{kl}} \quad \begin{array}{l} i = 1, \ldots, m \\ j = 1, \ldots, n \\ k = 1, \ldots, p \\ l = 1, \ldots, q \end{array}.$$

The question is how to arrange these derivatives. Different arrangements give rise to different concepts of derivatives in matrix calculus [see, for example, Magnus and Neudecker (1988), Graham (1981), Rogers (1980)]. Our approach is to consider the vectors $y = \text{vec } Y$ and $x = \text{vec } X$ and define a notion of a derivative of a vector y with respect to another vector x. Such a notion will accommodate all our needs in the future chapters.

In this chapter, no attempt has been made to give an exhaustive list of matrix calculus results. [For such a list one can do no better than refer to Lutkepohl (1996)]. Instead what is presented are results, some of which are new, that are most useful for our future applications.

4.2. BASIC DEFINITIONS

Let $y = (y_j)$ be an $m \times 1$ vector whose elements are differentiable functions of the elements of an $n \times 1$ vector $x = (x_i)$. We write $y = y(x)$ and say that y is a vector function of x. Then we have the following definition.

Definition 4.1. The derivative of y with respect to x, denoted by $\partial y/\partial x$, is the $n \times m$ matrix given by[1]

$$\frac{\partial y}{\partial x} = \begin{bmatrix} \frac{\partial y_1}{\partial x_1} & \cdots & \frac{\partial y_m}{\partial x_1} \\ \vdots & & \vdots \\ \frac{\partial y_1}{\partial x_n} & \cdots & \frac{\partial y_m}{\partial x_n} \end{bmatrix}.$$

Note that under this notion if y is a scalar so that $y(x)$ is a scalar function of x, the derivative $\partial y/\partial x$ is the $n \times 1$ vector given by

$$\frac{\partial y}{\partial x} = \begin{bmatrix} \frac{\partial y}{\partial x_1} \\ \vdots \\ \frac{\partial y}{\partial x_n} \end{bmatrix}.$$

Similarly, if x is a scalar and y is an $m \times 1$ vector, then the derivative $\partial y/\partial x$ is the $1 \times m$ vector

$$\frac{\partial y}{\partial x} = \begin{bmatrix} \frac{\partial y_1}{\partial x} & \cdots & \frac{\partial y_m}{\partial x} \end{bmatrix}.$$

For the general case in which y and x are $m \times 1$ and $n \times 1$ vectors, respectively, the jth column of the matrix $\partial y/\partial x$ is the derivative of a scalar function with respect to a vector, namely $\partial y_j/\partial x$, whereas the ith row of the matrix $\partial y/\partial x$ is the derivative of a vector with respect to a scalar, namely $\partial y/\partial x_i$.

[1] Magnus and Neudecker (1985) show that if one is to be mathematically formally correct one should define the derivative of y with respect to x as $\partial y/\partial x'$, rather than $\partial y/\partial x$, as we have.

Row vectors are accommodated by the following definition. By the symbol $\partial y/\partial x'$, we mean the $m \times n$ matrix defined by

$$\frac{\partial y}{\partial x'} = \left(\frac{\partial y}{\partial x}\right)',$$

and we define

$$\frac{\partial y'}{\partial x} = \frac{\partial y}{\partial x}.$$

4.3. SOME SIMPLE MATRIX CALCULUS RESULTS

The following simple matrix calculus results can be derived from our basic definitions.

Theorem 4.1. Let x be an $n \times 1$ vector and let A be a matrix of constants (i.e., the elements of A are not scalar functions of x). Then

$$\frac{\partial Ax}{\partial x} = A' \qquad \text{for } A,\ m \times n,$$

$$\frac{\partial x'A}{\partial x} = A, \qquad \text{for } A,\ n \times p,$$

$$\frac{\partial x'Ax}{\partial x} = (A + A')x \quad \text{for } A,\ n \times n.$$

Proof of Theorem 4.1. The jth element of Ax is $\sum_k a_{jk}x_k$, and so the jth column of $\partial Ax/\partial x$ is $A'_{j\bullet}$, where $A_{j\bullet}$ is the jth row of A and $\partial Ax/\partial x = A'$. Under our notation, $\partial x'A/\partial x = \partial A'x/\partial x = A$. The jth element of $\partial x'Ax/\partial x$ is $\sum_i a_{ij}x_i + \sum_k a_{jk}x_k$ so $\partial x'Ax/\partial x = (A + A')x$. □

4.4. MATRIX CALCULUS AND ZERO–ONE MATRICES

With the results of Theorem 4.1 in hand we can derive further results and we can see how zero-one matrices enter the picture. We saw in Subsection 3.3.1 of Chap. 3 that

$$\text{vec } X' = K_{nr} \text{ vec } X$$

for X, an $n \times r$ matrix, and

$$\text{vec } X = D \text{ vech } X$$

for X, a symmetric $n \times n$ matrix, where K_{nr} and D are a commutation matrix and a duplication matrix, respectively. It follows immediately that

$$\frac{\partial \text{ vec } X'}{\partial \text{ vec } X} = K'_{nr} = K_{rn} \tag{4.1}$$

for X, an $n \times r$ matrix, and

$$\frac{\partial \operatorname{vec} X}{\partial \operatorname{vech} X} = D'$$

for X, a symmetric $n \times n$ matrix. Moreover, as $\operatorname{vec} AXB = (B' \otimes A)\operatorname{vec} X$, it follows that

$$\frac{\partial \operatorname{vec} AXB}{\partial \operatorname{vec} X} = B \otimes A',$$

and

$$\frac{\partial \operatorname{vec} AX'B}{\partial \operatorname{vec} X} = K'_{nr}(B \otimes A') = K_{nr}(B \otimes A') \tag{4.2}$$

for X, an $n \times r$ matix. In subsection 3.3.3.1 of Chap. 3, we saw too that for X, an $n \times r$ matrix,

$$\operatorname{vec}(X \otimes I_G) = \left(I_r \otimes K_{nG}^{\tau_n}\right)\operatorname{vec} X,$$
$$\operatorname{vec}(I_G \otimes X) = \left(K_{rG}^{\tau_r} \otimes I_n\right)\operatorname{vec} X.$$

It follows that

$$\frac{\partial \operatorname{vec}(X \otimes I_G)}{\partial \operatorname{vec} X} = I_r \otimes K_{nG}^{\tau'_n} = I_r \otimes (K'_{nG})^{\bar{\tau}_n} = I_r \otimes K_{Gn}^{\bar{\tau}_n}, \tag{4.3}$$

$$\frac{\partial \operatorname{vec}(I_G \otimes X)}{\partial \operatorname{vec} X} = K_{Gr}^{\bar{\tau}_r} \otimes I_n. \tag{4.4}$$

Special cases of the last two results occur when X is an $n \times 1$ vector x. Then

$$\frac{\partial \operatorname{vec}(x \otimes I_G)}{\partial x} = K_{Gn}^{\bar{\tau}_n}, \tag{4.5}$$

$$\frac{\partial \operatorname{vec}(I_G \otimes x)}{\partial x} = \operatorname{devec} I_G \otimes I_n. \tag{4.6}$$

Moreover, as $(x \otimes a) = (I_n \otimes a)x$ and $(a \otimes x) = (a \otimes I_n)x$,

$$\frac{\partial (x \otimes a)}{\partial x} = I_n \otimes a', \tag{4.7}$$

$$\frac{\partial (a \otimes x)}{\partial x} = a' \otimes I_n. \tag{4.8}$$

4.5. THE CHAIN RULE AND THE PRODUCT RULE FOR MATRIX CALCULUS

Working out the derivatives of more complicated functions requires the application of the following lemmas that represent generalizations of the chain rule and the product rule of ordinary calculus.

Lemma 4.1. The Chain Rule. Let $x = (x_i)$, $y = (y_k)$, and $z = (z_j)$ be $n \times 1$, $r \times 1$, and $m \times 1$ vectors, respectively. Suppose z is a vector function of y and y itself is a vector function of x so that $z = z[y(x)]$. Then[2]

$$\frac{\partial z}{\partial x} = \frac{\partial y}{\partial x}\frac{\partial z}{\partial y}.$$

Proof of Lemma 4.1. The (ij)th element of the matrix $\partial z/\partial x$ is

$$\left(\frac{\partial z}{\partial x}\right)_{ij} = \frac{\partial z_j}{\partial x_i} = \sum_{k=1}^{r} \frac{\partial y_k}{\partial x_i}\frac{\partial z_j}{\partial y_k}$$

$$= \left(\frac{\partial y}{\partial x}\right)_{i\bullet}\left(\frac{\partial z}{\partial y}\right)_{\bullet j} = \left(\frac{\partial y}{\partial x}\frac{\partial z}{\partial x}\right)_{ij}.$$

Hence,

$$\frac{\partial z}{\partial x} = \frac{\partial y}{\partial x}\frac{\partial z}{\partial y}.$$ □

For our purposes it is useful to consider a generalization of the chain rule for matrix calculus for the case in which z is a vector function of two vectors. This generalization is given by the following lemma.

Lemma 4.2. Generalization of the Chain Rule. Let $z = (z_j)$ be an $m \times 1$ vector function of two vectors $u = (u_q)$ and $v = (u_p)$, which are $r \times 1$ and $s \times 1$, respectively. Suppose u and v are both vector functions of an $n \times 1$ vector $x = (x_i)$, so $z = z[u(x), v(x)]$. Then

$$\frac{\partial z}{\partial x} = \frac{\partial u}{\partial x}\frac{\partial z}{\partial u} + \frac{\partial v}{\partial x}\frac{\partial z}{\partial v}$$

$$= \left.\frac{\partial z}{\partial x}\right|_{v\text{ constant}} + \left.\frac{\partial z}{\partial x}\right|_{u\text{ constant}}.$$

[2] Note that the chain rule presented here is a backward one. If, however, one were to follow Magnus' notation then a forward chain rule could be obtained by

$$\frac{\partial z}{\partial x'} = \left(\frac{\partial z}{\partial x}\right)' = \left(\frac{\partial y}{\partial x}\frac{\partial z}{\partial y}\right)' = \frac{\partial z}{\partial y'}\frac{\partial y}{\partial x'}.$$

Proof of Lemma 4.2. The (ij)th element of the matrix $\partial z/\partial x$ is

$$\left(\frac{\partial z}{\partial x}\right)_{ij} = \frac{\partial z_j}{\partial x_i} = \sum_{q=1}^{r} \frac{\partial u_q}{\partial x_i}\frac{\partial z_j}{\partial u_q} + \sum_{p=1}^{s} \frac{\partial v_p}{\partial x_i}\frac{\partial z_j}{\partial v_p}$$

$$= \left(\frac{\partial u}{\partial r}\frac{\partial z}{\partial u}\right)_{ij} + \left(\frac{\partial v}{\partial x}\frac{\partial z}{\partial v}\right)_{ij}.$$

The result follows directly. □

Lemma 4.2 can be used to obtain a product rule for matrix calculus as presented in Lemma 4.3.

Lemma 4.3. Product Rule. Let X be an $m \times n$ matrix and let Y be an $n \times p$ matrix, and suppose that the elements of both matrices are scalar functions of a vector δ.

Then

$$\frac{\partial \operatorname{vec} XY}{\partial \delta} = \frac{\partial \operatorname{vec} X}{\partial \delta}(Y \otimes I_m) + \frac{\partial \operatorname{vec} Y}{\partial \delta}(I_p \otimes X').$$

Proof of Lemma 4.3. By Lemma 4.2, we have

$$\frac{\partial \operatorname{vec} XY}{\partial \delta} = \left.\frac{\partial \operatorname{vec} XY}{\partial \delta}\right|_{\substack{\operatorname{vec} Y\\ \text{constant}}} + \left.\frac{\partial \operatorname{vec} XY}{\partial \delta}\right|_{\substack{\operatorname{vec} X\\ \text{constant}}}$$

$$= \frac{\partial \operatorname{vec} X}{\partial \delta}\left.\frac{\partial \operatorname{vec} XY}{\partial \operatorname{vec} X}\right|_{\substack{\operatorname{vec} Y\\ \text{constant}}} + \frac{\partial \operatorname{vec} Y}{\partial \delta}\left.\frac{\partial \operatorname{vec} XY}{\partial \operatorname{vec} Y}\right|_{\substack{\operatorname{vec} X\\ \text{constant}}},$$

where the last equality follows from Lemma 4.1. We find that the result follows immediately by noting that $\operatorname{vec} XY = (Y' \otimes I_m)\operatorname{vec} X = (I_p \otimes X)\operatorname{vec} Y$, and by applying Theorem 4.1. □

Lemma 4.3 has the following useful corollary.

Corollary to Lemma 4.3. Let x be an $n \times 1$ vector, $f(x)$ be a scalar function of x, $u(x)$ and $v(x)$ be $m \times 1$ vector functions of x, and $A(x)$ and $B(x)$ be $p \times m$ and $m \times q$ matrices, respectively, whose elements are scalar functions of x. Then

$$\frac{\partial f(x)x}{\partial x} = f(x) \otimes I_n + \frac{\partial f(x)}{\partial x}x' = f(x)I_n + \frac{\partial f(x)}{\partial x}x',$$

$$\frac{\partial f(x)u(x)}{\partial x} = \frac{\partial u(x)}{\partial x}[f(x) \otimes I_m] + \frac{\partial f(x)}{\partial x}u(x)' = \frac{\partial u(x)}{\partial x}f(x) + \frac{\partial f(x)}{\partial x}u(x)',$$

$$\frac{\partial u(x)'v(x)}{\partial x} = \frac{\partial u(x)}{\partial x}v(x) + \frac{\partial v(x)}{\partial x}u(x),$$

$$\frac{\partial \operatorname{vec} u(x)v(x)'}{\partial x} = \frac{\partial u(x)}{\partial x}[v(x)' \otimes I_m] + \frac{\partial v(x)}{\partial x}[I_m \otimes u(x)'],$$

$$\frac{\partial A(x)\,u(x)}{\partial x} = \frac{\partial \operatorname{vec} A(x)}{\partial x}[u(x) \otimes I_p] + \frac{\partial u(x)}{\partial x}A(x)',$$

$$\frac{\partial \operatorname{vec} u(x)'B(x)}{\partial x} = \frac{\partial B(x)'u(x)}{\partial x} = \frac{\partial \operatorname{vec}[B(x)']}{\partial x}[u(x) \otimes I_q] + \frac{\partial u(x)}{\partial x}B(x).$$

Our definition, the simple results given in Theorem 4.1 and the lemmas representing generalization of the chain rule and product rule of ordinary calculus, allow us to derive derivatives for more complicated vector functions and scalar functions. These derivatives are represented as theorems under appropriate headings that make up the subsequent sections.

4.6. RULES FOR VECS OF MATRICES

Theorem 4.2. For a nonsingular $n \times n$ matrix X,

$$\frac{\partial \operatorname{vec} X^{-1}}{\partial \operatorname{vec} X} = -(X^{-1} \otimes X^{-1'}).$$

Proof of Theorem 4.2. Taking the vec of both sides of $XX^{-1} = I_n$, we have $\operatorname{vec} XX^{-1} = \operatorname{vec} I_n$.

Differentiating both sides with respect to vec X we have, by applying Lemma 4.3,

$$\frac{\partial \operatorname{vec} X}{\partial \operatorname{vec} X}(X^{-1} \otimes I_n) + \frac{\partial \operatorname{vec} X^{-1}}{\partial \operatorname{vec} X}(I_n \otimes X') = O.$$

Solving, we obtain

$$\frac{\partial \operatorname{vec} X^{-1}}{\partial \operatorname{vec} X} = -(X^{-1} \otimes I_n)(I_n \otimes X^{-1'}) = -(X^{-1} \otimes X^{-1'}). \qquad \square$$

Theorem 4.3. For A and B, $m \times n$ and $n \times p$ matrices of constants, respectively, and X, an $n \times n$ nonsingular matrix,

$$\frac{\partial \operatorname{vec} AX^{-1}B}{\partial \operatorname{vec} X} = -X^{-1}B \otimes X^{-1'}A'.$$

Proof of Theorem 4.3. From vec $AX^{-1}B = (B' \otimes A)\text{vec}\, X^{-1}$ we have, by using Lemma 4.1 and Theorem 4.2,

$$\frac{\partial \text{vec}\, AX^{-1}B}{\partial \text{vec}\, X} = \frac{\partial \text{vec}\, X^{-1}}{\partial \text{vec}\, X} \frac{\partial (B' \otimes A)\text{vec}\, X^{-1}}{\partial \text{vec}\, X^{-1}}$$
$$= -(X^{-1} \otimes X^{-1'})(B \otimes A')$$
$$= -X^{-1}B \otimes X^{-1'}A'.$$

□

The following results involve the commutation matrix K_{rr} and the matrix $N_r = \frac{1}{2}(I_{r^2} + K_{rr})$ and are derived for an $n \times r$ matrix X.

Theorem 4.4. Let A be an $n \times n$ matrix of constants. Then

$$\frac{\partial \text{vec}\, X'AX}{\partial \text{vec}\, X} = (I_r \otimes AX)K_{rr} + (I_r \otimes A'X).$$

Proof of Theorem 4.4. Applying Lemma 4.3, we have

$$\frac{\partial \text{vec}\, X'AX}{\partial \text{vec}\, X} = \frac{\partial \text{vec}\, X'}{\partial \text{vec}\, X}(AX \otimes I_r) + \frac{\partial \text{vec}\, AX}{\partial \text{vec}\, X}(I_r \otimes X).$$

However, as vec $AX = (I_r \otimes A)\text{vec}\, X$, by applying Theorem 4.1 we can write

$$\frac{\partial \text{vec}\, X'AX}{\partial \text{vec}\, X} = K_{nr}(AX \otimes I_r) + (I_r \otimes A'X).$$

However, from the properties of the commutative matrix, $K_{nr}(AX \otimes I_r) = (I_r \otimes AX)K_{rr}$.

□

Note that if A is the $n \times n$ identity matrix we have from the definition of N_r that

$$\frac{\partial \text{vec}\, X'X}{\partial \text{vec}\, X} = 2(I_r \otimes X)N_r.$$

Note also that if X is symmetric, then

$$\frac{\partial \text{vec}\, XAX}{\partial \text{vec}\, X} = (AX \otimes I_n) + (I_n \otimes A'X).$$

Theorem 4.5. Let B be an $r \times r$ matrix of constants. Then

$$\frac{\partial \text{vec}\, XBX'}{\partial \text{vec}\, X} = (BX' \otimes I_n) + (B'X' \otimes I_n)K_{nn}.$$

Proof of Theorem 4.5. Applying Lemma 4.3, we have

$$\frac{\partial \operatorname{vec} XBX'}{\partial \operatorname{vec} X} = \frac{\partial \operatorname{vec} X}{\partial \operatorname{vec} X}(BX' \otimes I_n) + \frac{\partial \operatorname{vec} BX'}{\partial \operatorname{vec} X}(I_n \otimes X').$$

However, from Eq. (4.2) we have

$$\frac{\partial \operatorname{vec} BX'}{\partial \operatorname{vec} X} = K_{rn}(I_n \otimes B'),$$

and hence

$$\begin{aligned}\frac{\partial \operatorname{vec} XBX'}{\partial \operatorname{vec} X} &= (BX' \otimes I_n) + K_{rn}(I_n \otimes B'X') \\ &= (BX' \otimes I_n) + (B'X' \otimes I_n)K_{nn}.\end{aligned}$$

□

Note that if B is the $r \times r$ identity matrix, we have

$$\frac{\partial \operatorname{vec} XX'}{\partial \operatorname{vec} X} = 2(X' \otimes I_n)N_n.$$

Theorem 4.6.

$$\frac{\partial \operatorname{vec}(X'X)^{-1}}{\partial \operatorname{vec} X} = -2[(X'X)^{-1} \otimes X(X'X)^{-1}]N_r.$$

Proof of Theorem 4.6. From Lemma 4.1,

$$\begin{aligned}\frac{\partial \operatorname{vec}(X'X)^{-1}}{\partial \operatorname{vec} X} &= \frac{\partial \operatorname{vec} X'X}{\partial \operatorname{vec} X}\frac{\partial \operatorname{vec}(X'X)^{-1}}{\partial \operatorname{vec} X'X} \\ &= -2(I_r \otimes X)N_r[(X'X)^{-1} \otimes (X'X)^{-1}].\end{aligned}$$

The result follows from the properties of N_r. □

Theorem 4.7.

$$\frac{\partial \operatorname{vec} X(X'X)^{-1}}{\partial \operatorname{vec} X} = [(X'X)^{-1} \otimes I_n] - 2[(X'X)^{-1} \otimes X(X'X)^{-1}]N_r(I_r \otimes X').$$

Proof of Theorem 4.7. Applying Lemma 4.3, we have

$$\frac{\partial \operatorname{vec} X(X'X)^{-1}}{\partial \operatorname{vec} X} = \frac{\partial \operatorname{vec} X}{\partial \operatorname{vec} X}[(X'X)^{-1} \otimes I_n] + \frac{\partial \operatorname{vec}(X'X)^{-1}}{\partial \operatorname{vec} X}(I_r \otimes X').$$

The result follows from Theorem 4.6. □

Note that by using the property that, for an $r \times r$ matrix A, $N_r(A \otimes A) = (A \otimes A)N_r = N_r(A \otimes A)N_r$, we can write

$$\begin{aligned}\frac{\partial \operatorname{vec} X(X'X)^{-1}}{\partial \operatorname{vec} X} &= [(X'X)^{-1} \otimes I_n] \\ &\quad - 2(I_r \otimes X)N_r[(X'X)^{-1} \otimes (X'X)^{-1}X'] \\ &= [(X'X)^{-1} \otimes I_n] \\ &\quad - 2(I_r \otimes X)N_r[(X'X)^{-1} \otimes (X'X)^{-1}]N_r(I_r \otimes X').\end{aligned}$$

Theorem 4.8.

$$\begin{aligned}\frac{\partial \operatorname{vec}(X'X)^{-1}X'}{\partial \operatorname{vec} X} &= K_{rn}[I_n \otimes (X'X)^{-1}] \\ &\quad - 2(I_r \otimes X)N_r[(X'X)^{-1}X' \otimes (X'X)^{-1}].\end{aligned}$$

Proof of Theorem 4.8. From Lemma 4.3,

$$\frac{\partial \operatorname{vec}(X'X)^{-1}X'}{\partial \operatorname{vec} X} = \frac{\partial \operatorname{vec}(X'X)^{-1}}{\partial \operatorname{vec} X}(X' \otimes I_r) + \frac{\partial \operatorname{vec} X'}{\partial \operatorname{vec} X}[I_n \otimes (X'X)^{-1}].$$

Applying Theorem 4.6 and Eq. (4.1), we can then write

$$\begin{aligned}\frac{\partial \operatorname{vec}(X'X)^{-1}X'}{\partial \operatorname{vec} X} &= -2(I_r \otimes X)N_r[(X'X)^{-1} \otimes (X'X)^{-1}](X' \otimes I_r) \\ &\quad + K_{rn}[I_n \otimes (X'X)^{-1}] \\ &= -2(I_r \otimes X)N_r[(X'X)^{-1}X' \otimes (X'X)^{-1}] \\ &\quad + K_{rn}[I_n \otimes (X'X)^{-1}].\end{aligned}$$ □

Again, we can obtain other expressions for this derivative by using the properties of the matrix N_r.

Theorem 4.9.

$$\frac{\partial \operatorname{vec} X(X'X)^{-1}X'}{\partial \operatorname{vec} X} = 2\{(X'X)^{-1}X' \otimes [I_n - X(X'X)^{-1}X']\}N_n.$$

Proof of Theorem 4.9. Applying Lemma 4.3, we write

$$\begin{aligned}\frac{\partial \operatorname{vec} X(X'X)^{-1}X'}{\partial \operatorname{vec} X} &= \frac{\partial \operatorname{vec} X(X'X)^{-1}}{\partial \operatorname{vec} X}(X' \otimes I_n) \\ &\quad + \frac{\partial \operatorname{vec} X'}{\partial \operatorname{vec} X}[I_n \otimes (X'X)^{-1}X'].\end{aligned} \tag{4.9}$$

From Theorem 4.7 and Eq. (4.1), we can write the right-hand side of Eq. (4.9) as

$$\{[(X'X)^{-1} \otimes I_n] - 2(I_r \otimes X)N_r[(X'X)^{-1} \otimes (X'X)^{-1}X']\}(X' \otimes I_n) + K_{rn}[I_n \otimes (X'X)^{-1}X'].$$

From the definition of N_r, we can rewrite this expression as

$$(X'X)^{-1}X' \otimes [I_n - X(X'X)^{-1}X'] - (I_r \otimes X)K_{rr}[(X'X)^{-1}X' \otimes (X'X)^{-1}X'] + K_{rn}[I_n \otimes (X'X)^{-1}X'].$$

However, by using the properties of the commutation matrix, we obtain

$$K_{rr}[(X'X)^{-1}X' \otimes (X'X)^{-1}X'] = [(X'X)^{-1}X' \otimes (X'X)^{-1}X']K_{nn},$$
$$K_{rn}[I_n \otimes (X'X)^{-1}X'] = [(X'X)^{-1}X' \otimes I_n]K_{nn},$$

and the result follows. □

The next two theorems involve the derivatives of vecs of Kronecker products and bring in the generalized devec of the commutation matrix.

Theorem 4.10. Let A be a $G \times s$ matrix of constants. Then

$$\frac{\partial \operatorname{vec}(X \otimes A)}{\partial \operatorname{vec} X} = I_r \otimes K_{Gn}^{\bar{\tau}_n}(A \otimes I_{nG}) = I_r \otimes (I_n \otimes a_1' \cdots I_n \otimes a_s'), \tag{4.10}$$

where a_j is the jth column of A.

Proof of Theorem 4.10. We write $\operatorname{vec}(X \otimes A) = \operatorname{vec}[(X \otimes I_G)(I_r \otimes A)] = (I_r \otimes A' \otimes I_{nG})\operatorname{vec}(X \otimes I_G)$, so by Theorem 4.1,

$$\frac{\partial \operatorname{vec}(X \otimes A)}{\partial \operatorname{vec} X} = \frac{\partial \operatorname{vec}(X \otimes I_G)}{\partial \operatorname{vec} X}(I_r \otimes A \otimes I_{nG}) = I_r \otimes K_{Gn}^{\bar{\tau}_n}(A \otimes I_{nG})$$

by Eq. (4.3). The last equality of Eq. (4.10) follows from Theorem 3.15 of Chap. 3. □

Theorem 4.11. Let A be a $G \times s$ matrix of constants. Then

$$\frac{\partial \operatorname{vec}(A \otimes X)}{\partial \operatorname{vec} X} = K_{sr}^{\bar{\tau}_r}(I_{sr} \otimes A') \otimes I_n = (I_r \otimes a_1' \cdots I_r \otimes a_s') \otimes I_n,$$

where a_j is the jth column of A.

Proof of Theorem 4.11. Write $\text{vec}(A \otimes X) = \text{vec}[(A \otimes I_n)(I_s \otimes X)] = (I_{sr} \otimes A \otimes I_n)\text{vec}(I_s \otimes X)$,
so, from Theorem 4.1,

$$\frac{\partial\,\text{vec}(A \otimes X)}{\partial\,\text{vec}\,X} = \frac{\partial\,\text{vec}(I_s \otimes X)}{\partial\,\text{vec}\,X}(I_{sr} \otimes A' \otimes I_n)$$
$$= K_{sr}^{\bar{\tau}_r}(I_{sr} \otimes A') \otimes I_n$$

by Eq. (4.4). Now

$$K_{sr}^{\bar{\tau}_r}(I_{sr} \otimes A') = \left(I_r \otimes e_1^{s'} \cdots I_r \otimes e_s^{s'}\right) \begin{bmatrix} I_r \otimes A' & & O \\ & \ddots & \\ O & & I_r \otimes A' \end{bmatrix}$$
$$= \left(I_r \otimes e_1^{s'} A' \cdots I_r \otimes e_s^{s'} A'\right)$$
$$= (I_r \otimes a_1' \cdots I_r \otimes a_s'). \qquad \square$$

Special cases of the last two theorems occur when X is an $n \times 1$ vector x. Then

$$\frac{\partial\,\text{vec}(x \otimes A)}{\partial x} = (I_n \otimes a_1' \cdots I_n \otimes a_s'),$$
$$\frac{\partial\,\text{vec}(A \otimes x)}{\partial x} = (a_1' \cdots a_s') \otimes I_n$$
$$= \text{devec}\,A' \otimes I_n,$$

which are generalizations of the results given by Eqs. (4.5) and (4.6).

4.7. RULES DEVELOPED FROM THE PROPERTIES OF K_{Gn}, $K_{Gn}^{\bar{\tau}_n}$, AND $K_{nG}^{\tau_n}$

Several derivatives can be derived by use of the properties of the commutation matrix and generalized vecs and devecs of commutation matrices, as the following theorems illustrate.

Theorem 4.12. Let x be an $n \times 1$ vector and let A be a $G \times n$ matrix of constants. Then

$$\frac{\partial (x \otimes I_G)Ax}{\partial x} = (I_n \otimes x'A') + A'(x' \otimes I_G).$$

Proof of Theorem 4.12. From the product rule, we have

$$\frac{\partial (x \otimes I_G)Ax}{\partial x} = \frac{\partial\,\text{vec}(x \otimes I_G)}{\partial x}(Ax \otimes I_{nG}) + \frac{\partial Ax}{\partial x}(x' \otimes I_G).$$
$$= K_{Gn}^{\bar{\tau}_n}(Ax \otimes I_{nG}) + A'(x' \otimes I_G)$$

from Eq. (4.5) and Theorem 4.1. However, by Theorem 2.8 of Chap. 2,

$$K_{Gn}^{\bar{\tau}_n}(Ax \otimes I_{nG}) = I_n \otimes x'A'. \qquad \square$$

Theorem 4.13. Let x be an $n \times 1$ vector and let A be a $G \times n$ matrix of constants. Then

$$\frac{\partial (I_G \otimes x)Ax}{\partial x} = (x'A' \otimes I_n) + A'(I_G \otimes x').$$

Proof of Theorem 4.13.

$$\begin{aligned}\frac{\partial (I_G \otimes x)Ax}{\partial x} &= \frac{\partial K_{Gn}(x \otimes I_G)Ax}{\partial x}\\ &= \frac{\partial (x \otimes I_G)Ax}{\partial x}K_{nG}.\end{aligned}$$

The result follows from Theorem 4.12 and the properties of the commutation matrix. $\square$

Theorem 4.14. Let x be an $n \times 1$ vector and let A be an $nG \times n$ matrix of constants. Then

$$\frac{\partial (I_G \otimes x')Ax}{\partial x} = (A^{\bar{\tau}_n} + A')(I_G \otimes x).$$

Proof of Theorem 4.14. From Theorem 3.8 of Chap. 3,

$$\begin{aligned}\frac{\partial (I_G \otimes x')Ax}{\partial x} &= \frac{\partial}{\partial x}K_{nG}^{\bar{\tau}_G}(x \otimes I_{nG})Ax\\ &= [(I_n \otimes x'A') + A'(x' \otimes I_{nG})]K_{Gn}^{\tau_G}\end{aligned}$$

from Theorems 4.12 and 4.1. However, from Theorem 3.8, $(x' \otimes I_{nG})K_{Gn}^{\tau_G} = I_G \otimes x$, and, from Theorem 3.10,

$$(I_n \otimes x'A')K_{Gn}^{\tau_G} = (Ax)^{\bar{\tau}_n} = A^{\bar{\tau}_n}(I_G \otimes x). \qquad \square$$

Theorem 4.15. Let x be an $n \times 1$ vector and let A be an $nG \times n$ matrix of constants. Then

$$\frac{\partial (x' \otimes I_G)Ax}{\partial x} = (I_n \otimes x')(A')^{\tau_G} + A'(x \otimes I_G).$$

Proof of Theorem 4.15. From Theorem 3.8,

$$\begin{aligned}\frac{\partial (x' \otimes I_G)Ax}{\partial x} &= \frac{\partial K_{nG}^{\bar{\tau}_G}}{\partial x}(I_{nG} \otimes x)Ax\\ &= [(x'A' \otimes I_n) + A'(I_{nG} \otimes x')]K_{Gn}^{\tau_G}\end{aligned}$$

from Theorems 4.13 and 4.14. From Theorem 3.8, $(I_{nG} \otimes x')K_{Gn}^{\tau_G} = x \otimes I_G$, and, from Theorem 3.11,

$$(x'A' \otimes I_n)K_{Gn}^{\tau_G} = (Ax)^{\bar{\tau}'_G} = (x'A')^{\tau_G} = (I_n \otimes x')(A')^{\tau_G}. \qquad \square$$

4.8. RULES FOR SCALAR FUNCTIONS OF A MATRIX

Suppose y is a scalar that is a differentiable function of the elements of an $n \times r$ matrix X. We say that y is a scalar function of the matrix X, and we write $y = y(X)$. Scalar functions that crop up a lot in the application of classical statistical procedures are traces and determinants, and derivatives for such functions are developed in the next two subsections.

4.8.1. Rules for Traces of Matrices

We can easily derive derivatives for scalar functions that are traces of matrices by using the result

$$\text{tr}\, AB = (\text{vec}\, A')'\text{vec}\, B$$

and then by applying the results we already obtained in Section 4.6 for vector functions that are vecs of matrices. In the next three theorems, we shall use the same notation as that we used previously and let X be an $n \times r$ matrix and A and B be $n \times n$ and $r \times r$ matrices of constants, respectively.

Theorem 4.16.

$$\frac{\partial\, \text{tr}\, AX}{\partial\, \text{vec}\, X} = \text{vec}\, A'.$$

Proof of Theorem 4.16. Write $\text{tr}\, AX = (\text{vec}\, A')'\text{vec}\, X$. Then the result follows from Theorem 4.1. $\square$

Theorem 4.17.

$$\frac{\partial\, \text{tr}\, X'AX}{\partial\, \text{vec}\, X} = \text{vec}(A'X + AX).$$

Proof of Theorem 4.17. We write $\text{tr}\, X'AX = \text{tr}\, AXX' = (\text{vec}\, A')'\text{vec}\, XX'$. Then, applying the chain rule given by Lemma 4.2, we obtain

$$\begin{aligned}\frac{\partial\, \text{tr}\, AXX'}{\partial\, \text{vec}\, X} &= \frac{\partial\, \text{vec}\, XX'}{\partial\, \text{vec}\, X}\text{vec}\, A' \\ &= [(X' \otimes I_n) + (X' \otimes I_n)K_{nn}]\text{vec}\, A'\end{aligned}$$

from Theorem 4.5. We find that the result follows by noting that $K_{nn}\, \text{vec}\, A' = \text{vec}\, A$. $\square$

Theorem 4.18.

$$\frac{\partial \operatorname{tr} XBX'A}{\partial \operatorname{vec} X} = \operatorname{vec}(AXB + A'XB')$$

Proof of Theorem 4.18. We write $\operatorname{tr} XBX'A = \operatorname{tr} BX'AX = (\operatorname{vec} B')'\operatorname{vec} X'AX$. Hence, by applying the chain rule, we obtain

$$\frac{\partial \operatorname{tr} XBX'A}{\partial \operatorname{vec} X} = \frac{\partial \operatorname{vec} X'AX}{\partial \operatorname{vec} X}\operatorname{vec} B'.$$

However, by Theorem 4.4, the right-hand side of the preceding equation can be written as

$$\begin{aligned}&[(I_r \otimes AX)K_{rr} + (I_r \otimes A'X)]\operatorname{vec} B'\\ &\quad = (I_r \otimes AX)\operatorname{vec} B + (I_r \otimes A'X)\operatorname{vec} B' = \operatorname{vec}(AXB + A'XB').\end{aligned}$$

□

4.8.2. Rules for Determinants of Matrices and Logs of Determinants

Again the results developed in Section 4.6 in conjunction with the chain rule allow us to obtain the derivatives of scalar functions that are determinants of matrices or logs of such determinants. However, before we follow such a procedure we prove the following theorem.

Theorem 4.19. Let X be a nonsingular $n \times n$ matrix and let $|X|$ denote the determinant of X. Then

$$\frac{\partial |X|}{\partial \operatorname{vec} X} = |X|\operatorname{vec}[(X^{-1})'].$$

Proof of Theorem 4.19. Expanding the determinant of X by using the jth column of X, we have $|X| = \sum_{i=1}^{n} c_{ij}x_{ij}$, where c_{ij} is the cofactor of the (ij)th element of X. If follows that $\partial|X|/\partial x_{ij} = c_{ij}$ and that the jth subvector of the column vector $\partial|X|/\operatorname{vec} X$ is

$$(c_{1j} \cdots c_{nj})' = (\text{adjoint } X')_{\bullet j}.$$

Hence,

$$\frac{\partial |X|}{\partial \operatorname{vec} X} = \operatorname{vec}[(\text{adjoint } X)'] = |X|\operatorname{vec}[(X^{-1})'].$$ □

Note that if $|X|$ is positive $\log |X|$ exists and the following result occurs directly from this theorem and the application of the chain rule:

$$\frac{\partial \log |X|}{\partial \operatorname{vec} X} = \operatorname{vec}(X^{-1'}).$$

With Theorem 4.19 and the results of Section 4.6 in hand, further derivatives for scalar functions that are determinants can easily be obtained, as the following theorems indicate.

Theorem 4.20. Let X be an $n \times r$ matrix, let A be an $n \times n$ matrix of constants, and suppose that $Y = X'AX$ is nonsingular. Then

$$\frac{\partial |Y|}{\partial \operatorname{vec} X} = |Y|[(Y^{-1'} \otimes A) + (Y^{-1} \otimes A')]\operatorname{vec} X.$$

Proof of Theorem 4.20. Applying the chain rule of Lemma 4.1, we have

$$\frac{\partial |Y|}{\partial \operatorname{vec} X} = \frac{\partial \operatorname{vec} Y}{\partial \operatorname{vec} X} \frac{\partial \operatorname{vec}|Y|}{\partial \operatorname{vec} Y},$$

so from Theorems 4.19 and 4.4, we have

$$\begin{aligned}\frac{\partial |Y|}{\partial \operatorname{vec} X} &= |Y|[(I_r \otimes AX)K_{rr} + (I_r \otimes A'X)]\operatorname{vec} Y^{-1'} \\ &= |Y|[(I_r \otimes AX)\operatorname{vec} Y^{-1} + (I_r \otimes A'X)\operatorname{vec} Y^{-1'}] \\ &= |Y|[\operatorname{vec} AXY^{-1} + \operatorname{vec} A'XY^{-1'}] \\ &= |Y|[(Y^{-1'} \otimes A) + (Y^{-1} \otimes A')]\operatorname{vec} X.\end{aligned}$$

□

Several obvious corollaries flow from this theorem. First, if A is the identity matrix, then

$$\frac{\partial |X'X|}{\partial \operatorname{vec} X} = 2|X'X|\operatorname{vec} X(X'X)^{-1},$$

provided, of course, that $X'X$ is nonsingular. Second, if $|Y|$ is positive so that $\log |Y|$ exists,

$$\frac{\partial \log |Y|}{\partial \operatorname{vec} X} = [(Y^{-1'} \otimes A) + (Y^{-1} \otimes A')]\operatorname{vec} X,$$

and if A is symmetric so Y is symmetric:

$$\frac{\partial \log |Y|}{\partial \operatorname{vec} X} = 2(Y^{-1} \otimes A)\operatorname{vec} X.$$

Third, suppose the elements of Y are themselves scalar functions of a $p \times 1$ vector δ . Then, by the chain rule,

$$\frac{\partial \log |Y|}{\partial \delta} = \frac{\partial \operatorname{vec} X}{\partial \delta}[(Y^{-1'} \otimes A) + (Y^{-1} \otimes A')]\operatorname{vec} X,$$

and, for symmetric A,

$$\frac{\partial \log |Y|}{\partial \delta} = 2\frac{\partial \operatorname{vec} X}{\partial \delta}(Y^{-1} \otimes A)\operatorname{vec} X.$$

Theorem 4.21. Let X be an $n \times r$ matrix, let B be an $r \times r$ matrix of constants, and suppose $Z = XBX'$ is nonsingular. Then

$$\frac{\partial |Z|}{\partial \operatorname{vec} X} = |Z|[(B \otimes Z^{-1'}) + (B' \otimes Z^{-1})]\operatorname{vec} X.$$

Proof of Theorem 4.21. This proof is similar to that of Theorem 4.20. □

Corollaries for this theorem corresponding to those derived for Theorem 4.20 are easily obtained; the details are left to the reader.

4.9. TABLES OF RESULTS

In this section, for easy reference, the results proved in this chapter are summarized in Tables 4.1–4.7.

Table 4.1. General Rules

Chain Rules

$$\frac{\partial z}{\partial x} = \frac{\partial y}{\partial x}\frac{\partial z}{\partial y}, \quad z = z[y(x)].$$

$$\frac{\partial z}{\partial x} = \frac{\partial u}{\partial x}\frac{\partial z}{\partial u} + \frac{\partial v}{\partial x}\frac{\partial z}{\partial v}, \quad z = z[u(x), v(x)].$$

Product Rule

$$\frac{\partial \operatorname{vec} XY}{\partial \delta} = \frac{\partial \operatorname{vec} X}{\partial \delta}(Y \otimes I_m) + \frac{\partial \operatorname{vec} Y}{\partial \delta}(I_p \otimes X'); \; X_{m \times n}, Y_{n \times p}.$$

Corollaries of Product Rule

$$\frac{\partial f(x)x}{\partial x} = f(x)I_n + \frac{\partial f(x)}{\partial x}x', \; f(x) \text{ is a scalar function of } n \times 1 \; x.$$

$$\frac{\partial f(x)u(x)}{\partial x} = \frac{\partial u(x)}{\partial x}f(x) + \frac{\partial f(x)}{\partial x}u(x)'; \; f(x) \text{ scalar function, } u(x) \text{ vector function.}$$

$$\frac{\partial u(x)'v(x)}{\partial x} = \frac{\partial u(x)}{\partial x}v(x) + \frac{\partial v(x)}{\partial x}u(x); \; u(x), v(x) \text{ vector functions.}$$

$$\frac{\partial \operatorname{vec} u(x)v(x)'}{\partial x} = \frac{\partial u(x)}{\partial x}[v(x)' \otimes I_m] + \frac{\partial v(x)}{\partial x}[I_m \otimes u(x)']; \; u(x), v(x) \, m \times 1 \text{ vector functions.}$$

$$\frac{\partial A(x)u(x)}{\partial x} = \frac{\partial \operatorname{vec} A(x)}{\partial x}[u(x) \otimes I_p] + \frac{\partial u(x)}{\partial x}A(x)'; \; u(x) \text{ vector function, } A(x) \; p \times m.$$

$$\frac{\partial \operatorname{vec} u(x)'B(x)}{\partial x} = \frac{\partial \operatorname{vec}[B(x)']}{\partial x}[u(x) \otimes I_q] + \frac{\partial u(x)}{\partial x}B(x); \; u(x) \text{ vector function, } B(x) \; m \times q.$$

Table 4.2. Simple Results

$$\frac{\partial Ax}{\partial x} = A'.$$

$$\frac{\partial x'A}{\partial x} = A.$$

$$\frac{\partial x'Ax}{\partial x} = (A + A')x.$$

$$\frac{\partial (x \otimes a)}{\partial x} = I_n \otimes a', \; x \text{ is an } n \times 1 \text{ vector.}$$

$$\frac{\partial (a \otimes x)}{\partial x} = a' \otimes I_n, \; x \text{ is an } n \times 1 \text{ vector.}$$

Table 4.3. Results for Vecs of Matrices

$$\frac{\partial \operatorname{vec} X'}{\partial \operatorname{vec} X} = K_{rn}.$$

$$\frac{\partial \operatorname{vec} X}{\partial \operatorname{vech} X} = D_n', \; X \text{ is a symmetric } n \times n \text{ matrix.}$$

$$\frac{\partial \operatorname{vec} AXB}{\partial \operatorname{vec} X} = B \otimes A'.$$

$$\frac{\partial \operatorname{vec} AX'B}{\partial \operatorname{vec} X} = K_{nr}(B \otimes A').$$

$$\frac{\partial \operatorname{vec}(X \otimes I_G)}{\partial \operatorname{vec} X} = I_r \otimes K_{Gn}^{\bar{\tau}_n}.$$

$$\frac{\partial \operatorname{vec}(I_G \otimes X)}{\partial \operatorname{vec} X} = K_{Gr}^{\bar{\tau}_r} \otimes I_n.$$

$$\frac{\partial \operatorname{vec}(x \otimes I_G)}{\partial x} = K_{Gn}^{\bar{\tau}_n}, \; x \text{ is an } n \times 1 \text{ vector.}$$

$$\frac{\partial \operatorname{vec}(I_G \otimes x)}{\partial x} = \operatorname{devec} I_G \otimes I_n, \; x \text{ is an } n \times 1 \text{ vector.}$$

$$\frac{\partial \operatorname{vec} X^{-1}}{\partial \operatorname{vec} X} = -(X^{-1} \otimes X^{-1'}), \; X \text{ is nonsingular.}$$

$$\frac{\partial \operatorname{vec} AX^{-1}B}{\partial \operatorname{vec} X} = -X^{-1}B \otimes X^{-1'}A', \; X \text{ is nonsingular.}$$

$$\frac{\partial \operatorname{vec} X'AX}{\partial \operatorname{vec} X} = (I_r \otimes AX)K_{rr} + (I_r \otimes A'X).$$

$$\frac{\partial \operatorname{vec} X'X}{\partial \operatorname{vec} X} = 2(I_r \otimes X)N_r.$$

$$\frac{\partial \operatorname{vec} XAX}{\partial \operatorname{vec} X} = (AX \otimes I_n) + (I_n \otimes A'X), \; X \text{ is a symmetric } n \times n \text{ matrix.}$$

$$\frac{\partial \operatorname{vec} XBX'}{\partial \operatorname{vec} X} = (BX' \otimes I_n) + (B'X' \otimes I_n)K_{nn}.$$

$$\frac{\partial \operatorname{vec} XX'}{\partial \operatorname{vec} X} = 2(X' \otimes I_n)N_n.$$

$$\frac{\partial \operatorname{vec}(X'X)^{-1}}{\partial \operatorname{vec} X} = -2[(X'X)^{-1} \otimes X(X'X)^{-1}]N_r.$$

$$\frac{\partial \operatorname{vec} X(X'X)^{-1}}{\partial \operatorname{vec} X} = [(X'X)^{-1} \otimes I_n] - 2[(X'X)^{-1} \otimes X(X'X)^{-1}]N_r(I_r \otimes X').$$

$$\frac{\partial \operatorname{vec}(X'X)^{-1}X'}{\partial \operatorname{vec} X} = K_{rn}[I_n \otimes (X'X)^{-1}] - 2(I_r \otimes X)N_r[(X'X)^{-1}X' \otimes (X'X)^{-1}].$$

$$\frac{\partial \operatorname{vec} X(X'X)^{-1}X'}{\partial \operatorname{vec} X} = 2\{(X'X)^{-1} \otimes [I_n - X(X'X)^{-1}X']\}N_n.$$

$$\frac{\partial \operatorname{vec}(X \otimes A)}{\partial \operatorname{vec} X} = I_r \otimes K_{Gn}^{\bar{\tau}_n}(A \otimes I_{nG}), \text{ } A \text{ is a } G \times s \text{ matrix.}$$

$$\frac{\partial \operatorname{vec}(A \otimes X)}{\partial \operatorname{vec} X} = K_{sr}^{\bar{\tau}_r}(I_{sr} \otimes A') \otimes I_n, \text{ } A \text{ is a } G \times s \text{ matrix.}$$

Note: Unless otherwise specified, X is an $n \times r$ matrix in these results.

Table 4.4. For x, an $n \times 1$ Vector

$$\frac{\partial(x \otimes I_G)Ax}{\partial x} = (I_n \otimes x'A') + A'(x' \otimes I_G), \text{ } A \text{ is a } G \times n \text{ matrix.}$$

$$\frac{\partial(I_G \otimes x)Ax}{\partial x} = (x'A' \otimes I_n) + A'(I_G \otimes x'), \text{ } A \text{ is a } Gn \times n \text{ matrix.}$$

$$\frac{\partial(I_G \otimes x')Ax}{\partial x} = (A^{\bar{\tau}_n} + A')(I_G \otimes x), \text{ } A \text{ is a } Gn \times n \text{ matrix.}$$

$$\frac{\partial(x' \otimes I_G)Ax}{\partial x} = (I_n \otimes x')(A')^{\tau_G} + A'(x \otimes I_G), \text{ } A \text{ is a } Gn \times n \text{ matrix.}$$

Table 4.5. Rules for Traces of Matrices

$$\frac{\partial \operatorname{tr} AX}{\partial \operatorname{vec} X} = \operatorname{vec} A'.$$

$$\frac{\partial \operatorname{tr} X'AX}{\partial \operatorname{vec} X} = \operatorname{vec}(A'X + AX).$$

$$\frac{\partial \operatorname{tr} XBX'A}{\partial \operatorname{vec} X} = \operatorname{vec}(AXB + A'XB').$$

Table 4.6. Rules for Determinants of Matrices

$$\frac{\partial|X|}{\partial \operatorname{vec} X} = |X|\operatorname{vec}[(X^{-1})'].$$

$$\frac{\partial|Y|}{\partial \operatorname{vec} X} = |Y|[(Y^{-1} \otimes A) + (Y^{-1} \otimes A')]\operatorname{vec} X \text{ for a nonsingular } Y = X'AX$$
$$= 2|Y|(Y^{-1} \otimes A)\operatorname{vec} X \text{ for symmetric } A.$$

$$\frac{\partial|Z|}{\partial \operatorname{vec} X} = |Z|[(B \otimes Z^{-1'}) + (B' \otimes Z^{-1})]\operatorname{vec} X \text{ for a nonsingular } Z = XBX'$$
$$= 2|Z|(B \otimes Z^{-1})\operatorname{vec} X \text{ for symmetric } B.$$

$$\frac{\partial|X'X|}{\partial \operatorname{vec} X} = 2|X'X|\operatorname{vec} X(X'X)^{-1}.$$

$$\frac{\partial|XX'|}{\partial \operatorname{vec} X} = 2|XX'|\operatorname{vec}(XX')^{-1}X.$$

Table 4.7. Rules for Logs

$$\frac{\partial \log|X|}{\partial \operatorname{vec} X} = \operatorname{vec}[(X^{-1})'].$$

$$\frac{\partial \log|Y|}{\partial \operatorname{vec} X} = [(Y^{-1'} \otimes A) + (Y^{-1} \otimes A')]\operatorname{vec} X \text{ for a nonsingular } Y = X'AX$$
$$= 2(Y^{-1} \otimes A)\operatorname{vec} X \text{ for symmetric } A.$$

$$\frac{\partial \log|Z|}{\partial \operatorname{vec} X} = [(B \otimes Z^{-1'}) + (B' \otimes Z^{-1})]\operatorname{vec} X \text{ for a nonsingular } Z = XBX'$$
$$= 2(B \otimes Z^{-1})\operatorname{vec} X \text{ for symmetric } B.$$

$$\frac{\partial \log|X'X|}{\partial \operatorname{vec} X} = 2 \operatorname{vec} X(X'X)^{-1}.$$

$$\frac{\partial \log|XX'|}{\partial \operatorname{vec} X} = 2 \operatorname{vec}(XX')^{-1}X.$$

5 Linear-Regression Models

5.1. INTRODUCTION

The linear-regression model is without doubt the best-known statistical model in both the material sciences and the social sciences. Because it is so well known, it provides us with a good starting place for the introduction of classical statistical procedures. Moreover, it furnishes an easy first application of matrix calculus that assuredly becomes more complicated in future models, and its inclusion ensures completeness in our sequence of statistical models.

The linear-regression model is modified in one way only to provide our basic model. Lagged values of the dependent variable will be allowed to appear on the right-hand side of the regression equation.

Far more worthy candidates of the mathematical tools presented in the preceding chapters are variations of the basic model that we achieve by allowing the disturbances to be correlated, forming either an autoregressive system or a moving-average system. These modifications greatly increase the complexity of the model. Lagged values of the dependent variable appearing among the independent variables when coupled with correlated disturbances make the asymptotic theory associated with the application of classical statistical procedures far more difficult. The same combination also makes the differentiation required in this application more difficult.

Our work then with these two variations of the basic linear-regression model require applications of the results and concepts discussed in the first four chapters. Particularly useful in this context will be the properties of shifting matrices and generalized vec operators discussed in Sections 3.7 and 2.4, respectively.

For notational convenience we drop the n from the generalized vec operator τ_n, so throughout this chapter S^{τ} will stand for S^{τ_n}, the generalized vec$_n$ of the matrix S. The asymptotic theory required in the evaluation of the information matrices is reserved for appendices at the end of the chapter in which the appropriate assumptions regarding the existence of various probability limits associated with the model are made.

5.2. THE BASIC LINEAR-REGRESSION MODEL

5.2.1. Assumptions of the Model

Consider the linear-regression model represented by the equation

$$y_t = \sum_{k=1}^{K} X_{tk}\beta_k + u_t, \quad t = 1, \ldots, n,$$

where we allow the possibility that some of the regressors X_k represent lagged values of the dependent variable y. In matrix notation we write this equation as

$$y = X\beta + u,$$

where y is the $n \times 1$ vector $y = (y_t)$, X is the $n \times K$ matrix $X = \{X_{tk}\}$, β is the $K \times 1$ vector $\beta = (\beta_k)$, and u is the $n \times 1$ vector $u = (u_t)$. We make the usual assumptions: The disturbances u_t are independently, identically normally distributed random variables with mean zero and variance σ^2 so $u \sim N(0, \sigma^2 I_n)$, $r(X) = K$ so $(X'X)^{-1}$ exists, and the variables in X that are not lagged dependent variables are constants. Additionally we assume that $p\lim X'X/n$ exists and is a positive-definite matrix and that there are no unit root problems. The last assumptions can be written more formally. Let y_{-j} be the $n \times 1$ vector whose elements are those of y except lagged j periods. Suppose $y_{-1}, \ldots, y_{-g}$ form the first g variables that go to make up the matrix X. Then we require that all the g roots of the polynominal equation

$$z^g - \beta_1 z^{g-1} - \cdots - \beta_g = 0$$

have absolute values of less than one.

We now wish to obtain the basic building blocks of classical statistical procedures, namely, the log-likelihood function, the score vector, the information matrix, and the Cramer–Rao lower bound.

5.2.2. The Log-Likelihood Function and the Score Vector

The parameters of our model are given by the $(K+1) \times 1$ vector $\theta = (\beta' \; \sigma^2)'$. The log-likelihood function, apart from a constant, is

$$l(\theta) = -\frac{n}{2}\log \sigma^2 - \frac{1}{2\sigma^2}u'u,$$

where in this function u is set equal to $y - X\beta$.

Obtaining the first component of the score vector, $\partial l/\partial\beta$, involves us in our first application of matrix calculus. By the chain rule

$$\frac{\partial u'u}{\partial \beta} = \frac{\partial u}{\partial \beta}\frac{\partial u'u}{\partial u} = -2X'u,$$

so

$$\frac{\partial l}{\partial \beta} = X'u/\sigma^2. \tag{5.1}$$

Clearly

$$\frac{\partial l}{\partial \sigma^2} = -\frac{n}{2\sigma^2} + \frac{u'u}{2\sigma^4}. \tag{5.2}$$

5.2.3. The Hessian Matrix, the Information Matrix, and the Cramer–Rao Lower Bound

The components of this matrix are easily obtained from Eqs. (5.1) and (5.2). They are

$$\frac{\partial^2 l}{\partial \beta \partial \beta'} = -\frac{X'X}{\sigma^2},$$
$$\frac{\partial^2 l}{\partial \beta \partial \sigma^2} = -\frac{X'u}{\sigma^4},$$
$$\frac{\partial^2 l}{\partial \sigma^{2^2}} = \frac{n}{2\sigma^4} - \frac{u'u}{\sigma^6}.$$

With standard asymptotic theory, $p \lim X'u/n = 0$ and $p \lim u'u/n = \sigma^2$, so the information matrix is

$$I(\theta) = p \lim \frac{1}{n\sigma^2} \begin{bmatrix} X'X & 0 \\ 0' & \dfrac{n}{2\sigma^2} \end{bmatrix},$$

and inverting this matrix gives the Cramer–Rao lower bound,

$$I^{-1}(\theta) = \sigma^2 p \lim n \begin{bmatrix} (X'X)^{-1} & 0 \\ 0' & \dfrac{2\sigma^2}{n} \end{bmatrix}.$$

5.2.4. Maximum-Likelihood Estimators

Equating $\partial l/\partial \beta$ to the null vector and $\partial l/\partial \sigma^2$ to zero gives the MLEs of θ:

$$\tilde{\beta} = (X'X)^{-1}X'y,$$
$$\tilde{\sigma}^2 = \tilde{u}'\tilde{u}/n.$$

The MLE of β is the ordinary-least-squares (OLS) estimator. This estimator is consistent and asymptotically efficient, so

$$\sqrt{n}(\tilde{\beta} - \beta) \xrightarrow{d} N(0, I^{\beta\beta}),$$

where, from the Cramer–Rao lower bound $I^{-1}(\theta)$,

$$I^{\beta\beta} = \sigma^2(p \lim X'X/n)^{-1}.$$

This, by the way, is the only occasion on which we can actually obtain an algebraic expression for the MLE of the parameters of primary interest. In future models, we shall have to be content with an iterative interpretation of the MLE we obtain by setting the score vector equal to the null vector.

5.3. THE LINEAR-REGRESSION MODEL WITH AUTOREGRESSIVE DISTURBANCES

5.3.1. The Model, the Matrix $M(\alpha)$ and the Log-Likelihood Function

Consider the linear-regression equation

$$y_t = \sum_{k=1}^{K} X_{tk}\beta_k + u_t, \quad t = 1, \dots, n,$$

where, as in Section 5.2, we allow the possibility that some of the regressors X_k represent lagged values of the dependent variable y. We also assume that the disturbances are subject to an autoregressive system of the order of p so

$$u_t + \alpha_1 u_{t-1} + \cdots + \alpha_p u_{t-p} = \varepsilon_t, \quad t = 1, \dots, n,$$

where $p < n$. The ε_ts are assumed to be independently, identically normally distributed random variables with mean zero and covariance σ^2. We assume that there are no unit roots problems.

In matrix notation, we write the autoregressive process as

$$u + \alpha_1 u_{-1} + \cdots + \alpha_p u_{-p} = \varepsilon,$$

where

$$u = \begin{pmatrix} u_1 \\ \vdots \\ u_n \end{pmatrix}, \quad \varepsilon = \begin{pmatrix} \varepsilon_1 \\ \vdots \\ \varepsilon_n \end{pmatrix}, \quad u_{-j} = \begin{pmatrix} u_{-j+1} \\ \vdots \\ u_0 \\ u_1 \\ \vdots \\ u_{n-j} \end{pmatrix}.$$

As far as our asymptotic theory is concerned, all presample values may be replaced with zeros without affecting our asymptotic results. We saw in

Subsection 3.7.6 that if we do this at the start of our analysis we can write

$$u_{-j} = \begin{pmatrix} 0 \\ \vdots \\ 0 \\ u_1 \\ \vdots \\ u_{n-j} \end{pmatrix} = S_j u,$$

where S_j is the shifting matrix

$$S_j = \begin{matrix} \\ j\left\{ \begin{matrix} \\ \\ \\ \end{matrix} \right. \\ \\ \\ \\ \end{matrix} \begin{bmatrix} 0 & & & & & \\ \vdots & \ddots & & O & & \\ 0 & & \ddots & & & \\ 1 & \ddots & & \ddots & & \\ & \ddots & \ddots & & \ddots & \\ O & & 1 & 0 & \dots & 0 \end{bmatrix},$$

and we can write the autoregressive process as

$$u + \alpha_1 S_1 u + \cdots + \alpha_p S_p u = \varepsilon,$$

or

$$u + U_p \alpha = \varepsilon,$$

where α is the $p \times 1$ vector $(\alpha_1 \cdots \alpha_p)'$,

$$U_p = (S_1 u \cdots S_p u) = S(I_p \otimes u), \tag{5.3}$$

and S is the $n \times np$ matrix $S = (S_1 \cdots S_p)$.

Considering

$$S(I_p \otimes u)\alpha = S \operatorname{vec} u\alpha' = S(\alpha \otimes I_n)u,$$

we can write the autoregressive process as

$$M(\alpha)u = \varepsilon, \tag{5.4}$$

where

$$M(\alpha) = I_n + S(\alpha \otimes I_n). \tag{5.5}$$

From case 1 in Subsection 3.7.5,

$$M(\alpha) = \begin{bmatrix} 1 & & & & & \\ \alpha_1 & \ddots & & & O & \\ \vdots & \ddots & \ddots & & & \\ \alpha_p & & \ddots & \ddots & & \\ & \ddots & & \ddots & \ddots & \\ O & & \alpha_p & \cdots & \alpha_1 & 1 \end{bmatrix}. \tag{5.6}$$

[1]

By using Theorem 3.24 we can write

$$M(\alpha) = I_n + \bar{S}(I_n \otimes \mathcal{S}\alpha),$$

where $\bar{S} = (I_n \; S_1 \cdots S_{n-1})$ and $\mathcal{S}$ is the selection matrix $(e_2^n \cdots e_{p+1}^n)$. Clearly

$$\text{vec}\, \bar{S}(I_n \otimes \mathcal{S}\alpha) = \bar{S}^{\tau} \mathcal{S}\alpha,$$

and

$$\text{vec}\, M(\alpha) = \text{vec}\, I_n + \bar{S}^{\tau} \mathcal{S}\alpha. \tag{5.7}$$

Therefore, by replacing presample values with zeros, we can write our model succinctly in matrix notation as

$$y = X\beta + u,$$
$$M(\alpha)u = \varepsilon,$$
$$\varepsilon \sim N(0, \sigma^2 I),$$

where $M(\alpha)$ is the matrix given by Eqs. (5.5) and (5.6). The parameters of our model are $\theta = (\beta' \; \alpha' \; \sigma^2)'$, and the log-likelihood function (apart from a constant) is

$$l(\theta) = -\frac{n}{2}\log \sigma^2 - \frac{1}{2\sigma^2}\varepsilon'\varepsilon,$$

where in this function ε is set equal to $M(\alpha)(y - X\beta)$. In applying matrix calculus to help us work out the derivatives of this function, we need $\partial\varepsilon/\partial\alpha$ and $\partial\,\text{vec}\, M(\alpha)/\partial\alpha$. Both these expressions can be written simply in terms of our shifting matrices. Clearly

$$\varepsilon = u + S(\alpha \otimes I_n)u = u + S\,\text{vec}\, u\alpha' = u + S(I_p \otimes u)\alpha,$$

[1] The matrix $M(\alpha)$ was originally used by Phillips (1966) and appears in the works of other authors such as Pagan (1974) and Godfrey (1978a).

so

$$\frac{\partial \varepsilon}{\partial \alpha} = (I_p \otimes u')S' = U_p'. \tag{5.8}$$

From Eq. (5.7), we see that

$$\frac{\partial \operatorname{vec} M(\alpha)}{\partial \alpha} = \mathcal{S}'\bar{\mathcal{S}}^{\tau'}. \tag{5.9}$$

5.3.2. The Score Vector $\partial l/\partial \theta$ and the Hessian Matrix $\partial^2 l/\partial \theta \partial \theta'$

If we use the derivatives given by Eqs. (5.8) and (5.9) it is a simple matter to obtain the score vector of our model. The components of this vector are as follows:

$$\frac{\partial l}{\partial \beta} = X'M(\alpha)'\varepsilon/\sigma^2, \tag{5.10}$$

$$\frac{\partial l}{\partial \alpha} = -(I_p \otimes u')S'\varepsilon/\sigma^2 = -U_p'\varepsilon/\sigma^2, \tag{5.11}$$

$$\frac{\partial l}{\partial \sigma^2} = -n/2\sigma^2 + \varepsilon'\varepsilon/2\sigma^4. \tag{5.12}$$

In a similar manner, certain components of the Hessian matrix are easily obtained with Eqs. (5.8) and (5.9). They are

$$\frac{\partial^2 l}{\partial \beta \partial \beta'} = -X'M(\alpha)'M(\alpha)X/\sigma^2,$$

$$\frac{\partial^2 l}{\partial \beta \partial \sigma^2} = -X'M(\alpha)'\varepsilon/\sigma^4 = \left(\frac{\partial^2 l}{\partial \sigma^2 \partial \beta'}\right)',$$

$$\frac{\partial^2 l}{\partial \alpha \partial \sigma^2} = (I_p \otimes u')S'\varepsilon/\sigma^4 = \left(\frac{\partial^2 l}{\partial \sigma^2 \partial \alpha'}\right)',$$

$$\frac{\partial^2 l}{\partial \alpha \partial \alpha'} = -(I_p \otimes u')S'S(I_p \otimes u)/\sigma^2 = -U_p'U_p/\sigma^2,$$

$$\frac{\partial^2 l}{\partial \sigma^{2^2}} = n/2\sigma^4 - \varepsilon'\varepsilon/\sigma^6.$$

The remaining derivative, namely $\partial^2 l/\partial \beta \partial \alpha'$, requires a bit more work. From

Eq. (5.10) we can write

$$\frac{\partial l}{\partial \beta} = X'M(\alpha)'M(\alpha)u/\sigma^2 = (u' \otimes X')\operatorname{vec} M(\alpha)'M(\alpha)/\sigma^2.$$

Now, using the backward chain rule, we have

$$\begin{aligned}\frac{\partial \operatorname{vec} M(\alpha)'M(\alpha)}{\partial \alpha} &= \frac{\partial \operatorname{vec} M(\alpha)}{\partial \alpha}\frac{\partial \operatorname{vec} M(\alpha)'M(\alpha)}{\partial \operatorname{vec} M(\alpha)} \\ &= 2S'\bar{S}^{\tau'}[I_n \otimes M(\alpha)]N_n,\end{aligned}$$

where $N_n = \frac{1}{2}(I_{n^2} + K_{nn})$ and K_{nn} is a commutation matrix. It follows that

$$\begin{aligned}\frac{\partial X'M(\alpha)'M(\alpha)u}{\partial \alpha} &= 2S'\bar{S}^{\tau'}[I_n \otimes M(\alpha)]N_n(u \otimes X) \\ &= S'\bar{S}^{\tau'}[I_n \otimes M(\alpha)][(X \otimes u) + (u \otimes X)] \\ &= S'\bar{S}^{\tau'}\{(X \otimes \varepsilon) + [u \otimes M(\alpha)X]\} \\ &= S'\bar{S}^{\tau'}[(I_n \otimes \varepsilon) + (u \otimes I_n)M(\alpha)]X.\end{aligned}$$

However, from Theorem 3.24 we have

$$\begin{aligned}&S'\bar{S}^{\tau'}(I_n \otimes \varepsilon) = (I_p \otimes \varepsilon')S^{\tau}, \\ &S'\bar{S}^{\tau'}(u \otimes I_n) = [S(I_p \otimes u)]' = U_p'.\end{aligned}$$

If follows then that

$$\frac{\partial^2 l}{\partial \beta \partial \alpha'} = \frac{1}{\sigma^2}[X'S^{\tau'}(I_p \otimes \varepsilon) + X'M(\alpha)'U_p] = \left(\frac{\partial^2 l}{\partial \alpha \partial \beta'}\right)'.$$

5.3.3. The Information Matrix $I(\theta) = -p \lim \frac{1}{n}\frac{\partial^2 l}{\partial \theta \partial \theta'}$

The probability limits required for forming this matrix are worked out in Appendix 5.A. By using these limits we can write the information matrix as

$$I(\theta) = p \lim \frac{1}{n\sigma^2}\begin{bmatrix} \bar{X}'\bar{X} & -\bar{X}'U_p & O \\ -U_p'\bar{X} & U_p'U_p & O \\ 0' & 0' & \frac{n}{2\sigma^2}\end{bmatrix}, \tag{5.13}$$

where $\bar{X} = M(\alpha)X$. For the special case in which X is exogenous and contains no lagged dependent variables, the information matrix simplifies

$$I(\theta) = p\lim \frac{1}{n\sigma^2} \begin{bmatrix} \bar{X}'\bar{X} & O & 0 \\ O & U_p'U_p & 0 \\ 0' & 0' & \dfrac{n}{2\sigma^2} \end{bmatrix}. \tag{5.14}$$

5.3.4. The Cramer–Rao Lower Bound $I^{-1}(\theta)$

Inverting the information matrix is straightforward. We obtain

$$I^{-1}(\theta) = \sigma^2 p\lim n \begin{bmatrix} (\bar{X}'M_p\bar{X})^{-1} & (\bar{X}'M_p\bar{X})^{-1}\bar{X}'U_p(U_p'U_p)^{-1} & 0 \\ (U_p'U_p)^{-1}U_p'\bar{X}(\bar{X}'M_p\bar{X})^{-1} & (U_p'\bar{M}U_p)^{-1} & 0 \\ 0' & 0' & \dfrac{2\sigma^2}{n} \end{bmatrix}, \tag{5.15}$$

for the general case, in which

$$M_p = I_n - U_p(U_p'U_p)^{-1}U_p', \quad \bar{M} = I_n - \bar{X}(\bar{X}'\bar{X})^{-1}\bar{X}',$$

and

$$I^{-1}(\theta) = \sigma^2 p\lim n \begin{bmatrix} (\bar{X}'\bar{X})^{-1} & O & 0 \\ O & (U_p'U_p)^{-1} & 0 \\ 0' & 0' & \dfrac{2\sigma^2}{n} \end{bmatrix} \tag{5.16}$$

for the case in which X is exogenous.

5.3.5. Statistical Inference from the Score Vector and the Information Matrix

We have seen in the preceding subsections how the use of shifting matrices and matrix calculus greatly facilitates the obtaining of the score vector and information matrix of our model. With these matrices in hand, we can easily derive statistical results from them. These results, most of which are well known, are listed in this section.

5.3.5.1. Maximum-Likelihood Estimators as Iterative Generalized-Least-Squares Estimators

Using the score vector given by Eqs. (5.10)–(5.12), we can obtain an interpretation of the MLE of β as an iterative generalized-least-squares (GLS) estimator for the model with autoregressive disturbances. Returning to the score vector, we see that

$$\partial l/\partial\sigma^2 = 0 \text{ gives } \tilde{\sigma}^2 = \tilde{\varepsilon}'\tilde{\varepsilon}/n = \tilde{u}'M(\tilde{\alpha})'M(\tilde{\alpha})\tilde{u}/n,$$

and

$$\partial l/\partial\beta = 0 \text{ gives } X'M(\alpha)'M(\alpha)(y - X\beta) = 0,$$

which yields

$$\tilde{\beta} = [X'M(\tilde{\alpha})'M(\tilde{\alpha})X]^{-1}X'M(\tilde{\alpha})'M(\tilde{\alpha})y.$$

Finally,

$$\partial l/\partial\alpha = 0 \text{ gives } U_p'\varepsilon = 0,$$

but

$$\begin{aligned} U_p'\varepsilon &= U_p' \operatorname{vec} M(\alpha)u = U_p'(u' \otimes I_n) \operatorname{vec} M(\alpha) \\ &= U_p'(u' \otimes I_n)(\operatorname{vec} I_n + \bar{S}^\tau S\alpha). \end{aligned}$$

Now

$$U_p'(u' \otimes I_n) \operatorname{vec} I_n = U_p'u,$$

and, by using Theorem 3.24, we obtain

$$U_p'(u' \otimes I_n)\bar{S}^\tau S\alpha = U_p'S(I_p \otimes u)\alpha = U_p'U_p\alpha.$$

Therefore,

$$\partial l/\partial\alpha = 0$$

gives rise to the equations

$$\begin{aligned} &-U_p'U_p\alpha = U_p'u, \\ &\tilde{\alpha} = -(\tilde{U}_p'\tilde{U}_p)^{-1}\tilde{U}_p'\tilde{u}. \end{aligned}$$

Clearly the solution we have obtained for the MLEs is iterative as $\tilde{\alpha}$ still contains $\tilde{\beta}$ through U_p and $\tilde{\beta}$ clearly contains $\tilde{\alpha}$.

5.3.5.2. Asymptotic Efficiency

Suppose α was known. Then from Eq. (5.13) the information matrix would be

$$I\begin{pmatrix}\beta \\ \sigma^2\end{pmatrix} = p\lim \frac{1}{n\sigma^2}\begin{bmatrix} \bar{X}'\bar{X} & 0 \\ 0' & \dfrac{n}{2\sigma^2} \end{bmatrix}$$

and the asymptotic Cramer–Rao lower bound for a consistent estimator of β would be $p\lim \sigma^2(\bar{X}'\bar{X}/n)^{-1}$. The GLS estimator $\bar{\beta} = (\bar{X}'\bar{X})^{-1}\bar{X}'\bar{y}$ would, for example, obtain this bound. From Eq. (5.14) it is clear that, even if α is unknown, provided that X is exogenous and does not contain lagged values of the dependent variable, the Cramer–Rao lower bound for a consistent estimator of β is still $p\lim \sigma^2(\bar{X}'\bar{X}/n)^{-1}$. The GLS estimator

$$\tilde{\tilde{\beta}} = (\hat{\hat{X}}'\hat{\hat{X}})^{-1}\hat{\hat{X}}'\hat{\hat{y}},$$

where $\hat{\hat{X}} = M(\hat{\alpha})X$, $\hat{\hat{y}} = M(\hat{\alpha})y$, and $\hat{\alpha}$ is a consistent estimator of α, for this special case would be as efficient asymptotically as $\tilde{\beta}$. However, from Eq. (5.15) it is clear that, if X contains lagged values of y, the Cramer–Rao lower bound for a consistent estimator of β is now $\sigma^2\ p\lim(\bar{X}'M_p\bar{X}/n)^{-1}$. The GLS estimator $\tilde{\tilde{\beta}}$ still attains this bound so it is still asymptotically efficient but is less efficient than $\tilde{\beta}$.

5.3.5.3. Classical Tests for the Null Hypothesis $H_0: \alpha = 0$

LAGRANGIAN MULTIPLIER TEST STATISTIC FOR $H_0: \alpha = 0$. We wish to obtain the Lagrangian multiplier test (LMT) statistic for the null hypothesis $H_0: \alpha = 0$ against the alternative $H_A: \alpha \neq 0$. Recall from Chap. 1 that the LMT statistic can be written as

$$T_1 = \frac{1}{n}\left.\frac{\partial l}{\partial \alpha}\right|_{\hat{\theta}}' \quad I^{\alpha\alpha}(\hat{\theta})\left.\frac{\partial l}{\partial \alpha}\right|_{\hat{\theta}},$$

where $I^{\alpha\alpha}$ refers to that part of the Cramer–Rao lower bound corresponding to α and $\hat{\theta}$ refers to the constrained MLE of θ; that is, in forming $\hat{\theta}$, we set α equal to 0 and β and σ^2 equal to $\hat{\beta}$ and $\hat{\sigma}^2$, the constrained MLEs of β and σ^2 obtained after we impose $H_0: \alpha = 0$ on our model. However, with $\alpha = 0$, and $y = X\beta + \varepsilon$, $\varepsilon \sim N(0, \sigma^2 I)$, so we are confronted with the linear-regression model with the sole modification that X may contain lagged values of y. It follows that the constrained MLEs are the OLS estimators $\hat{\beta} = (X'X)^{-1}X'y$, and $\hat{\sigma}^2 = y'My/n$, where $M = I_n - X(X'X)^{-1}X'$. Finally, under H_0, u equates to ε so

$$\left.\frac{\partial l}{\partial \alpha}\right|_{\hat{\theta}} = -\hat{U}'_p\hat{u}/\hat{\sigma}^2,$$

where $\hat{U}_p$ is formed from the elements of OLS residual vector $\hat{u} = My$. We are now in a position to form the LMT statistic. We do this for both the case in which X is exogenous and for the more general case in which X contains lagged values of the dependent variable y.

First, when X is exogenous, we have seen that

$$I^{\alpha\alpha} = \sigma^2(p\lim U'_pU_p/n)^{-1},$$

so if we ignore the probability limit,

$$I^{\alpha\alpha}(\hat{\theta}) = \hat{\sigma}^2(\hat{U}'_p\hat{U}_p/n)^{-1}.$$

The LMT statistic for this special case would be

$$T_1' = \hat{u}'\hat{U}_p(\hat{U}_p'\hat{U}_p')^{-1}\hat{U}_p'\hat{u}/\hat{\sigma}^2.$$

Clearly T_1' is the ratio of the explained variation to the unexplained variation of a regression of $\hat{u}$ on $\hat{U}_p$. Under H_0, T_1' asymptotically has a χ^2 distribution with p degrees of freedom, and the upper tail of this distribution would be used to find the appropriate critical region.

Second, with X containing lagged values of y, we have seen that $I^{\alpha\alpha}$ is more complicated. Now it is given by

$$I^{\alpha\alpha} = \sigma^2(p \lim U_p' \bar{M} U_p/n)^{-1}.$$

Under H_0, $\bar{X} = X$ and $\bar{M} = M$, so again we ignore the probability limit

$$I^{\alpha\alpha}(\hat{\theta}) = \hat{\sigma}^2(\hat{U}_p' M \hat{U}_p/n)^{-1},$$

and the LMT statistic now becomes

$$T_1 = \hat{u}'\hat{U}_p(\hat{U}_p' M \hat{U}_p)^{-1}\hat{U}_p'\hat{u}/\hat{\sigma}^2.$$

This test statistic was first obtained by Godfrey (1978a), and, under H_0, T_1 asymptotically has a χ^2 distribution with p degrees of freedom. Godfrey shows that this test statistic is asymptotically equivalent to p times the usual F test statistic one would form for the null hypothesis in the regression

$$y = X\beta - \hat{U}_p\alpha + \eta,$$

the only difference in the two test statistics being the consistent estimator used for σ^2.

Wald test statistic for $H_0\colon \alpha = 0$. As in the first part of this subsection, let $\tilde{\theta} = (\tilde{\beta}' \; \tilde{\alpha}' \; \tilde{\sigma}^2)'$ be the MLE of θ. By using these estimators, we could form $M(\tilde{\alpha})$, $\tilde{\bar{X}} = M(\tilde{\alpha})X$, $\tilde{\bar{M}} = I_n - \tilde{\bar{X}}(\tilde{\bar{X}}'\tilde{\bar{X}})^{-1}\tilde{\bar{X}}'$, $\tilde{u} = y - X\tilde{\beta}$, and $\tilde{U}_p$. The Wald test statistic would be

$$T_2' = \tilde{\alpha}'\tilde{U}_p'\tilde{U}_p\tilde{\alpha}/\tilde{\sigma}^2 \tag{5.17}$$

for the case in which X is exogenous and

$$T_2 = \tilde{\alpha}'\tilde{U}_p'\tilde{\bar{M}}\tilde{U}_p\tilde{\alpha}/\tilde{\sigma}^2 \tag{5.18}$$

for the more general case in which X contains lagged values of y. The difficulty with these test statistics is in obtaining an algebraic expression for the MLE $\tilde{\theta}$. We find the MLE $\tilde{\theta}$ by solving the system of equations $\partial l/\partial\theta = 0$ for θ, but a casual glance at the score vector shows that this system of equations is highly nonlinear. However, these days, numerical techniques with the aid of fast computers should ensure that we can come up with the maximum-likelihood estimates of θ and thus the observed value of the Wald test statistics T_2' and T_2.

We can then determine whether the observed values fall in the appropriate critical region and act accordingly.

This being said, it is still possible for comparison purposes to get some insights into the Wald test statistics by use of the iterative solution for $\tilde{\alpha}$ obtained in Subsection 5.3.5.1, namely

$$\tilde{\alpha} = -(\tilde{U}'_p\tilde{U}_p)^{-1}\tilde{U}'_p\tilde{u}.$$

Substituting this iterative solution into Eq. (5.17), we get

$$T_2' \equiv \tilde{u}'\tilde{U}_p(\tilde{U}'_p\tilde{U}_p)^{-1}\tilde{U}'_p\tilde{u}/\tilde{\sigma}^2,$$

where the symbol $\equiv$ stands for "is asymptotically equivalent to." Comparing T_2' with T_1', we see that the test statistic T_2' essentially has the same format as that of the LMT statistic T_1', the difference being that the former works with the unconstrained MLEs whereas the latter uses the OLS estimators.

For the more general case in which X contains lagged values of y, we have

$$T_2 \equiv \tilde{u}'\tilde{U}_p(\tilde{U}'_p\tilde{U}_p)^{-1}(\tilde{U}'_p\tilde{\tilde{M}}\tilde{U}_p)(\tilde{U}'_p\tilde{U}_p)^{-1}\tilde{U}'_p\tilde{u}/\tilde{\sigma}^2. \tag{5.19}$$

Noting that for the LMT statistic T_1, as $\hat{U}'_p\hat{U}_p = \hat{U}'_pM\hat{U}_p$, we could write

$$T_1 = \hat{u}'\hat{U}_p(\hat{U}'_p\hat{U}_p)^{-1}(\hat{U}'_pM\hat{U}_p)(\hat{U}'_p\hat{U}_p)^{-1}\hat{U}'_p\hat{u}/\hat{\sigma}^2,$$

so again the Wald test statistic essentially has the same format as that of the LMT statistic. The difference between the two test statistics is that the former works with the MLE in forming $\tilde{u}$ and $\tilde{U}_p$ whereas the LMT statistic uses the OLS estimators and the (equivalent) Wald test statistic uses $\tilde{\tilde{M}}$ in the covariance matrix whereas the LMT statistic uses M.

THE LIKELIHOOD RATIO TEST STATISTIC FOR H_0. The likelihood ratio test (LRT) statistic is

$$T_3 = 2[l(\tilde{\theta}) - l(\hat{\theta})].$$

In obtaining an explicit expression for this test statistic, we are faced with the same difficulty as we had with the Wald test statistic in that both test statistics work with the MLE $\tilde{\theta}$. However, as with the Wald test statistic we can get some insight into the nature of the LRT statistic by using the iterative solution $\tilde{\alpha} \equiv -(\tilde{U}'\tilde{U}_p)^{-1}\tilde{U}'_p\tilde{u}$. Clearly $\tilde{\varepsilon} = \tilde{u} + \tilde{U}_p\tilde{\alpha}$, so substituting our iterative solution for $\tilde{\alpha}$ into this equation allows us to write

$$\tilde{\varepsilon} \equiv \tilde{M}_p\tilde{u} \text{ with } \tilde{M}_p = I_n - \tilde{U}_p(\tilde{U}'_p\tilde{U}_p)^{-1}\tilde{U}'_p.$$

Our iterative solution for σ^2 is $\tilde{\sigma}^2 \equiv \tilde{\varepsilon}'\tilde{\varepsilon}/n$, so substituting the above expression for $\tilde{\varepsilon}$ we write

$$\tilde{\sigma}^2 \equiv \tilde{u}'\tilde{M}_p\tilde{u}/n. \tag{5.20}$$

By substituting expression (5.20) into the log-likelihood function we get, apart from a constant,

$$l(\tilde{\theta}) \equiv -\frac{n}{2}\log\tilde{\sigma}^2,$$

and an equivalent test for the LRT statistic would be

$$T_3 \equiv -n \log \tilde{\sigma}^2/\hat{\sigma}^2.$$

As log is a monotonic function, the LRT statistic is equivalent to

$$\bar{T}_3 = n\tilde{\sigma}^2/\hat{\sigma}^2 = [\tilde{u}'\tilde{u} - \tilde{u}'\tilde{U}'_p(\tilde{U}'_p\tilde{U}_p)^{-1}\tilde{U}'_p\tilde{u}]/\hat{\sigma}^2.$$

Note from Eq. (5.19) that we can write

$$T_2 \equiv [\tilde{u}'\tilde{u} - \tilde{u}'\tilde{U}_p(\tilde{U}'_p\tilde{U}_p)^{-1}(\tilde{U}'_p\tilde{\tilde{N}}\tilde{U}_p)(\tilde{U}'_p\tilde{U}_p)^{-1}\tilde{U}'_p\tilde{u}]/\tilde{\sigma}^2,$$

with

$$\tilde{\tilde{N}} = \tilde{\tilde{X}}(\tilde{\tilde{X}}'\tilde{\tilde{X}})^{-1}\tilde{\tilde{X}}',$$

and we can obtain an equivalent expression for T_1. Again, we see the essential similarities between the test statistics.

For example, the numerator in the test statistic equivalent to T_2 would be the same as that of $\bar{T}_3$ except that the former uses $\tilde{\tilde{N}}$ in forming the matrix in the quadratic form whereas the latter is the identity matrix.

5.4. LINEAR-REGRESSION MODEL WITH MOVING-AVERAGE DISTURBANCES

5.4.1. The Model, the Log-Likelihood Function, and Important Derivatives

Consider the linear-regression equation

$$y_t = \sum_{k=1}^{K} X_{tk}\beta_k + u_t, \quad t = 1, \dots, n,$$

where again we allow for the possibility that some of the regressors X_k represent lagged values of the dependent variable y. Now we assume that the disturbances are subject to a moving-average process of the order of p, which we write as

$$u_t = \varepsilon_t + \alpha_1\varepsilon_{t-1} + \cdots + \alpha_p\varepsilon_{t-p},$$

where $p < n$. The ε_ts are assumed to be independently, identically normally distributed random variables with mean zero and variance σ^2. Again, we assume that there are no unit root problems arising from lagged dependent variables. Putting this process in matrix notation and replacing presample values with zeros, we clearly can write the process

$$u = M(\alpha)\varepsilon.$$

Clearly, as $|M(\alpha)| = 1$ $M(\alpha)$ is nonsingular, we can write

$$\varepsilon = M(\alpha)^{-1}u.$$

We assume that the disturbance process is invertable. In matrix notation, then we can write our model succinctly as

$$\begin{aligned} y &= X\beta + u, \\ u &= M(\alpha)\varepsilon, \\ \varepsilon &\sim N(0, \sigma^2 I). \end{aligned}$$

Again, the parameters of our model are $\theta = (\beta' \; \alpha' \; \sigma^2)'$ and the log-likelihood function is

$$l(\theta) = -\frac{n}{2}\log\sigma^2 - \frac{1}{2\sigma^2}\varepsilon'\varepsilon,$$

except now ε is set equal to $M(\alpha)^{-1}(y - X\beta)$ in this function. As in the preceding model, we need to acquire an expression for $\partial\varepsilon/\partial\alpha$. To do this, we write

$$\varepsilon = \text{vec}\, M(\alpha)^{-1}u = (u' \otimes I_n)\text{vec}\, M(\alpha)^{-1}.$$

Using the backward chain rule, we then have

$$\begin{aligned} \frac{\partial\varepsilon}{\partial\alpha} &= \frac{\partial\, \text{vec}\, M(\alpha)}{\partial\alpha} \frac{\partial\, \text{vec}\, M(\alpha)^{-1}}{\partial\, \text{vec}\, M(\alpha)} \frac{\partial(u' \otimes I_n)\, \text{vec}\, M(\alpha)^{-1}}{\partial\, \text{vec}\, M(\alpha)^{-1}} \\ &= -S'\bar{S}^{\tau'}[M(\alpha)^{-1} \otimes M(\alpha)^{-1'}](u \otimes I_n) \\ &= -S'\bar{S}^{\tau'}(\varepsilon \otimes I_n)M(\alpha)^{-1'}. \end{aligned}$$

However, from Theorem 3.24,

$$S'\bar{S}^{\tau'}(\varepsilon \otimes I_n) = (I_p \otimes \varepsilon')S' = E_p',$$

where

$$E_p = S(I_p \otimes \varepsilon). \tag{5.21}$$

It follows that

$$\frac{\partial\varepsilon}{\partial\alpha} = -E_p' M(\alpha)^{-1'}. \tag{5.22}$$

Note that this derivative is more complicated than the corresponding one for the autoregressive model in that $\partial\varepsilon/\partial\alpha$ now involves $M(\alpha)^{-1}$. This means in turn that certain components of the Hessian matrix $\partial^2 l/\partial\theta\partial\theta'$ will of necessity be more complicated. However, again by use of our results on shifting matrices, these derivatives are obtainable.

5.4.2. The Score Vector $\partial l/\partial\theta$ and the Hessian Matrix $\partial^2 l/\partial\theta\partial\theta'$

By using the derivative $\partial\varepsilon/\partial\alpha$ given by Eq. (5.22) and the derivative $\partial \operatorname{vec} M(\alpha)/\partial\alpha$ given by Eq. (5.9), it is a simple matter to obtain the score vector. Its components are

$$\frac{\partial l}{\partial\beta} = X'M(\alpha)^{-1'}\varepsilon/\sigma^2, \tag{5.23}$$

$$\frac{\partial l}{\partial\alpha} = (I_p \otimes \varepsilon')S'M(\alpha)^{-1'}\varepsilon/\sigma^2 = E_p'M(\alpha)^{-1'}\varepsilon/\sigma^2, \tag{5.24}$$

$$\frac{\partial l}{\partial\sigma^2} = -n/2\sigma^2 + \varepsilon'\varepsilon/2\sigma^4. \tag{5.25}$$

As with the preceding model certain components of this matrix are easily obtained with Eqs. (5.22) and (5.9). They are

$$\frac{\partial^2 l}{\partial\beta'\partial\beta'} = -X'M(\alpha)^{-1'}M(\alpha)^{-1}X/\sigma^2,$$

$$\frac{\partial^2 l}{\partial\beta\partial\sigma^2} = -X'M(\alpha)^{-1'}\varepsilon/\sigma^2 = \left(\frac{\partial^2 l}{\partial\sigma^2\partial\beta'}\right)',$$

$$\frac{\partial^2 l}{\partial\alpha\partial\sigma^2} = -E_p'M(\alpha)^{-1'}\varepsilon/\sigma^4,$$

$$\frac{\partial^2 l}{\partial\sigma^{2^2}} = n/2\sigma^4 - \varepsilon'\varepsilon/\sigma^6.$$

The remaining derivatives, namely $\partial^2 l/\partial\beta\partial\alpha'$ and $\partial^2 l/\partial\alpha\partial\alpha'$, require extra effort and will again involve our using our results on shifting matrices.

Consider first obtaining $\partial^2 l/\partial\beta\partial\alpha'$. To this end write

$$\begin{aligned} X'M(\alpha)^{-1'}M(\alpha)^{-1}u &= X' \operatorname{vec} M(\alpha)^{-1'}M(\alpha)^{-1}u \\ &= X'(u' \otimes I_n)\operatorname{vec} M(\alpha)^{-1'}M(\alpha)^{-1}. \end{aligned}$$

Now,

$$\begin{aligned} \frac{\partial \operatorname{vec} M(\alpha)^{-1'}M(\alpha)^{-1}}{\partial\alpha} &= \frac{\partial \operatorname{vec} M(\alpha)}{\partial\alpha}\frac{\partial \operatorname{vec} M(\alpha)^{-1}}{\partial \operatorname{vec} M(\alpha)}\frac{\partial \operatorname{vec} M(\alpha)^{-1'}M(\alpha)^{-1}}{\partial \operatorname{vec} M(\alpha)^{-1}} \\ &= -2S'\bar{S}^{\tau'}[M(\alpha)^{-1} \otimes M(\alpha)^{-1'}][I_n \otimes M(\alpha)^{-1}]N_n, \end{aligned}$$

so

$$\begin{aligned} \frac{\partial X' \operatorname{vec} M(\alpha)^{-1'}M(\alpha)^{-1}u}{\partial\alpha} &= -S'\bar{S}^{\tau'}[M(\alpha)^{-1} \otimes M(\alpha)^{-1'}M(\alpha)^{-1}] \\ &\quad \times [(I_n \otimes u) + (u \otimes I_n)]X \\ &= -S'\bar{S}^{\tau'}\{[I_n \otimes M(\alpha)^{-1'}\varepsilon] + (\varepsilon \otimes I_n) \\ &\quad \times M(\alpha)^{-1'}\}M(\alpha)^{-1}X. \end{aligned}$$

However, from Theorem 3.24,

$$S'\bar{S}^{\tau'}[I_n \otimes M(\alpha)^{-1'}\varepsilon] = [I_p \otimes \varepsilon' M(\alpha)^{-1}]S^{\tau},$$
$$S'\bar{S}^{\tau'}(\varepsilon \otimes I_n) = (I_p \otimes \varepsilon')S' = E_p',$$

so

$$\frac{\partial^2 l}{\partial\beta\partial\alpha'} = -X'M(\alpha)^{-1'}\{S^{\tau'}[I_p \otimes M(\alpha)^{-1'}\varepsilon] + M(\alpha)^{-1}E_p\}/\sigma^2$$
$$= \left(\frac{\partial^2 l}{\partial\alpha\partial\beta'}\right)'.$$

The most difficult derivative to derive is $\partial^2 l/\partial\alpha\partial\alpha'$. Using the product rule of matrix calculus and referring to Eq. (5.24), we write

$$\frac{\partial}{\partial\alpha}(I_p \otimes \varepsilon')S'M(\alpha)^{-1'}\varepsilon = \frac{\partial \operatorname{vec}(I_p \otimes \varepsilon')S'}{\partial\alpha}[M(\alpha)^{-1'}\varepsilon \otimes I_p] + \frac{\partial M(\alpha)^{-1'}\varepsilon}{\partial\alpha}S(I_p \otimes \varepsilon). \tag{5.26}$$

Using the backward chain rule, we have

$$\frac{\partial \operatorname{vec}(I_p \otimes \varepsilon')S'}{\partial\alpha} = \frac{\partial\varepsilon}{\partial\alpha}\frac{\partial \operatorname{vec} S(I_p \otimes \varepsilon)}{\partial\varepsilon}\frac{\partial \operatorname{vec}(I_p \otimes \varepsilon')S'}{\partial \operatorname{vec} S(I_p \otimes \varepsilon)},$$

and, as

$$\operatorname{vec} S(I_p \otimes \varepsilon) = S^{\tau}\varepsilon, \quad \partial \operatorname{vec} S(I_p \otimes \varepsilon)/\partial\varepsilon = S^{\tau'},$$

we have

$$\frac{\partial \operatorname{vec}(I_p \otimes \varepsilon')S'}{\partial\alpha} = -E_p'M(\alpha)^{-1'}S^{\tau'}K_{np}, \tag{5.27}$$

where K_{np} is a commutation matrix.

Again, using the product rule, we have

$$\frac{\partial M(\alpha)^{-1'}\varepsilon}{\partial\alpha} = \frac{\partial \operatorname{vec} M(\alpha)^{-1'}}{\partial\alpha}(\varepsilon \otimes I_n) + \frac{\partial\varepsilon}{\partial\alpha}M(\alpha)^{-1},$$
$$\frac{\partial \operatorname{vec} M(\alpha)^{-1'}}{\partial\alpha} = \frac{\partial \operatorname{vec} M(\alpha)}{\partial\alpha}\frac{\partial \operatorname{vec} M(\alpha)'}{\partial \operatorname{vec} M(\alpha)}\frac{\partial \operatorname{vec} M(\alpha)^{-1'}}{\partial \operatorname{vec} M(\alpha)'}$$
$$= -S'\bar{S}^{\tau'}K_{nn}[M(\alpha)^{-1'} \otimes M(\alpha)^{-1}],$$

so

$$\frac{\partial M(\alpha)^{-1}\varepsilon}{\partial\alpha} = -S'\bar{S}^{\tau}K_{nn}[M(\alpha)^{-1'}\varepsilon \otimes M(\alpha)^{-1}] - E_p'M(\alpha)^{-1'}M(\alpha)^{-1}. \tag{5.28}$$

Using Eqs. (5.27) and (5.28) in Eq. (5.26), we obtain

$$\frac{\partial^2 l}{\partial\alpha\partial\alpha'} = -\{E_p' M(\alpha)^{-1'} S^{\tau'} K_{np}[M(\alpha)^{-1'}\varepsilon \otimes I_p]$$
$$+ S'\bar{S}^{\tau'} K_{nn}[M(\alpha)^{-1'}\varepsilon \otimes M(\alpha)^{-1}]E_p$$
$$+ E_p' M(\alpha)^{-1'} M(\alpha)^{-1} E_p\}/\sigma^2. \tag{5.29}$$

From the definition of E_p given by Eq. (5.21) and the properties of the commutation matrix, we can write the first matrix on the right-hand side of Eq. (5.29) as $-(I_p \otimes \varepsilon')S'M(\alpha)^{-1'} S^{\tau'}[I_p \otimes M(\alpha)^{-1'}\varepsilon]/\sigma^2$. Again using the properties of the commutation matrix, we can write the second matrix on the right-hand side of Eq. (5.29) as $-S'\bar{S}^{\tau'}[I_n \otimes M(\alpha)^{-1'}\varepsilon]M(\alpha)^{-1}S(I_p \otimes \varepsilon)/\sigma^2$. However, by Theorem 3.24, this matrix is equal to $-[I_p \otimes \varepsilon' M(\alpha)^{-1}]S^{\tau} M(\alpha)^{-1} S(I_p \otimes \varepsilon)/\sigma^2$, so we can write

$$\frac{\partial^2 l}{\partial\alpha\partial\alpha'} = -((I_p \otimes \varepsilon')S'M(\alpha)^{-1'}S^{\tau'}[I_p \otimes M(\alpha)^{-1'}\varepsilon]$$
$$+ \{(I_p \otimes \varepsilon')S'M(\alpha)^{-1'}S^{\tau'}[I_p \otimes M(\alpha)^{-1'}\varepsilon]\}'$$
$$+ E_p' M(\alpha)^{-1'} M(\alpha)^{-1} E_p)/\sigma^2.$$

5.4.3. The Information Matrix $I(\theta) = -p\lim \frac{1}{n}\partial^2 l/\partial\theta\partial\theta'$

The probability limits required for forming this matrix are worked out in Appendix 5.B. Using these limits, we can write the information matrix as

$$I(\theta) = p\lim \frac{1}{n\sigma^2}\begin{bmatrix} X^{*\prime}X^* & X^{*\prime}M(\alpha)^{-1}E_p & 0 \\ E_p' M(\alpha)^{-1'}X^* & E_p' M(\alpha)^{-1'}M(\alpha)^{-1}E_p & 0 \\ 0' & 0' & \frac{n}{2\sigma^2} \end{bmatrix}, \tag{5.30}$$

where $X^* = M(\alpha)^{-1}X$. For the special case in which X is exogenous and contains no lagged dependent variables, the information matrix simplifies to

$$I(\theta) = p\lim \frac{1}{n\sigma^2}\begin{bmatrix} X^{*\prime}X^* & O & 0 \\ O & E_p' M(\alpha)^{-1'}M(\alpha)^{-1}E_p & 0 \\ 0' & 0' & \frac{n}{2\sigma^2} \end{bmatrix}. \tag{5.31}$$

5.4.4. The Cramer–Rao Lower Bound $I^{-1}(\theta)$

Inverting the information matrix is straightforward. We obtain

$$I^{-1}(\theta) = \sigma^2 p \lim n \begin{bmatrix} (X^{*\prime} M_F X^*)^{-1} & -(X^{*\prime} M_F X^*)^{-1} X^{*\prime} F (F'F)^{-1} & 0 \\ -(F'F)^{-1} F' X^* (X^{*\prime} M_F X^*)^{-1} & (F' M^* F)^{-1} & 0 \\ 0' & 0' & \dfrac{2\sigma^2}{n} \end{bmatrix}, \tag{5.32}$$

where $F = M(\alpha)^{-1} E_p$, $M_F = I_n - F(F'F)^{-1} F'$, and $M^* = I_n - X^* (X^{*\prime} X^*)^{-1} X^{*\prime}$ for the general case, and

$$I^{-1}(\theta) = \sigma^2 p \lim n \begin{bmatrix} (X^{*\prime} X^*)^{-1} & O & 0 \\ O & (F'F)^{-1} & 0 \\ 0' & 0' & \dfrac{2\sigma^2}{n} \end{bmatrix} \tag{5.33}$$

for the case in which X is exogenous.

5.4.5. Statistical Inference from the Score Vector and the Information Matrix

As with the preceding model, the score vector and the information matrix can be used to obtain statistical results for our model, and this is the purpose of this subsection.

5.4.5.1. Maximum-Likelihood Estimators as Iterative Generalized-Least-Square Estimators

In Subsection 5.3.5.1. we saw that we could obtain iterative solutions for the MLEs $\tilde{\beta}$, $\tilde{\alpha}$, and $\tilde{\sigma}$ in the autoregressive case and that these solutions gave an iterative GLS interpretation for the MLE of β. Interestingly enough, a similar interpretation for the MLE of θ in the moving-average disturbances case does not appear to be available. Consider the score vector for this model given by Eqs. (5.23)–(5.25). Solving $\partial l/\partial \beta = 0$ gives

$$\tilde{\beta} = [X' M(\tilde{\alpha})^{-1\prime} M(\tilde{\alpha})^{-1} X]^{-1} X' M(\tilde{\alpha})^{-1\prime} M(\alpha)^{-1} y,$$

as expected, but the difficulty arises from $\partial l/\partial \alpha = 0$. Unlike in the autoregressive case, we cannot extract α from this equation. The problem is that whereas vec $M(\alpha)$ is linear in α [see Eq. (5.7)], vec $M(\alpha)^{-1}$ is highly nonlinear in α.

5.4.5.2. Asymptotic Efficiency

Suppose α is known. Then the information matrix would be

$$I\begin{pmatrix}\beta \\ \sigma^2\end{pmatrix} = p\lim \frac{1}{n\sigma^2}\begin{bmatrix} X^{*\prime}X^* & 0 \\ 0' & \frac{n}{2\sigma^2}\end{bmatrix},$$

and the asymptotic Cramer–Rao lower bound for a consistent estimator of β would be $\sigma^2 p\lim(X^{*\prime}X^*/n)^{-1}$. The GLS estimator $\tilde{\beta} = (X^{*\prime}X^*)^{-1}X^{*\prime}y^*$ would attain this bound. From Eq. (5.33) it is clear that, even if α is unknown, provided that X is exogenous and does not contain lagged values of the dependent variable, the Cramer–Rao lower bound for a consistent estimator of β is still $p\lim\sigma^2(X^{*\prime}X^*/n)^{-1}$. The GLS estimator

$$\tilde{\tilde{\beta}} = (\hat{X}^{*\prime}\hat{X}^*)^{-1}\hat{X}^{*\prime}\hat{y}^*,$$

where $\hat{X}^* = M(\hat{\alpha})^{-1}X$, $\hat{y}^* = M(\hat{\alpha})^{-1}y$, and $\hat{\alpha}$ is a consistent estimator of α, for this special case would be as efficient asymptotically as $\tilde{\beta}$. However, from Eq. (5.32) it is clear that, if X contains lagged values of y, the Cramer–Rao lower bound for a consistent estimator of β is now $\sigma^2 p\lim(X^{*\prime}M_F X^*/n)^{-1}$. The GLS estimator $\tilde{\tilde{\beta}}$ still attains the bound so it is still asymptotically efficient but is less efficient than $\tilde{\beta}$.

5.4.5.3. Classical Tests for the Null Hypothesis $H_0 : \alpha = 0$

LAGRANGIAN MULTIPLIER TEST STATISTIC FOR $H_0 : \alpha = 0$. Godfrey (1978) showed that the LMT statistic was incapable of distinguishing between autoregressive disturbances and moving-average disturbances. With the score vectors and the information matrices in hand for the two models, we can easily see why this is the case. We form the LMT statistic by using $\partial l \partial\alpha$ and the information matrix evaluated at $\alpha = 0$. If we do this, then, for both models,

$$\left.\frac{\partial l}{\partial \alpha}\right|_{\alpha=0} = \pm U_p' u/\sigma^2,$$

$$I(\theta)\Big|_{\alpha=0} = p\lim\frac{1}{n\sigma^2}\begin{bmatrix} X'X & \pm X'U_p & 0 \\ \pm U_p'X & U_p'U_p & 0 \\ 0' & 0' & \frac{n}{2\sigma^2}\end{bmatrix},$$

so the LMT statistic must be the same for both models.

THE WALD TEST STATISTIC AND THE LIKELIHOOD RATIO TEST STATISTIC FOR $H_0 : \alpha = 0$. As before let $\tilde{\theta} = (\tilde{\beta}'\ \tilde{\alpha}'\ \tilde{\sigma}^2)'$ be the MLE of θ and let $\hat{\sigma}^2 = y'My/n$. If we had these estimators in hand we could form $M(\tilde{\alpha})^{-1}$, $\tilde{X}^* = M(\tilde{\alpha})^{-1}X$, $\tilde{y}^* = M(\tilde{\alpha})^{-1}y$, $\tilde{\varepsilon} = \tilde{y}^* - \tilde{X}^*\tilde{\beta}$, and thus $\tilde{E}_p$, $\tilde{F}$, and $\tilde{M}^*$. The Wald test statistic would then be

$$T_2' = \tilde{\alpha}'\tilde{F}'\tilde{F}\tilde{\alpha}/\tilde{\sigma}^2$$

for the case in which X is exogenous and

$$T_2 = \tilde{\alpha}'\tilde{F}'\tilde{M}^*\tilde{F}\tilde{\alpha}/\tilde{\sigma}^2$$

for the more general case in which X contains lagged values of y. The LRT statistic would be

$$T_3 = 2\,[l(\tilde{\theta}) - l(\theta)].$$

As with the autoregressive process, the difficulty in obtaining algebraic expressions for these test statistics lies in the fact that the system of equations $\partial l/\partial\theta = 0$ is highly nonlinear in θ. Again, numerical techniques with the aid of computers ensure that we can at least obtain the maximum-likelihood estimates and thus the observed values of these test statistics. However, unlike in the autoregressive process, we cannot get comparative insights into our classical test statistics by using an iterative solution for the MLE $\tilde{\theta}$ as we have seen in Subsection 5.4.5.1 that no such iterative solution is available.

APPENDIX 5.A. PROBABILITY LIMITS ASSOCIATED WITH THE INFORMATION MATRIX FOR THE AUTOREGRESSIVE DISTURBANCES MODEL

p lim $X'M(\alpha)'\varepsilon/n$: The easiest way of obtaining this probability limit is to consider the transformed equation

$$\bar{y} = \bar{X}\beta + \varepsilon, \tag{5.A.1}$$

where $\bar{y} = M(\alpha)y$ and $\bar{X} = M(\alpha)X$. If α is known, then we would obtain a consistent estimator of β, regardless of whether X contains lagged values of y, by applying ordinary least squares to Eq. (5.A.1), to obtain

$$\bar{\beta} = (\bar{X}'\bar{X})^{-1}\bar{X}'\bar{y} = \beta + (\bar{X}'\bar{X}/n)^{-1}\bar{X}'\varepsilon/n.$$

We assume that $p\lim X'M(\alpha)'M(\alpha)X/n$ exists, so

$$p\lim X'M(\alpha)'\varepsilon/n = 0.$$

p lim $U'_p\varepsilon/n$: Consider the artificial equation

$$u = -U_p\alpha + \varepsilon \tag{5.A.2}$$

and suppose for the moment that the us are known. Then we could obtain a consistent estimator of α by applying ordinary least square to Eq. (5.A.2) to obtain

$$\tilde{\alpha} = -\left(U'_pU_p\right)^{-1}U'_pu = \alpha - \left(U'_pU_p/n\right)^{-1}U'_p\varepsilon/n.$$

Again, we assume that $p\lim U'_pU_p/n$ exists, so $p\lim U'_p\varepsilon/n = 0$.

$\boldsymbol{p}\,\mathbf{lim}\,\boldsymbol{X}'\boldsymbol{S}^{\tau'}(\boldsymbol{I}_p \otimes \boldsymbol{\varepsilon})/\boldsymbol{n}$: This probability limit involves our looking at $p\lim X'S_j'\varepsilon/n$. Let x_k be the k column of X and consider

$$x_k'S_j'\varepsilon = \sum_{t=1}^{n-j} x_{tk}\varepsilon_{t+j}, \quad j = 1, \cdots, p.$$

Clearly, $p\lim x_k'S_j'\varepsilon/n = 0$ even if x_k refers to lagged values of the dependent variable.

$\boldsymbol{p}\,\mathbf{lim}\,\boldsymbol{X}'\boldsymbol{M}(\boldsymbol{\alpha})'\boldsymbol{S}(\boldsymbol{I}_p \otimes \boldsymbol{u})/\boldsymbol{n}$: Consider the jth component of this matrix, namely $p\lim X'M(\alpha)'S_ju/n$. Clearly, if X is exogenous, this $p\lim$ is equal to the null vector. Suppose, however, that X contains lagged values of the dependent variable. This $p\lim$ may not be equal to the null vector at least for some j. Suppose, for example, that $x_k = y_{-1}$. Then, as $M(\alpha)'$ is upper triangular with ones down the main diagonal, $x_k'M(\alpha)'S_1u$ would involve $\sum_t u_{t-1}u_t$, and so the $p\lim X'M(\alpha)'S_1u/n$ would not be the null vector.

APPENDIX 5.B. PROBABILITY LIMITS ASSOCIATED WITH THE INFORMATION MATRIX FOR THE MOVING-AVERAGE DISTURBANCES MODEL

$\boldsymbol{p}\,\mathbf{lim}\,\boldsymbol{X}'\boldsymbol{M}(\boldsymbol{\alpha})^{-1'}\boldsymbol{\varepsilon}/\boldsymbol{n}$: We proceed as in Appendix 5.A and consider the transformed equation

$$y^* = X^*\beta + \varepsilon, \tag{5.B.1}$$

where $y^* = M(\alpha)^{-1}y$ and $X^* = M(\alpha)^{-1}X$. If α is known, then we would obtain a consistent estimator of β, regardless of whether X contains lagged values of y, by applying ordinary least squeres to Eq. (B.5.1.) to obtain

$$\tilde{\beta} = (X^{*\prime}X^*)^{-1}X^{*\prime}y^* = \beta + (X^{*\prime}X^*/n)^{-1}X^{*\prime}\varepsilon/n.$$

We assume that $p\lim X'M(\alpha)^{-1'}M(\alpha)^{-1}X/n$ exists, so $p\lim X'M(\alpha)^{-1'}\varepsilon/n = 0$.

$\boldsymbol{p}\,\mathbf{lim}\,\boldsymbol{E}_p'\boldsymbol{M}(\boldsymbol{\alpha})^{-1'}\boldsymbol{\varepsilon}/\boldsymbol{n}$: We write

$$E_p'M(\alpha)^{-1'}\varepsilon = (I \otimes \varepsilon')S'M(\alpha)^{-1'}\varepsilon = [\varepsilon'M(\alpha)^{-1}S_1\varepsilon \cdots \varepsilon'M(\alpha)^{-1}S_p\varepsilon]'$$

and consider the typical quadratic form of this vector, say $\varepsilon'S_j'M(\alpha)^{-1'}\varepsilon$. Now $M(\alpha)^{-1'}$ is upper triangular and we have seen from Subsection 3.7.4.2 that $S_j'M(\alpha)^{-1'}$ is strictly upper triangular with zeros in the $j-1$ diagonals above the main diagonal. It follows that $\varepsilon'S_j'M(\alpha)^{-1'}\varepsilon$ is of the form $\sum_t \varepsilon_t a_{tt+j}\varepsilon_{t+j}$, and so $p\lim \varepsilon'S_j'M(\alpha)^{-1'}\varepsilon/n$ is zero and the $p\lim E_p'M(\alpha)^{-1'}\varepsilon/n$ is the null vector.

$\boldsymbol{p}\,\mathbf{lim}\,\boldsymbol{X}'\boldsymbol{M}(\boldsymbol{\alpha})^{-1'}\boldsymbol{S}^{\tau'}[\boldsymbol{I}_p \otimes \boldsymbol{M}(\boldsymbol{\alpha})^{-1'}\boldsymbol{\varepsilon}]/\boldsymbol{n}$: Clearly,

$$X'M(\alpha)^{-1'}\{S^{\tau'}[I_p \otimes M(\alpha)^{-1'}\varepsilon]\} = X'M(\alpha)^{-1'}[S_1'M(\alpha)^{-1'}\varepsilon \cdots S_p'M(\alpha)^{-1'}\varepsilon].$$

Consider the typical submatrix, say

$$X'M(\alpha)^{-1'}S_j'M(\alpha)^{-1'}\varepsilon.$$

As $M(\alpha)^{-1'}$ is upper triangular, we have seen from Subsection 3.7.4.2 that $S_j'M(\alpha)^{-1'}$ is strictly upper triangular with zeros along the $j-1$ diagonals above the main diagonal. Let $A = M(\alpha)^{-1'}S_j'M(\alpha)^{-1'}$. Then, as $M(\alpha)^{-1'}$ is upper triangular, A is strictly upper triangular with the same configuration as that of $S_j'M(\alpha)^{-1'}$. Let $X = (x_1 \cdots x_K)$ and consider

$$x_k'A\varepsilon = \sum_t x_{tk}a_{tt+j}\varepsilon_{t+j}.$$

Clearly, if the independent variables are exogenous, then $p\lim x_k'A\varepsilon/n = 0$. However, this is also true if x_k refers to lagged values of the dependent variable. Suppose, for example, that $x_k = y_{-1}$ so $x_{tk} = y_{t-1}$. As y_{t-1} depends on ε_{t-1} and the ε_ts are, by assumption, independent, it follows that $p\lim x_k'A\varepsilon/n$ is still zero. Hence, regardless of whether X contains lagged values of y,

$$p\lim X'M(\alpha)^{-1'}S^{\tau'}[I_p \otimes M(\alpha)^{-1'}\varepsilon]/n = 0.$$

$\boldsymbol{p\lim(I_p \otimes \varepsilon')S'M(\alpha)^{-1'}S^{\tau'}[I_p \otimes M(\alpha)^{-1'}\varepsilon]/n}$: Clearly, the matrix in this probability limit can be written as

$$\begin{bmatrix} \varepsilon'S_1'M(\alpha)^{-1'}S_1'M(\alpha)^{-1'}\varepsilon & \dots & \varepsilon'S_1'M(\alpha)^{-1'}S_p'M(\alpha)^{-1'}\varepsilon \\ \vdots & & \vdots \\ \varepsilon'S_p'M(\alpha)^{-1'}S_1'M(\alpha)^{-1'}\varepsilon & \dots & \varepsilon'S_p'M(\alpha)^{-1'}S_p'M(\alpha)^{-1'}\varepsilon \end{bmatrix}.$$

Consider the typical quadratic form of this matrix, say

$$\varepsilon'S_j'M(\alpha)^{-1'}S_i'M(\alpha)^{-1'}\varepsilon.$$

We have seen that $S_j'M(\alpha)^{-1'}$ is strictly upper triangular with zeros along the $j-1$ diagonals above the main diagonal. Let $B = S_j'M(\alpha)^{-1'}S_i'M(\alpha)^{-1'}$ and suppose, without loss of generality, that we assume that $j > i$. Then B is also strictly upper triangular with the same configuration as that of $S_j'M(\alpha)^{-1'}$, so this quadratic form can be written as

$$\sum_t \varepsilon_t b_{tt+j}\varepsilon_{t+j},$$

and, as the ε_ts are assumed to be independent random variables, $p\lim \sum_t \varepsilon_t b_{tt+j}\varepsilon_{t+j}/n$ is zero. It follows then that

$$p\lim(I_p \otimes \varepsilon')S'M(\alpha)^{-1'}S^{\tau'}[I_p \otimes M(\alpha)^{-1'}\varepsilon]/n = 0.$$

6 Seemingly Unrelated Regression Equations Models

6.1. INTRODUCTION

On a scale of statistical complexity, the seemingly unrelated regression equations (SURE) model is one step up from the linear-regression model. The essential feature that distinguishes the two models is that in the former model the disturbances are contemporaneously correlated whereas in the latter model the disturbances are assumed independent.

In this chapter, we apply classical statistical procedures to three variations of the SURE model: First we look at the standard model; then, as we did with the linear-regression model, we look at two versions of the model in which the disturbances are subject to vector autoregressive processes and vector moving-average processes. In our analysis, we shall find that our work on generalized vecs and devecs covered in Sections 2.4 and 4.7 particularly relevant. The duplication matrix discussed in Section 3.5 will make an appearance as will elimination matrices (Section 3.4).

From the practice established in the previous chapter, the asymptotic analysis needed in the evaluation of information matrices is given in Appendix 6.A at the end of the chapter, in which appropriate assumptions are made about the existence of certain probability limits. We can obtain the matrix calculus rules used in the differentiation of this chapter by referring to the tables at the end of Chap. 4.

6.2. THE STANDARD SURE MODEL

6.2.1. The Model and the Log-Likelihood Functions

We consider a system of G linear-regression equations, which we write as

$$\begin{aligned} y_1 &= X_1\delta_1 + u_1 \\ &\vdots \\ y_G &= X_G\delta_G + u_G \end{aligned}$$

or more succinctly as

$$y = X\delta + u,$$

where y is the $nG \times 1$ vector $y = (y_1' \cdots y_G')'$, X is the block diagonal matrix with X_i in the ith block diagonal position, $\delta = (\delta_1' \cdots \delta_G')'$, and $u = (u_1' \cdots u_G')'$. We assume that the disturbances have zero expectations and are contemporaneously correlated so

$$\begin{aligned} \mathcal{E}(u_{ti}u_{sj}) &= 0, \quad t \neq s, \\ &= \sigma_{ij}, \quad t = s, \end{aligned}$$

and the covariance matrix of u is given by

$$V(u) = \Sigma \otimes I_n,$$

where Σ is the $G \times G$ matrix whose (ij)th element is σ_{ij}.

Finally, we assume that the disturbance vector u has a multivariate normal distribution with mean vector 0 and covariance matrix $V(u) = \Sigma \otimes I_n$.

Thus we write our model as

$$\begin{aligned} y &= X\delta + u, \\ u &\sim N(0, \Sigma \otimes I_n). \end{aligned}$$

The parameters of the model are given by $\theta = (\delta'\nu')'$, where $\nu = \text{vech}\, \Sigma$ and the log-likelihood function, apart from a constant, is

$$l(\theta) = -\frac{n}{2} \log \det \Sigma - \frac{1}{2} u'(\Sigma^{-1} \otimes I_n)u, \tag{6.1}$$

where in this function u is set equal to $y - X\delta$. Alternatively, we can write this function as

$$l(\theta) = -\frac{n}{2} \log \det \Sigma - \frac{1}{2} \text{tr}\, \Sigma^{-1} U'U, \tag{6.2}$$

where U is the $n \times G$ matrix $(u_1 \cdots u_G)$.

Usually δ contains the parameters of primary interest, and $\nu = \text{vech}\, \Sigma$ are the nuisance parameters. This is not always the case, however, as later on in the section we wish to develop the LMT statistic for the null hypothesis $H_0 : \sigma_{ij} = 0, i \neq j$. Then ν would represent the parameters of primary interest and δ the nuisance parameters. However, treating δ as the parameter of primary interest for the moment, we obtain the concentrated log-likelihood function $l^*(\delta)$.

From the log-likelihood function $l(\theta)$, written as Eq. (6.2) we have

$$\frac{\partial l}{\partial \nu} = -\frac{n}{2} \frac{\partial \log \det \Sigma}{\partial \nu} - \frac{1}{2} \frac{\partial\, \text{tr}\, \Sigma^{-1} U'U}{\partial \nu},$$

and we deal with each component of this derivative in turn. First, by the chain rule,

$$\frac{\partial \log\det\Sigma}{\partial \nu} = \frac{\partial \operatorname{vec}\Sigma}{\partial \nu}\frac{\partial \log\det\Sigma}{\partial \operatorname{vec}\Sigma} = D'\operatorname{vec}\Sigma^{-1},$$

where D is the $G^2 \times (1/2)\, G(G+1)$ duplication matrix associated with a $G \times G$ symmetric matrix. Next

$$\begin{aligned}\frac{\partial \operatorname{tr}\Sigma^{-1}U'U}{\partial \nu} &= \frac{\partial \operatorname{vec}\Sigma}{\partial \nu}\frac{\partial \operatorname{vec}\Sigma^{-1}}{\partial \operatorname{vec}\Sigma}\frac{\partial \operatorname{tr}\Sigma^{-1}U'U}{\partial \operatorname{vec}\Sigma^{-1}}\\ &= -D'(\Sigma^{-1}\otimes\Sigma^{-1})\operatorname{vec}U'U.\end{aligned}$$

It follows that

$$\frac{\partial l}{\partial \nu} = \frac{D'}{2}(\operatorname{vec}\Sigma^{-1}U'U\Sigma^{-1} - n\operatorname{vec}\Sigma^{-1}). \tag{6.3}$$

Clearly, this derivative is equal to the null vector only if we set

$$\Sigma = \tilde{\Sigma} = U'U/n.$$

Substituting back for Σ in Eq. (6.2), we find that the concentrated log-likelihood function is, apart from a constant,

$$l^*(\delta) = -\frac{n}{2}\log\det\tilde{\Sigma}, \tag{6.4}$$

with $\tilde{\Sigma}$ set equal to $U'U/n$.

6.2.2. The Score Vector $\partial l/\partial\theta$ and the Hessian matrix $\partial^2 l/\partial\theta\partial\theta'$

By using the rules of matrix calculus listed in the tables at the end of Chap. 4, we can easily carry out the differentiation required for obtaining the score vector and the Hessian matrix of the log likelihood.

The first component of the score vector is

$$\frac{\partial l}{\partial \delta} = -\frac{1}{2}\frac{\partial u}{\partial \delta}\frac{\partial u'(\Sigma^{-1}\otimes I_n)u}{\partial u} = X'(\Sigma^{-1}\otimes I_n)u. \tag{6.5}$$

The second component of the score vector was derived in the previous subsection and is

$$\frac{\partial l}{\partial \nu} = \frac{D'}{2}(\operatorname{vec}\Sigma^{-1}U'U\Sigma^{-1} - n\operatorname{vec}\Sigma^{-1}). \tag{6.6}$$

The first component of the Hessian matrix[1] is

$$\frac{\partial l}{\partial \delta\partial \delta'} = \frac{\partial}{\partial \delta}\frac{\partial l}{\partial \delta} = \frac{\partial u}{\partial \delta}\frac{\partial X'(\Sigma^{-1}\otimes I_n)u}{\partial u} = -X'(\Sigma^{-1}\otimes I_n)X.$$

[1] We need not take the transpose here as $\partial l/\partial\delta\partial\delta'$ is symmetric.

The derivative $\partial^2 l/\partial\delta\partial\nu'$ is the transpose of

$$\frac{\partial}{\partial\nu}\left(\frac{\partial l}{\partial\delta}\right) = \frac{\partial}{\partial\nu}X' \operatorname{vec} U\Sigma^{-1} = \frac{\partial \operatorname{vec}\Sigma}{\partial\nu}\frac{\partial \operatorname{vec} U\Sigma^{-1}}{\partial \operatorname{vec}\Sigma}X$$
$$= -D'(\Sigma^{-1}\otimes\Sigma^{-1}U')X,$$

so

$$\frac{\partial^2 l}{\partial\delta\partial\nu'} = -X'(\Sigma^{-1}\otimes U\Sigma^{-1})D.$$

Finally, from Eq. (6.6)

$$\frac{\partial^2 l}{\partial\nu\partial\nu'} = \left(\frac{\partial \operatorname{vec}\Sigma^{-1}U'U\Sigma^{-1}}{\partial\nu} - n\frac{\partial \operatorname{vec}\Sigma^{-1}}{\partial\nu}\right)\frac{D}{2},$$

with

$$\begin{aligned}\frac{\partial \operatorname{vec}\Sigma^{-1}U'U\Sigma^{-1}}{\partial\nu} &= \frac{\partial \operatorname{vec}\Sigma}{\partial\nu}\frac{\partial \operatorname{vec}\Sigma^{-1}}{\partial \operatorname{vec}\Sigma}\frac{\partial \operatorname{vec}\Sigma^{-1}U'U\Sigma^{-1}}{\partial \operatorname{vec}\Sigma^{-1}}\\ &= -D'(\Sigma^{-1}\otimes\Sigma^{-1})[(I_G\otimes U'U\Sigma^{-1})K_{GG}\\ &\quad +(I_G\otimes U'U\Sigma^{-1})]\\ &= -2D'(\Sigma^{-1}\otimes\Sigma^{-1})(I_G\otimes U'U\Sigma^{-1})N,\end{aligned}$$

and

$$\frac{\partial \operatorname{vec}\Sigma^{-1}}{\partial\nu} = \frac{\partial \operatorname{vec}\Sigma}{\partial\nu}\frac{\partial \operatorname{vec}\Sigma^{-1}}{\partial \operatorname{vec}\Sigma} = -D'(\Sigma^{-1}\otimes\Sigma^{-1}),$$

where $N = (1/2)(I_{G^2} + K_{GG})$. It follows that

$$\frac{\partial^2 l}{\partial\nu\partial\nu'} = D'(\Sigma^{-1}\otimes\Sigma^{-1})\left[\frac{n}{2}I_{G^2} - (I_G\otimes U'U\Sigma^{-1})\right]D,$$

as $ND = D$.

6.2.3. The Information Matrix $I(\theta) = -p\lim\frac{1}{n}\partial^2 l/\partial\theta\partial\theta'$ and the Cramer–Rao Lower Bound $I^{-1}(\theta)$

Under our assumptions, $p\lim U'U/n = \Sigma$ and $p\lim X'(I_n\otimes U)/n = O$ regardless of whether X contains lagged values of the dependent variables. The information matrix is then

$$I\begin{pmatrix}\delta\\ \nu\end{pmatrix} = \begin{bmatrix} p\lim X(\Sigma^{-1}\otimes I_n)X/n & O\\ O & \frac{1}{2}D'(\Sigma^{-1}\otimes\Sigma^{-1})D\end{bmatrix}, \tag{6.7}$$

and from the properties of the duplication matrix given in Section 3.5 the Cramer–Rao lower bound is

$$I^{-1} = \begin{bmatrix} [p\lim X'(\Sigma^{-1} \otimes I_n)X/n]^{-1} & O \\ O & 2LN(\Sigma \otimes \Sigma)NL' \end{bmatrix},$$

where L is the $(1/2)G(G+1) \times G^2$ elimination matrix.

6.2.4. Statistical Inference from the Score Vector and the Information Matrix

6.2.4.1. Maximum-Likelihood Estimators as Iterative Joint-Generalized-Least-Squares Estimators

Let $\hat{\delta}$ be a consistent estimator of δ and suppose that $\sqrt{n}(\hat{\delta} - \delta) \xrightarrow{d} N(0, V)$. Then, in order for $\hat{\delta}$ to be a best asymptotically normally distributed estimator (which is shortened to BAN estimator), V must equal the Cramer–Rao lower bound $[p\lim X'(\Sigma^{-1} \otimes I_n)X/n]^{-1}$. One such estimator that does this is the joint-generalized-least-squares (JGLS) estimator

$$\hat{\delta} = [X'(\hat{\Sigma}^{-1} \otimes I_n)X]^{-1}X'(\hat{\Sigma}^{-1} \otimes I_n)y, \tag{6.8}$$

where $\hat{\Sigma} = \hat{U}'\hat{U}/n$ and $\hat{U}$ is formed from the OLS residual vectors $\hat{u}_j = [I_n - X_j(X_j'X_j)^{-1}X_j']y_j$.

The MLE has an iterative JGLS interpretation as when we equate the score vector to the null vector we get

$$\frac{\partial l}{\partial \delta} = X'(\Sigma^{-1} \otimes I_n)(y - X\delta) = 0,$$

which implies that

$$\tilde{\delta} = [X'(\Sigma^{-1} \otimes I_n)X]^{-1}X'(\Sigma^{-1} \otimes I_n)y,$$

and

$$\frac{\partial l}{\partial v} = \frac{D'}{2}(\text{vec}\,\Sigma^{-1}U'U\Sigma^{-1} - n\,\text{vec}\,\Sigma^{-1}) = 0,$$

which implies that

$$\hat{\Sigma} = \hat{U}'\hat{U}/n. \tag{6.9}$$

These solutions are clearly iterative rather than explicit as $\hat{\delta}$ still depends on Σ and $\hat{\Sigma}$ depends on δ through U.

6.2.4.2. The Lagrangian Multiplier Test Statistic for $H_0 : \sigma_{ij} = 0, i \neq j$

As we mentioned at the start of this chapter, what distinguishes the SURE model from the linear-regression model is the assumption that the disturbances are contemporaneously correlated. It is this assumption that induces us to regard the equations as one large system $y = X\delta + u$ and to estimate δ by using the JGLS estimator given by Eq. (6.8). If, however, the disturbances are not contemporaneously correlated there is no point in doing this. Instead, efficient estimating would merely require the application of ordinary least squares to each equation.

We would then like to develop a classical test statistic for the null hypothesis:

$$H_0 : \sigma_{ij} = 0, \quad i \neq j \quad \text{against } H_A : \sigma_{ij} \neq 0,$$

or, in vector notation,

$$H_0 : \bar{\nu} = 0 \text{ against } H_A : \bar{\nu} \neq 0,$$

where $\bar{\nu} = \bar{\nu}(\Sigma)$ is defined in Subsection 2.3.4. The most amenable test statistic for this case is the LMT statistic, which would be

$$T = \frac{1}{n} \frac{\partial l}{\partial \bar{\nu}}\bigg|_{\hat{\theta}}' I^{\bar{\nu}\bar{\nu}}(\hat{\theta}) \frac{\partial l}{\partial \bar{\nu}}\bigg|_{\hat{\theta}},$$

where $I^{\bar{\nu}\bar{\nu}}$ refers to that part of the Cramer–Rao lower bound corresponding to $\bar{\nu}$ and in forming $\hat{\theta}$ we set $\bar{\nu}$ equal to the null vector and evaluate all other parameters at the constrained MLEs, i.e., at the OLS estimators.

In forming T the first task is to obtain $\partial l/\partial \bar{\nu}$ and $I^{\bar{\nu}\bar{\nu}}$ under H_0 from $\partial l \partial \nu$ and $I^{\nu\nu}$, which we already have in hand. We do this by means of an appropriate selection matrix $\mathcal{S}$, which has the property

$$\bar{\nu} = \mathcal{S}\nu$$

However, $\nu = L \operatorname{vec} \Sigma$ and $\bar{\nu} = \bar{L} \operatorname{vec} \Sigma$, where L and $\bar{L}$ are $(1/2)G(G+1) \times G^2$ and $(1/2)G(G-1) \times G^2$ elimination matrices, defined in Section 3.4, so it must be true that $\mathcal{S}L = \bar{L}$. Now consider $\partial l/\partial \bar{\nu}$. As the matrix $\mathcal{S}$ selects from the vector ν the elements that belong to $\bar{\nu}$ it follows that

$$\frac{\partial l}{\partial \bar{\nu}} = \mathcal{S}\frac{\partial l}{\partial \nu} = \mathcal{S}\frac{D'D}{2}[\nu(\Sigma^{-1}U'U\Sigma^{-1}) - n\nu(\Sigma^{-1})],$$

where we use the property that for a symmetric matrix A, $D\nu(A) = \operatorname{vec} A$. Moreover, from the properties of zero-one matrices given in Section 3.6,

$$\mathcal{S}D'D = 2\mathcal{S} - \mathcal{S}LK_{GG}L' = 2\mathcal{S} - \bar{L}K_{GG}L' = 2\mathcal{S}.$$

Also, if H_0 is true, $\mathcal{S}\nu(\Sigma^{-1}) = \bar{\nu}(\Sigma^{-1}) = 0$ so

$$\frac{\partial l}{\partial \bar{\nu}} = \mathcal{S}\nu(A) = \bar{\nu}(A),$$

where $A = \Sigma^{-1}U'U\Sigma^{-1}$, which itself under H_0 is

$$A = \begin{bmatrix} \rho_{11} & \cdots & \rho_{1G} \\ \vdots & & \vdots \\ \rho_{G1} & \cdots & \rho_{GG} \end{bmatrix},$$

with $\rho_{ij} = u_i' u_j / \sigma_{ii}\sigma_{jj}$. Finally then, under H_0,

$$\frac{\partial l}{\partial \bar{\nu}} = \begin{pmatrix} \rho_{21} \\ \vdots \\ \rho_{G1} \\ \rho_{32} \\ \vdots \\ \rho_{G2} \\ \vdots \\ \rho_{GG-1} \end{pmatrix}.$$

Next we evaluate $I^{\bar{\nu}\bar{\nu}}$ under H_0. As $\bar{\nu} = \mathcal{S}\nu$ it follows that $I^{\bar{\nu}\bar{\nu}} = \mathcal{S}I^{\nu\nu}\mathcal{S}'$, where

$$I^{\nu\nu} = 2LN(\Sigma \otimes \Sigma)NL',$$

and under H_0, Σ is diagonal so from Theorem 3.16, $I^{\nu\nu}$ will then be the diagonal matrix given by

$$I^{\nu\nu} = \begin{bmatrix} 2\sigma_{11}^2 & & & & & & & & & O \\ & \sigma_{11}\sigma_{22} & & & & & & & & \\ & & \ddots & & & & & & & \\ & & & \sigma_{11}\sigma_{GG} & & & & & & \\ & & & & 2\sigma_{22}^2 & & & & & \\ & & & & & \sigma_{22}\sigma_{33} & & & & \\ & O & & & & & \ddots & & & \\ & & & & & & & \sigma_{22}\sigma_{GG} & & \\ & & & & & & & & \ddots & \\ & & & & & & & & & 2\sigma_{GG}^2 \end{bmatrix}.$$

Selecting the appropriate elements from this matrix, we have that, under H_0,

$$I^{\overline{vv}} = \begin{bmatrix} \sigma_{11}\sigma_{22} & & & & & & & \\ & \ddots & & & & & O & \\ & & \sigma_{11}\sigma_{GG} & & & & & \\ & & & \sigma_{22}\sigma_{33} & & & & \\ & & & & \ddots & & & \\ & O & & & & \sigma_{22}\sigma_{GG} & & \\ & & & & & & \ddots & \\ & & & & & & & \sigma_{G-1G-1}\sigma_{GG} \end{bmatrix}.$$

Marrying the two components of the LMT statistic together, we obtain

$$T = n\sum_{i=2}^{G}\sum_{j=1}^{i-1} r_{ij}^2,$$

where $r_{ij}^2 = \hat{\sigma}_{ij}^2/\hat{\sigma}_{ii}\hat{\sigma}_{jj}$, $\hat{\sigma}_{ij} = \hat{u}_i'\hat{u}_j/n$, and $\hat{u}_i$ is the OLS residual vector obtained from the ith equation. This test statistic was first obtained by Breusch and Pagan (1980). Under H_0, T tends in distribution to a χ^2 random variable with $(1/2)G(G-1)$ degrees of freedom so the upper tail of this distribution is used to find the appropriate critical region.

6.3. THE SURE MODEL WITH VECTOR AUTOREGRESSIVE DISTURBANCES

6.3.1. The Model

As in the preceding, section we consider a system of G linear-regression equations

$$\begin{aligned} y_1 &= X_1\delta_1 + u_1 \\ &\vdots \\ y_G &= X_G\delta_G + u_G \end{aligned}$$

or a one-equation system

$$y = X\delta + u.$$

We now assume that the disturbances are subject to a vector autoregressive system of the order of p. Let $\mathbf{u}_t$ be the $G \times 1$ vector containing the tth values of the G disturbances. Then we have

$$\mathbf{u}_t + R_1\mathbf{u}_{t-1} + \cdots + R_p\mathbf{u}_{t-p} = \varepsilon_t, \quad t = 1, \ldots, n, \tag{6.10}$$

where each matrix R_j is a $G \times G$ matrix of unknown parameters and the ε_t are assumed to independently identically normally distributed random vectors with mean 0 and a positive-definite covariance matrix Σ. We assume that there are no unit root problems. Let U and E be the $n \times G$ matrices $U = (u_1 \cdots u_G)$ and $E = (\varepsilon_1 \cdots \varepsilon_G)$, so under this notation $\boldsymbol{\varepsilon}_t$ is the tth row of E, and let U_{-l} denote the matrix U but with values that are lagged l periods. Then we can write the disturbances system (6.10) as

$$U + U_{-1}R_1' + \cdots + U_{-p}R_p' = E,$$

or

$$U + U_p R' = E \tag{6.11}$$

where R is the $G \times Gp$ matrix $R = (R_1 \cdots R_p)$ and U_p is the $n \times Gp$ matrix $U_p = (U_{-1} \cdots U_{-p})$. In the application of asymptotic theory, presample values are replaced with zeros without affecting our results. Suppose we do this at the start of our analysis. Then we can write

$$U_{-j} = S_j U, \quad j = 1, \ldots, p,$$

where S_j is the appropriate $n \times n$ shifting matrix and

$$U_p = S(I_p \otimes U),$$

where S is the $n \times np$ matrix given by $S = (S_1 \cdots S_p)$. Taking the vec of both sides of Eq. (6.11), we have

$$u + (R \otimes I_n)\text{vec}\, U_p = \varepsilon,$$

where

$$u = \text{vec}\, U, \quad \varepsilon = \text{vec}\, E.$$

However,

$$\text{vec}\, U_p = \begin{pmatrix} \text{vec}\, S_1 U \\ \vdots \\ \text{vec}\, S_p U \end{pmatrix} = \begin{pmatrix} I_G \otimes S_1 \\ \vdots \\ I_G \otimes S_p \end{pmatrix} u = Cu,$$

where C is a $Gpn \times nG$ matrix given by

$$C = \begin{pmatrix} I_G \otimes S_1 \\ \vdots \\ I_G \otimes S_p \end{pmatrix},$$

so we can write our disturbances systems as

$$M(r)u = \varepsilon,$$

where $M(r) = I_{Gn} + N(r)$, and $N(r)$ is the $nG \times nG$ matrix given by

$$N(r) = (R \otimes I_n)C.$$

Therefore, after this mathematical maneuvering, we can write our model as

$$
\begin{aligned}
& y = X\delta + u, \\
& M(r)u = \varepsilon, \\
& \varepsilon \sim N(0, \Sigma \otimes I_n).
\end{aligned}
$$

6.3.2. Properties of the Matrices $N(r)$ and $M(r)$

The matrices $N(r)$ and $M(r)$ play a crucial role in the statistical analysis of our model that follows. As such, it pays us to consider some of the properties of these matrices.

Clearly,

$$N(r) = (R_1 \otimes S_1) + \cdots + (R_p \otimes S_p).$$

Let

$$R_l = \left\{ r_{ij}^l \right\} \quad \text{for } l = 1, \ldots, p.$$

Then

$$N(r) = \begin{bmatrix} r_{11}^1 S_1 & \cdots & r_{1G}^1 S_1 \\ \vdots & & \vdots \\ r_{G1}^1 S_1 & \cdots & r_{GG}^1 S_1 \end{bmatrix} + \cdots + \begin{bmatrix} r_{11}^p S_p & \cdots & r_{1G}^p S_p \\ \vdots & & \vdots \\ r_{G1}^p S_p & \cdots & r_{GG}^p S_p \end{bmatrix}.$$

Consider the $n \times n$ submatrix of $N(r)$ in the $(1, 1)$ position as typical. Letting N_{11} denote this matrix, we have

$$
\begin{aligned}
N_{11} &= r_{11}^1 S_1 + r_{11}^2 S_2 + \cdots + r_{11}^p S_p \\
&= \begin{bmatrix} 0 & & & & \\ r_{11}^1 & \ddots & & O & \\ & \ddots & \ddots & & \\ & & \ddots & \ddots & \\ & O & & r_{11}^1 & 0 \end{bmatrix} + \begin{bmatrix} 0 & & & & & \\ 0 & \ddots & & & O & \\ r_{11}^2 & & \ddots & \ddots & & \\ & \ddots & & \ddots & \ddots & \\ O & & & r_{11}^2 & 0 & 0 \end{bmatrix} + \cdots + \begin{bmatrix} 0 & & & & & & \\ O & \ddots & & & & & \\ r_{11}^p & & \ddots & \ddots & & & \\ & \ddots & & \ddots & \ddots & \ddots & \\ O & & & & r_{11}^p & O & 0 \end{bmatrix} \\
&= \begin{bmatrix} 0 & & & & & & \\ r_{11}^1 & \ddots & & & O & & \\ r_{11}^2 & \ddots & \ddots & & & & \\ \vdots & \ddots & \ddots & \ddots & & & \\ & & \ddots & \ddots & \ddots & & \\ r_{11}^p & & & \ddots & \ddots & \ddots & \\ & \ddots & & & \ddots & \ddots & \ddots \\ O & & r_{11}^p & \cdots & \cdots & r_{11}^2 & r_{11}^1 & 0 \end{bmatrix},
\end{aligned}
$$

which is clearly a Toeplitz matrix that is strictly lower triangular and a band matrix. Therefore, if we write

$$N(r) = \begin{bmatrix} N_{11} & \cdots & N_{1G} \\ \vdots & & \vdots \\ N_{G1} & \cdots & N_{GG} \end{bmatrix},$$

then each submatrix N_{ij} is $n \times n$, Toeplitz strictly lower triangular, and band. Now if we write

$$M(r) = I_{Gn} + N(r) = \begin{bmatrix} M_{11} & \cdots & M_{1G} \\ \vdots & & \vdots \\ M_{G1} & \cdots & M_{GG} \end{bmatrix},$$

then it follows that each M_{ii}, $i = 1, \ldots, G$, is $n \times n$, Toeplitz lower triangular, and band with ones along its main diagonal whereas each M_{ij}, $i \neq j$, is $n \times n$, Toeplitz, strictly lower triangular, and band.

6.3.3. The Matrix J and Derivatives $\partial \operatorname{vec} N(r)/\partial r$, $\partial \varepsilon/\partial r$

Important derivatives for our work are $\partial \operatorname{vec} N(r)/\partial r$ and $\partial \varepsilon/\partial r$. These derivatives bring generalized vecs and devecs into the analysis and are derived in this section. For notational convenience we use superscripts τ and $\bar{\tau}$ to denote the generalized vec_G and devec_G operators, respectively.

THE MATRIX J AND THE DERIVATIVE $\partial \operatorname{VEC} N(r)/\partial r$. Now

$$N(r) = (R \otimes I_n)C,$$

so

$$\operatorname{vec} N(r) = (C' \otimes I_{nG})\operatorname{vec}(R \otimes I_n).$$

By Eq. (3.6)

$$\operatorname{vec}(R \otimes I_n) = \left(I_{pG} \otimes K^{\tau}_{Gn}\right)r,$$

where $r = \operatorname{vec} R$ and we can write

$$\operatorname{vec} N(r) = Jr, \tag{6.12}$$

where J is an $n^2G^2 \times pG^2$ matrix given by

$$J = (C' \otimes I_{nG})\left(I_{pG} \otimes K^{\tau}_{Gn}\right). \tag{6.13}$$

Clearly then

$$\frac{\partial \operatorname{vec} N(r)}{\partial r} = J',$$

and, as $(K_{Gn}^{\tau})' = (K_{Gn}')^{\bar{\tau}} = K_{nG}^{\bar{\tau}}$,

$$J' = \left(I_{pG} \otimes K_{nG}^{\bar{\tau}}\right)(C \otimes I_{nG}). \tag{6.14}$$

PROPERTIES OF THE MATRIX J. The matrix J is used extensively throughout the rest of this chapter. As such, we need to know some of its properties. These properties can be derived from the theorems concerning $K_{nG}^{\bar{\tau}}$ in Subsection 3.3.3 and are given in the following propositions, where u, U_p, and C are defined in Section 6.3.1.

Proposition 6.1.

$$J'(u \otimes I_{nG}) = K_{pG,G}(I_G \otimes U_p').$$

Proof of Proposition 6.1. As vec $U_p = Cu$, we can write

$$J'(u \otimes I_{nG}) = \left(I_{pG} \otimes K_{nG}^{\bar{\tau}}\right)(\operatorname{vec} U_p \otimes I_{nG}). \tag{6.15}$$

However, applying Theorem 3.9, we can write the right-hand side of Eq. (6.15) as

$$K_{pG,G}(I_G \otimes U_p'). \qquad \square$$

Proposition 6.2.

$$J' K_{nG,nG} = K_{pG,G}\left(I_G \otimes K_{n,pG}^{\bar{\tau}_{pG}}\right)(I_{nG} \otimes C).$$

Proof of Proposition 6.2. Using the properties of the commutation matrix, we can write

$$J' K_{nG,nG} = \left(I_{pG} \otimes K_{nG}^{\bar{\tau}}\right) K_{pGn,nG}(I_{nG} \otimes C).$$

We find that the result follows by applying Theorem 3.12. $\square$

Proposition 6.3.

$$J'(I_{nG} \otimes u) = (I_{pG} \otimes U')C.$$

Proof of Proposition 6.3. From the definition of J

$$J'(I_{nG} \otimes u) = \left(I_{pG} \otimes K_{nG}^{\bar{\tau}}\right)(C \otimes u) = \left(I_{pG} \otimes K_{nG}^{\bar{\tau}}\right)(I_{pGn} \otimes u)C.$$

Now,

$$(I_{pG} \otimes K_{nG}^{\bar{\tau}})(I_{pGn} \otimes u) = I_{pG} \otimes K_{nG}^{\bar{\tau}}(I_n \otimes u) = I_{pG} \otimes U',$$

by Theorem 3.10. □

THE DERIVATIVE $\partial\varepsilon/\partial r$. Next, as $\varepsilon = M(r)u = (u' \otimes I_{nG})\text{vec}\, M(r)$, we have, by using the backward chain rule of matrix calculus,

$$\frac{\partial\varepsilon}{\partial r} = \frac{\partial\, \text{vec}\, N(r)}{\partial r}(u \otimes I_{nG}) = J'(u \otimes I_{nG}).$$

However, applying Proposition 6.1, we have

$$\frac{\partial\varepsilon}{\partial r} = J'(u \otimes I_{nG}) = K_{pG,G}(I_G \otimes U_p'). \tag{6.16}$$

6.3.4. The Parameters of the Model, the Log-Likelihood Function, and the Score Vector

The parameters of the model are given by $\theta = (\delta'\, r'\, \nu')'$, where $\nu = \text{vech}\, \Sigma$ and the log-likelihood function, apart from a constant, is

$$l(\theta) = -\frac{n}{2}\log\det\Sigma - \frac{1}{2}\varepsilon'(\Sigma^{-1} \otimes I_n)\varepsilon, \tag{6.17}$$

where in this function we set ε equal to $M(r)(y - X\delta)$. We can obtain the first and the third components of the score vector by adapting Eqs. (6.5) and (6.6) of Subsection 6.2.2. They are

$$\frac{\partial l}{\partial\delta} = X^{d'}(\Sigma^{-1} \otimes I_n)\varepsilon, \tag{6.18}$$

$$\frac{\partial l}{\partial\nu} = \frac{D'}{2}(\text{vec}\,\Sigma^{-1}E'\,E\,\Sigma^{-1} - n\,\text{vec}\,\Sigma^{-1}), \tag{6.19}$$

where $X^d = M(r)X$ and D is the $G^2 \times (1/2)G(G+1)$ duplication matrix. Using the derivative given by Eq. (6.16), we easily obtain the second component of the score vector as follows:

$$\frac{\partial l}{\partial r} = -\frac{1}{2}\frac{\partial\varepsilon}{\partial r}\frac{\partial\varepsilon'(\Sigma^{-1} \otimes I_n)\varepsilon}{\partial\varepsilon} = -K_{pG,G}(\Sigma^{-1} \otimes U_p')\varepsilon. \tag{6.20}$$

6.3.5. The Hessian Matrix $\partial^2 l / \partial\theta\partial\theta'$

We can also obtain several components of the Hessian matrix by adapting the derivatives of Section 6.2.2. They are listed here for convenience:

$$\frac{\partial^2 l}{\partial\delta\partial\delta'} = -X^{d'}(\Sigma^{-1} \otimes I_n)X^d, \tag{6.21}$$

$$\frac{\partial^2 l}{\partial\delta\partial v'} = -X^{d'}(\Sigma^{-1} \otimes E\,\Sigma^{-1})D, \tag{6.22}$$

$$\frac{\partial^2 l}{\partial v\partial v'} = D'(\Sigma^{-1} \otimes \Sigma^{-1})\left[\frac{nI_{G^2}}{2} - (I_G \otimes E'E\,\Sigma^{-1})\right]D. \tag{6.23}$$

The derivatives involving r are obtained each in turn.
$\boldsymbol{\partial^2 l / \partial\delta\partial r'}$: We derive this derivative from $\partial l / \partial r$, which, from Eq. (6.20), we write as

$$\frac{\partial l}{\partial r} = -K_{pG,G}(\Sigma^{-1} \otimes I_{pG})\text{vec}\, U_p' E.$$

Using a product rule of matrix calculus, we have

$$\frac{\partial\, \text{vec}\, U_p' E}{\partial\delta} = \frac{\partial\, \text{vec}\, U_p'}{\partial\delta}(E \otimes I_{pG}) + \frac{\partial\varepsilon}{\partial\delta}(I_G \otimes U_p).$$

However, $\text{vec}\, U_p' = K_{n,pG}\, C(y - X\delta)$, so $\partial\, \text{vec}\, U_p' / \partial\delta = -X'C'K_{pG,n}$, and

$$\frac{\partial\, \text{vec}\, U_p' E}{\partial\delta} = -X'C'\, K_{pG,n}(E \otimes I_{pG}) - X^{d'}(I_G \otimes U_p).$$

Our derivative follows directly and is given by

$$\begin{aligned}\frac{\partial^2 l}{\partial\delta\partial r'} &= X'C'\, K_{pG,n}(E\,\Sigma^{-1} \otimes I_{pG})K_{G,pG} + X^{d'}(\Sigma^{-1} \otimes U_p)K_{G,pG} \\ &= X'C'(I_{pG} \otimes E\,\Sigma^{-1}) + X^{d'}(\Sigma^{-1} \otimes U_p)K_{G,pG}.\end{aligned} \tag{6.24}$$

$\boldsymbol{\partial^2 l / \partial r\, \partial v'}$: Again, we derive this derivative from $\partial l / \partial r$, which we now write as

$$\frac{\partial l}{\partial r} = -K_{pG,G}(I_G \otimes U_p' E)\text{vec}\, \Sigma^{-1}.$$

As $\partial\, \text{vec}\, \Sigma^{-1} / \partial v = -D'(\Sigma^{-1} \otimes \Sigma^{-1})$, it follows that our derivative is given by

$$\frac{\partial^2 l}{\partial r \partial v'} = K_{pG,G}(\Sigma^{-1} \otimes U_p' E\,\Sigma^{-1})D.$$

$\partial^2 l \partial r \partial r'$: From Eqs. (6.20) and (6.16), we have

$$\frac{\partial^2 l}{\partial r \partial r'} = -K_{pG,G}(\Sigma^{-1} \otimes U_p' U_p) K_{G,pG} = -(U_p' U_p \otimes \Sigma^{-1}). \tag{6.25}$$

6.3.6. The Information Matrix $I(\theta) = -p \lim \frac{1}{n} \partial^2 l / \partial\theta \partial\theta'$

Clearly, under appropriate assumptions, $p \lim E'E/n = \Sigma$, $p \lim U_p' E/n = O$, and $p \lim X'C'(I_{pG} \otimes E)/n = O$, so our information matrix can be written as

$$I(\theta) = p \lim \frac{1}{n} \begin{bmatrix} X^{d'}(\Sigma^{-1} \otimes I_n) X^d & -X^{d'}(\Sigma^{-1} \otimes U_p) K_{G,pG} & O \\ -K_{pG,G}(\Sigma^{-1} \otimes U_p') X^d & U_p' U_p \otimes \Sigma^{-1} & O \\ O & O & \frac{n}{2} D'(\Sigma^{-1} \otimes \Sigma^{-1}) D \end{bmatrix}. \tag{6.26}$$

If the matrix X does not contain lagged values of dependent variables, then $p \lim X^{d'}(I_G \otimes U_p)/n = 0$, and for this special case the information matrix simplifies to

$$I(\theta) = p \lim \frac{1}{n} \begin{bmatrix} X^{d'}(\Sigma^{-1} \otimes I_n) X^d & O & O \\ O & U_p' U_p \otimes \Sigma^{-1} & O \\ O & O & \frac{n}{2} D'(\Sigma^{-1} \otimes^{-1}) D \end{bmatrix}. \tag{6.27}$$

6.3.7. The Cramer-Rao Lower Bound $I^{-1}(\theta)$

Inverting the information matrix is straightforward. For the general case let

$$I^{-1}(\theta) = \begin{bmatrix} I^{\delta\delta} & I^{\delta r} & I^{\delta v} \\ I^{r\delta} & I^{rr} & I^{rv} \\ I^{v\delta} & I^{vr} & I^{vv} \end{bmatrix}.$$

Then

$$I^{\delta\delta} = [p \lim X^{d'}(\Sigma^{-1} \otimes M_p) X^d / n]^{-1}, \tag{6.28}$$

$$I^{\delta r} = (I^{r\delta})' = I^{\delta\delta} p \lim X^{d'} [I_G \otimes U_p (U_p' U_p)^{-1}] K_{G,pG}, \tag{6.29}$$

$$I^{\delta v} = (I^{\delta v})' = O, \tag{6.30}$$

$$\begin{aligned} I^{rr} &= K_{pG,G} p \lim \{\Sigma \otimes (U_p' U_p / n)^{-1} + [I_G \otimes (U_p' U_p)^{-1} U_p'] \\ &\quad \times X^d I^{\delta\delta} X^{d'} \times [I_G \otimes U_p (U_p' U_p)^{-1}]\} K_{G,pG} \\ &= p \lim n \{U_p' U_p \otimes \Sigma^{-1} - K_{pG,G}(\Sigma^{-1} \otimes U_p') X^d \\ &\quad \times [X^{d'}(\Sigma^{-1} \otimes I_n) X^d]^{-1} X^{d'}(\Sigma^{-1} \otimes U_p) K_{G,pG}\}^{-1}, \end{aligned} \tag{6.31}$$

$$I^{rv} = (I^{vr}) = O, \tag{6.32}$$

$$I^{vv} = 2NL(\Sigma \otimes \Sigma)NL', \tag{6.33}$$

where $M_p = I_n - U_p(U_p'U_p)^{-1}U_p'$, $N = (1/2)(I_{G^2} + K_{GG})$ and L is the $(1/2)G(G+1) \times G^2$ elimination matrix.

For the special case in which X is exogenous and contains no lagged dependent variables,

$$I^{-1}(\theta) = p\lim n \begin{pmatrix} [X^{d'}(\Sigma^{-1} \otimes I_n)X^d]^{-1} & O & O \\ O & (U_p'U_p)^{-1} \otimes \Sigma & O \\ O & O & 2LN(\Sigma \otimes \Sigma)NL'/n \end{pmatrix}. \tag{6.34}$$

6.3.8. Statistical Inference from the Score Vector and the Information Matrix

6.3.8.1. Efficient Estimation of δ

1. Case in which R is known. Consider the equation

$$y^d = X^d\delta + \varepsilon, \tag{6.35}$$

where $y^d = M(r)X$ and $X^d = M(r)X$. Clearly this equation satisfies the assumptions of the SURE model without vector autoregressive disturbances. With R known, we can form y^d and X^d and an asymptotically efficient estimation of δ would be the JGLS estimator applied to Eq. (6.35); that is,

$$\hat{\delta} = [X^{d'}(\hat{\Sigma}^{-1} \otimes I_n)X^d]^{-1}X^{d'}(\hat{\Sigma}^{-1} \otimes I_n)y^d, \tag{6.36}$$

where $\hat{\Sigma} = \hat{E}'\hat{E}'/n$, $\hat{E} = \text{devec}_n\,\hat{\varepsilon}$, and $\hat{\varepsilon}$ is the OLS residual vector. As $\hat{\delta}$ is a BAN estimator, we have

$$\sqrt{n}(\hat{\delta} - \delta) \xrightarrow{d} N(0, V_1),$$

where V_1 is the Cramer–Rao lower bound referring to δ. With r known, our unknown parameters would $(\delta'v')'$ and the information matrix, both for the case in which X is exogenous and for the case in which X contains lagged dependent variables would be

$$I^*\begin{pmatrix}\delta \\ v\end{pmatrix} = p\lim \frac{1}{n}\begin{bmatrix} X^{d'}(\Sigma^{-1} \otimes I_n)X^d & O \\ O & \frac{n}{2}D'(\Sigma^{-1} \otimes \Sigma^{-1})D \end{bmatrix}.$$

The asymptotic covariance matrix of $\hat{\delta}$ would then be

$$V_1 = [p\lim X^{d'}(\Sigma^{-1} \otimes I_n)X^d/n]^{-1}.$$

2. Case in which R is unknown. The estimator $\hat{\delta}$ is not available to us in the more realistic case in which R is unknown. However, an asymptotically efficient estimator for δ may be obtained from the following procedure.[2]

1. Apply joint generalized least square to $y = X\delta + u$, ignoring the vector autoregression, to obtain estimator $\bar{\delta}$, say, and the residual vector $\hat{u} = y - X\bar{\delta}$. From $\hat{u}$, form $\hat{U} = \text{devec}_n\, \hat{U}$ and $\hat{U}_p = S(I_p \otimes \hat{U})$.
2. Compute

$$R' = -(\hat{U}_p'\hat{U}_p)^{-1}\hat{U}_p'\hat{U},\ \hat{r} = \text{vec}\,\hat{R} \text{ and } M(\hat{r}),$$
$$\hat{E} = \hat{U} + \hat{U}_p\hat{R}',$$
$$\hat{y}^d = M(\hat{r})y,$$
$$\hat{X}^d = M(\hat{r})X,$$
$$\hat{\Sigma} = \hat{E}'\hat{E}/n.$$

3. Compute

$$\hat{\hat{\delta}} = [\hat{X}^{d'}(\hat{\Sigma}^{-1} \otimes I_n)\hat{X}^d]^{-1}\hat{X}^{d'}(\hat{\Sigma}^{-1} \otimes I_n)\hat{y}. \tag{6.37}$$

The estimator $\hat{\hat{\delta}}$ is asymptotically efficient for both the case in which X is exogenous and for the case in which X contains lagged values of the dependent variables. However, as in the case of GLS estimators in dynamic linear-regression models, the efficiency of $\hat{\hat{\delta}}$ differs in the two cases.

First, consider the case in which X is exogenous. As $\hat{\hat{\delta}}$ is a BAN estimator,

$$\sqrt{n}(\hat{\hat{\delta}} - \delta) \xrightarrow{d} N(0, V_2),$$

where V_2 is the appropriate Cramer–Rao lower bound obtained from $I^{-1}(\theta)$ given by Eq. (6.34). Therefore, we see that

$$V_2 \equiv V_1 = [p \lim X^{d'}(\Sigma^{-1} \otimes I_n)X^d/n]^{-1}.$$

This means that the JGLS estimator $\hat{\hat{\delta}}$ with unknown R is as asymptotically efficient as the JGLS estimator $\hat{\delta}$ with known R. As in the linear-regression model, not knowing R cost us nothing in terms of asymptotic efficiency.

Next, consider the case in which X contains lagged dependent variables. For this case $I^{-1}(\theta)$ is given by Eqs. (6.28)–(6.33) so the asymptotic covariance matrix of $\hat{\hat{\delta}}$ is

$$V_2 \equiv I^{\delta\delta} = [p \lim X^{d'}(\Sigma^{-1} \otimes M_p)X^d/n]^{-1}.$$

[2] The formal proof that this procedure does indeed lead to an asymptotically efficient estimator may be obtained along the lines of a similar proof presented in Subsection 7.3.5.1.

It is easily seen that now $V_1^{-1} - V_2^{-1}$ is positive semidefinite so $V_2 - V_1$ is also positive semidefinite.

The JGLS estimator $\hat{\delta}$ that can be formed with known R is asymptotically more efficient than the JGLS estimator $\hat{\hat{\delta}}$ with unknown R. Not knowing R, now costs us in terms of asymptotic efficiency, just as it did in the equivalent linear-regression case.

6.3.8.2. Maximum-Likelihood Estimators as Iterative Joint-Generalized-Least-Squares Estimators

Using the score vector given by Eqs. (6.18)–(6.20) makes it possible to obtain an interpretation of the MLE of δ as an iterative JGLS estimator. Returning to the score vector, we see that $\partial l/\partial r = 0$ gives $K_{pG,G}\text{vec}\, U_p' E\Sigma = 0$, which implies that $U_p' E = O$, so from Eq. (6.11),

$$\tilde{R}' = -(U_p' U_p)^{-1} U_p' U. \tag{6.38}$$

Next, $\partial l/\partial v = 0$ gives

$$\tilde{\Sigma} = E'E/n, \tag{6.39}$$

and solving $\partial l/\partial \delta = 0$ for δ yields

$$\tilde{\delta} = [X^{d'}(\Sigma^{-1} \otimes I_n)X^d]^{-1} X^{d'}(\Sigma^{-1} \otimes I_n)y^d.$$

This interpretation of the MLE is clearly iterative as $\tilde{R}$ still contains $\tilde{\delta}$ through U_p whereas $\tilde{\delta}$ contains $\tilde{R}$ through X^d. However, this interpretation clearly points to the estimation procedure outlined above.

6.3.8.3. Classical Test Statistics for Hypotheses Concerning the Disturbances

1. THE HYPOTHESIS $H_0 : \sigma_{ij} = 0,\ i \neq j$. Two hypotheses are of interest regarding the disturbances of this model: that the disturbance εs are in fact contemporaneously correlated and that the disturbances are in fact subject to an autoregressive process.

The first is easily dealt with. The appropriate null hypothesis is

$$H_0 : \sigma_{ij} = 0, \quad i \neq j.$$

Compare Eqs. (6.26) and (6.27) with Eq. (6.7). Clearly, as the information matrix $I(\theta)$ for this model is block diagonal, both for the case in which X is exogenous and for the case in which X contains lagged dependent variables, the LMT statistic for H_0 is the Breusch–Pagan test statistic discussed in Subsection 6.2.4.2 with the proviso that we now work with the εs rather than with the us. This proviso complicates procedures in that

$$\varepsilon = y^d - X^d \delta,$$

and, as $y^d = M(r)y,\ X^d = M(r)X$, and r is unknown, y^d and X^d are unknown and must be predicted before we start. We could do this by ignoring the vector autoregressive process, assuming the εs are contemporaneously uncorrelated and applying ordinary least squares to $y = X\delta + u$. With the OLS residual vector we would obtain a consistent estimator $\hat{r}$ of r by following the procedure outlined in Subsection 6.3.8.1 and then form predictors $\hat{y}^d$ and $\hat{X}^d$. Then $\hat{\varepsilon}$ would be the residual vector from the regression of $\hat{y}^d$ on $\hat{X}^d$ and the LMT statistic would be formed as in Subsection 6.2.5.2 but with $\hat{\varepsilon}$ in place of $\hat{u}$.

It is unlikely that testing $H_0 : \sigma_{ij} = 0, i \neq j$, would play a significant role in this model as it would in the standard model, the reason being that imposing $\sigma_{ij} = 0,\ i \neq j$, on the model does not simplify the estimation procedure all that much. We would still have to follow steps like those provided in Subsection 6.3.8.1, starting with an OLS estimator rather that a JGLS estimator in step 1, and the estimator we would end up with is simpler only to the extent that $\hat{\Sigma}$ is now diagonal. This does not lead to great computational savings as X^d is not block diagonal.

A better diagnostic procedure would be first to test the null hypothesis $H_0 : r = 0$. If this is accepted, we could then aim at greater simplification by testing $H_0 : \sigma_{ij} = 0, i \neq j$, by using the basic LMT statistic of Subsection 6.2.4.2.

2. THE LMT STATISTIC FOR $H_0 : r = 0$. The second more important hypothesis then concerns the autoregressive process.

If the disturbances of the SURE model are not subject to vector autoregression then, rather than using the estimator $\hat{\hat{\delta}}$ given by Eq. (6.37), we would use the JGLS estimator obtained from $y = X\delta + u$, namely

$$\bar{\delta} = [X'(\hat{\Sigma}^{-1} \otimes I_n)X]^{-1} X'(\hat{\Sigma}^{-1} \otimes I)y.$$

It is of interest to us then to develop a test statistic for the null hypothesis $H_0 : r = 0$ against the alternative $H_A : r \neq 0$. As in the linear model, the most amenable classical test statistic is the LMT statistic, which is given by

$$T_1 = \frac{1}{n} \frac{\partial l}{\partial r}\bigg|_{\hat{\theta}}' I^{rr}(\hat{\theta}) \frac{\partial l}{\partial r}\bigg|_{\hat{\theta}},$$

where, in forming $\hat{\theta}$, we put r equal to the null vector and evaluate all other parameters at the constrained MLEs, the MLEs we get for δ and ν after we set r equal to the null vector. Asymptotically the constrained MLE for δ is equivalent to $\bar{\delta}$.

The actual test statistic itself will depend on the case before us. We have seen that $I(\theta)$ and therefore $I^{rr}(\theta)$ differ, depending on whether X is exogenous or X contains lagged dependent variables. Of course for both cases in which $r = 0,\ M(r) = I_{nG},\ X^d = X,\ p\lim U_p'U_p/n = I_p \otimes \Sigma$. We consider each case in turn.

First, when X is exogenous

$$I^{rr}(\theta)|_{r=0} = I_p \otimes \Sigma^{-1} \otimes \Sigma.$$

It follows that for this case the LMT statistic is

$$\begin{aligned}
T_1' &= \frac{1}{n} u'(\Sigma^{-1} \otimes U_p) K_{G,pG}[I_p \otimes \Sigma^{-1} \otimes \Sigma] K_{pG,G}(\Sigma^{-1} \otimes U_p')u|_{\hat{\theta}} \\
&= \frac{1}{n} u'[\Sigma^{-1} \otimes U_p(I_p \otimes \Sigma^{-1})U_p']u|_{\hat{\theta}} \\
&= n\,\hat{u}'\{(\hat{U}'\hat{U})^{-1} \otimes \hat{U}_p[I_p \otimes (\hat{U}'\hat{U})^{-1}]\hat{U}_p'\}\hat{u}, \qquad (6.40)
\end{aligned}$$

where $\hat{u}$ is the constrained MLE residual vector, $\hat{U} = \text{devec}_n\,\hat{U}$ and $\hat{U}_p = S(I_p \otimes \hat{U})$. (An asymptotically equivalent test statistic would use the JGLS estimator residuals formed from $\bar{\delta}$). Under H_0, T_1' has a limiting χ^2 distribution with pG^2 degrees of freedom, so the upper tail of this distribution is used to obtain the appropriate critical region.

This LMT statistic, like several other such test statistics, has an intuitive interpretation in terms of an F test associated with an underlying regression. Suppose for the moment that U and U_p are known and consider the artificial regression

$$u = (I_G \otimes U_p)\rho + \varepsilon,$$

where $\rho = \text{vec}\, R'$. This equation would not satisfy the assumptions of the linear-regression model as $V(\varepsilon) = \Sigma \otimes I_n$ rather than a scalar matrix. However, suppose further that Σ is known and consider the nonsingular matrix $\mathcal{P}$ such that $\mathcal{P}'\mathcal{P} = \Sigma^{-1}$. Then the transformed equation

$$\bar{u} = \bar{U}_p\rho + \bar{\varepsilon},$$

with $\bar{u} = (\mathcal{P} \otimes I_n)u$, $\bar{\varepsilon} = (\mathcal{P} \otimes I_n)\varepsilon$ and $\bar{U}_p = \mathcal{P} \otimes U_p$ would satisfy the Gauss–Markov assumptions. We could then apply the usual F test for the null hypothesis $H_0 : \rho = 0$, obtaining the test statistic

$$F = \frac{(\bar{u}'\bar{u} - \bar{u}'\bar{M}_p\bar{u})/pG^2}{\bar{u}'\bar{M}_p\bar{u}/(n - pG^2)}$$

with $\bar{M}_p = I_{nG} - \bar{U}_p(\bar{U}_p'\bar{U}_p)^{-1}\bar{U}_p'$. However, it is easily seen that the numerator of this artificial F test statistic, apart from the constant, is

$$u'[\Sigma^{-1} \otimes U_p(U_p'U_p)^{-1}U_p']u.$$

Noting that, under H_0, $p\lim U_p'U_p/n = I_p \otimes p\lim U'U/n$ and that $U'U/n$ is a consistent estimator of Σ, we see that the LMT statistic is asymptotically equivalent to n times this numerator after we have placed caps on u and U.

Second, we consider the more complicated case in which X contains lagged dependent variables. From Eq. (6.31) we can write

$$\begin{aligned} I^{rr}(\theta)|_{r=0} = {} & K_{pG,G}(\Sigma \otimes I_p \otimes \Sigma^{-1})K_{G,pG} + p\lim n^2 K_{pG,G} \\ & \times [I_G \otimes (I_p \otimes \Sigma^{-1})U_p'] \\ & \times X(X'\{\Sigma^{-1} \otimes [I_n - U_p(I_p \otimes \Sigma^{-1})U_p']\}X)^{-1} \\ & \times X'[I_G \otimes U_p(I_p \otimes \Sigma^{-1})]K_{G,pG}. \end{aligned}$$

Now, as $\left.\frac{\partial l}{\partial r}\right|_{r=0} = -K_{pG,G}(\Sigma^{-1} \otimes U_p')u$ and as $K_{pG,G}^{-1} = K_{pG,G}' = K_{G,pG}$, we can write the LMT statistic, ignoring the $p\lim$, as

$$\begin{aligned} T_1 = {} & T_1' + nu'[\Sigma^{-1} \otimes U_p(I_p \otimes \Sigma^{-1})U_p'] \\ & \times X(X'(\Sigma^{-1} \otimes [I_n - U_p(I_p \otimes \Sigma^{-1})U_p'])X)^{-1}X' \\ & \times [\Sigma^{-1} \otimes U_p(I_p \otimes \Sigma^{-1})U_p']u|_{\hat{\theta}} \end{aligned} \qquad (6.41)$$

In the evaluation at $\hat{\theta}$, we put $\hat{u}, \hat{U}'\hat{U}/n$, and $\hat{U}_p$ in place of u, Σ, and U_p, respectively, where $\hat{u}$ is the constrained MLE residual vector, $\hat{U} = \text{devec}_n\, \hat{u}$, and $\hat{U}_p = S(I_p \otimes \hat{U})$.

3. The Wald test statistic for $H_0 : r = 0$. The other classical statistic that is worth considering in this context is the Wald test statistic. Suppose $\tilde{\theta} = (\tilde{\delta}'\tilde{r}'\tilde{\nu}')'$ is the MLE of θ. Then the Wald test statistic would be based on

$$T_2 = n\tilde{r}'[I^{rr}(\tilde{\theta})]^{-1}\tilde{r},$$

where

$$I^{rr}(\theta) = (p\lim U_p'U_p/n)^{-1} \otimes \Sigma$$

for the case in which X is exogenous, and

$$\begin{aligned} I^{rr}(\theta) = {} & p\lim n\{U_p'U_p \otimes \Sigma^{-1} + K_{pG,G}(\Sigma^{-1} \otimes U_p')X^d \\ & \times [X^{d\prime}(\Sigma^{-1} \otimes I_n)X^d]^{-1}X^{d\prime}(\Sigma^{-1} \otimes U_p)K_{G,pG}\}^{-1} \end{aligned}$$

for the case in which X contains lagged values of the dependent variables.

An analysis similar to that conducted in Subsection 5.3.5.3 can now be conducted for the Wald test statistic here. As in the dynamic linear-regression case, we have difficulty in obtaining an explicit expression for the Wald statistic as the system of equations $\partial l/\partial\theta = 0$ is nonlinear in θ, although numerical techniques with the aid of computers should ensure that we can obtain the observed value of our test statistic.

It is also possible in this case to gain some comparative insight into the Wald test statistic by using the iterative solution for the MLEs obtained in

Subsection 6.3.8.2. There we show that the iterative solution for $\tilde{R}$ is given by $\tilde{R}' = -(U_p'U_p)^{-1}U_p'U$, so vec $\tilde{R}' = -[I_G \otimes (U_p'U_p)^{-1}U_p']u$ and

$$\tilde{r} = K_{pG,G}\,\text{vec}\tilde{R}' = -K_{pG,G}[I_G \otimes (U_p'U_p)^{-1}U_p']u.$$

For the case in which X is exogenous, the Wald test statistic essentially looks at

$$T_2' = nu'[I_G \otimes U_p(U_p'U_p)^{-1}]K_{G,pG}(U_p'U_p/n \otimes \Sigma^{-1})K_{pG,G} \\ \times [I_G \otimes (U_p'U_p)^{-1}U_p']u|_{\tilde{\theta}} = u'(\Sigma^{-1} \otimes \mathcal{N}_p)u|_{\tilde{\theta}} \quad (6.42)$$

with $\mathcal{N}_p = U_p(U_p'U_p)^{-1}U_p'$.

Comparing Eq. (6.42) with Eq. (6.40), we see that essentially the Wald test statistic has the same format as that of the LMT statistic, the difference being that the former evaluates u, Σ^{-1}, and U_p by using the (unconstrained) MLE whereas the latter evaluates these components by using the constrained MLEs.

Note that from Eqs. (6.38) and (6.39)

$$\tilde{\Sigma} = \tilde{E}'\tilde{E}/n, \quad \tilde{E} = \tilde{M}_p\tilde{U}, \quad (6.43)$$

where $\tilde{M}_p = I_p - \tilde{\mathcal{N}}_p$ so we can write T_2' out in full as

$$T_2' = u[(\tilde{U}'\tilde{M}_p\tilde{U}/n)^{-1} \otimes \tilde{U}_p(\tilde{U}_p'\tilde{U}_p)^{-1}\tilde{U}_p']\tilde{u},$$

where $\tilde{u} = y - X\tilde{\delta}$, $\tilde{\delta}$ is the MLE of δ, and $\tilde{U} = \text{devec}_n\,\tilde{u}$.

For the more complicated case in which X contains lagged dependent variables, the Wald test statistic is equivalent to

$$T_2 = u'[I_G \otimes U_p(U_p'U_p)^{-1}]K_{G,pG}\{(U_p'U_p \otimes \Sigma^{-1}) \\ + K_{pG,G}(\Sigma^{-1} \otimes U_p')X^d[X^{d'}(\Sigma^{-1} \otimes I_n)X^d]^{-1}X^{d'} \\ \times (\Sigma^{-1} \otimes U_p)K_{G,pG}\}K_{pG,G}[I_G \otimes (U_p'U_p)^{-1}U_p']u|_{\tilde{\theta}}.$$

Using the properties of the commutation matrix, we can simplify this expression to

$$T_2 = T_2' + u'(\Sigma^{-1} \otimes \mathcal{N}_p)X^d[X^{d'}(\Sigma^{-1} \otimes I_n)X^d]^{-1}X^{d'}(\Sigma^{-1} \otimes \mathcal{N}_p)u|_{\tilde{\theta}}.$$

Compare this with the corresponding case for the LMT given by Eq. (6.41), which we can write as

$$T_1 = T_1' + u'(\Sigma^{-1} \otimes \mathcal{N}_p)X^d[X^{d'}(\Sigma^{-1} \otimes M_p)X^d]^{-1}X^{d'}(\Sigma^{-1} \otimes \mathcal{N}_p)u|_{\tilde{\theta}}.$$

We have already noted the similarities between T_1' and T_2'. The second part of the two test statistics clearly involves a quadratic form of the vector

$X^{d'}(\Sigma^{-1} \otimes \mathcal{N}_p)u$, the difference being that for T_2 the matrix used in the quadratic form is $[X^{d'}(\Sigma^{-1} \otimes I_n)X^d]^{-1}$ whereas in T_1 it is $[X^{d'}(\Sigma^{-1} \otimes M_p)X^d]^{-1}$.

Needless to say, T_2 evaluates everything at the (unconstrained) MLE whereas T_1 evaluates everything at the constrained MLE.

4. THE LRT STATISTIC FOR $H_0 : r = 0$. Again using our iterative interpretation of the MLEs of Σ, both for the case in which we have no vector autoregression disturbances (Subsection 6.2.4.1) and for the case in which such disturbances exist (Subsection 6.3.8.2), and the log-likelihood function given by Eq. (6.17), we see that the LRT statistic is equivalent to

$$T_3 = -\frac{n}{2} \log \frac{\det \tilde{\Sigma}}{\det \hat{\Sigma}},$$

where $\tilde{\Sigma}$ and $\hat{\Sigma}$ are given by Eqs. (6.39) and (6.9), respectively. This expression clearly is a monotonic function of $\det \tilde{\Sigma} / \det \hat{\Sigma}$, but given the complicated nature of the determinant of a matrix, it is difficult to make further comparisons with the other two test statistics. Unlike in the linear-regression case, our iterative solutions do not help in this context.

6.4. THE SURE MODEL WITH VECTOR MOVING-AVERAGE DISTURBANCES

6.4.1. The Model

In this section, we assume that the disturbances of the model given are now subject to the moving-average process

$$\mathbf{u}_t = \varepsilon_t + R_1\varepsilon_{t-1} + \cdots + R_p\varepsilon_{t-1}.$$

Again, we assume that there are no unit root problems arising from lagged dependant variables. Following a similar analysis to that of Subsection 6.3.1, we write the model as

$$y = X\beta + u,$$
$$u = M(r)\varepsilon,$$
$$\varepsilon \sim N(0, \Sigma \otimes I_n).$$

Assuming invertability, we write

$$\varepsilon = M(r)^{-1}u.$$

It is the presence of the inverse matrix $M(r)^{-1}$ that makes the differentiation of the log likelihood far more complicated for the case of moving-average disturbances, but again the mathematics is greatly facilitated by use of generalized vecs and devecs. Before we commence this differentiation it pays us to look at some of the properties of $M(r)^{-1}$, properties that we shall need in the application of our asymptotic theory.

6.4.2. The Matrix $M(r)^{-1}$

Recall from Subsection 6.3.2 that if we write

$$M(r) = \begin{bmatrix} M_{11} & \cdots & M_{1G} \\ \vdots & & \vdots \\ M_{G1} & \cdots & M_{GG} \end{bmatrix},$$

then each $M_{ii},\ i = 1 \cdots G$, is an $n \times n$ Toeplitz lower-triangular band matrix with ones along its main diagonal whereas each $M_{ij},\ i \neq j$, is an $n \times n$ Toeplitz matrix that is strictly lower triangular and band. Suppose we write

$$M(r)^{-1} = \begin{bmatrix} M^{11} & \cdots & M^{1G} \\ \vdots & & \vdots \\ M^{G1} & \cdots & M^{GG} \end{bmatrix},$$

where each submatrix is $n \times n$. Then Theorem 2.6 of Chap. 2 allows us to conclude that each M^{ij} has characteristics similar to those of M_{ij}; that is, $M^{ii},\ i = 1 \cdots G$, is a lower-triangular matrix with ones down its main diagonal whereas $M^{ij},\ i \neq j$, is strictly lower triangular.

However, we can go further than this with regards to the properties of $M(r)^{-1}$. Recall that

$$M(r) = I_{nG} + (R \otimes I_n)C,$$

where R is the $G \times Gp$ matrix $R = (R_1 \cdots R_p)$ and C is the $Gnp \times Gn$ matrix given by

$$C = \begin{pmatrix} I_G \otimes S_1 \\ \vdots \\ I_G \otimes S_p \end{pmatrix}.$$

From the work we did in Subsection 3.7.4.3, it follows that it is possible to write

$$M(r)^{-1} = I_{nG} + (\bar{R} \otimes I_n)\bar{C}, \tag{6.44}$$

where $\bar{R}$ is a $G \times G(n-1)$ matrix whose elements are products of the elements of R and $\bar{C}$ is the $Gn(n-1) \times Gn$ matrix given by

$$\bar{C} = \begin{pmatrix} I_G \otimes S_1 \\ \vdots \\ I_G \otimes S_{n-1} \end{pmatrix}.$$

In other words, each submatrix M^{ii} of the inverse is a Toeplitz matrix of the form

$$I_n + a_1 S_1 + \cdots + a_{n-1} S_{n-1}$$

for $i = 1, \ldots, G$, whereas each submatrix $M^{ij}, i \neq j$, of the inverse is a Toeplitz matrix of the form

$$b_1 S_1 + \cdots + b_{n-1} S_{n-1}$$

for suitable a_is and b_js that are functions of the elements of R.
Now consider, say,

$$M(r)^{-1'} = \begin{bmatrix} M^{11'} & \cdots & M^{G1'} \\ \vdots & & \vdots \\ M^{1G'} & \cdots & M^{GG'} \end{bmatrix} = \begin{bmatrix} \mathcal{M}_{11} & \cdots & \mathcal{M}_{1G} \\ \vdots & & \vdots \\ \mathcal{M}_{G1} & \cdots & \mathcal{M}_{GG} \end{bmatrix}.$$

It follows that each $\mathcal{M}_{ii}, i = 1 \cdots G$, is an $n \times n$ upper-triangular matrix with ones as its main diagonal elements whereas each $\mathcal{M}_{ij},\ i \neq j$, is strictly upper triangular. In fact, each $\mathcal{M}_{ii}$ is a Toeplitz matrix of the form

$$I_n + a_1 S_1' + \cdots + a_{n-1} S_{n-1}',$$

whereas each $\mathcal{M}_{ij},\ i \neq j$, is a Toeplitz matrix of the form

$$b_1 S_1' + \cdots + b_{n-1} S_{n-1}'$$

for suitable a_is and b_js.

6.4.3. The Derivative $\partial\varepsilon/\partial r$

Just as in the analysis of the preceding model we shall need the derivative $\partial\varepsilon/\partial r$.
We write

$$\varepsilon = M(r)^{-1} u = (u' \otimes I_G) \text{vec}\, M(r)^{-1},$$

and

$$\partial \text{ vec}\, M(r)^{-1}/\partial r = \frac{\partial \text{ vec}\, N(r)}{\partial r} \frac{\partial \text{ vec} M(r)^{-1}}{\partial \text{ vec} M(r)} = -J'[M(r)^{-1} \otimes M(r)^{-1'}], \tag{6.45}$$

so

$$\frac{\partial\varepsilon}{\partial r} = -J'(\varepsilon \otimes I_{nG}) M(r)^{-1'}.$$

However, we can obtain an alternative way of writing this derivative by using the properties of J as we did in Eq. (6.16) of Subsection 6.3.3 to get

$$\frac{\partial\varepsilon}{\partial r} = -J'(\varepsilon \otimes I_{nG}) M(r)^{-1'} = -K_{pG,Gp}(I_G \otimes E_p') M(r)^{-1'}, \tag{6.46}$$

where

$$E_p = S(I_p \otimes E).$$

6.4.4. The Parameters of the Model, the Log-Likelihood Function, and the Score Vector

The parameters of the model are given by $\theta = (\delta' r' v')'$ and the log-likelihood function, apart from a constant, is

$$l(\theta) = -\frac{n}{2} \log \det \Sigma - \frac{1}{2}\varepsilon'(\Sigma^{-1} \otimes I_n)\varepsilon,$$

where in this function we set ε equal to $y^* - X^*\delta$, with $y^* = M(r)^{-1}y$ and $X^* = M(r)^{-1}X$. The first and the third components of the score vector are given by Eqs. (6.18) and (6.19), with X^* in place of X^d. Using Eq. (6.46), we find that the second component of the score vector is given by

$$\frac{\partial l}{\partial r} = K_{pG,G}\,(I_G \otimes E_p')\,M(r)^{-1'}(\Sigma^{-1} \otimes I_n)\varepsilon. \qquad (6.47)$$

6.4.5. The Hessian matrix $\partial^2 l/\partial\theta\partial\theta'$

The components of the Hessian matrix $\partial^2 l/\partial\delta\partial\delta'$, $\partial^2 l/\partial\delta\partial v'$, and $\partial^2 l/\partial v\partial v'$ are given by Eqs. (6.21), (6.22), and (6.23), respectively, but with X^* in place of X^d. The derivative $\partial l/\partial r\partial v'$ is obtained in much the same way as for the preceding model. We get

$$\frac{\partial^2 l}{\partial r\partial v'} = -K_{pG,G}\,(I_G \otimes E_p')M(r)^{-1'}(\Sigma^{-1} \otimes E\Sigma^{-1})D.$$

The last two components of the Hessian matrix, namely $\partial^2 l/\partial\delta\partial r'$ and $\partial^2 l/\partial r\partial r'$, require more effort to obtain and draw heavily on the properties of the matrix J given by Propositions 6.1 and 6.2 of Subsection 6.3.3.1 and the Theorem 3.11 of Subsection 3.3.3 concerning $K_{nG}^{\bar{\tau}}$. Each is handled in turn.

$\partial^2 l/\partial\delta\partial r'$: We start from $\partial l/\partial r$, which we write as

$$\frac{\partial l}{\partial r} = J'(\varepsilon \otimes I_{nG})\mathcal{A}\varepsilon,$$

where $\mathcal{A} = M(r)^{-1'}(\Sigma^{-1} \otimes I_n)$. Using the backward chain rule of matrix calculus, we find that it follows that

$$\frac{\partial^2 l}{\partial\delta\partial r'} = -\frac{\partial\varepsilon}{\partial\delta}\frac{\partial}{\partial\varepsilon}[J'(\varepsilon \otimes I_{nG})\mathcal{A}\varepsilon]. \qquad (6.48)$$

However, in Chap. 4, from our table of matrix calculus results,

$$\frac{\partial(\varepsilon \otimes I_{nG})\mathcal{A}\varepsilon}{\partial\varepsilon} = \mathcal{A}'(\varepsilon' \otimes I_{nG}) + (I_{nG} \otimes \varepsilon'\mathcal{A}'),$$

and, as $\partial\varepsilon/\partial\delta = -X^{*\prime}$, we have referring to Eq. 6.48

$$\frac{\partial^2 l}{\partial\delta\partial r'} = -X^{*\prime}\{(\Sigma^{-1}\otimes I_n)M(r)^{-1}(\varepsilon'\otimes I_{nG}) + [I_{nG}\otimes(\text{vec}E\,\Sigma^{-1})'M(r)^{-1}]\}J. \tag{6.49}$$

We now want to write this derivative in terms of commutation matrices. We do this by using the properties of J. By Proposition 6.1 of Subsection 6.3.3.1.,

$$J'(\varepsilon\otimes I_{nG}) = K_{pG,G}(I_G\otimes E'_p). \tag{6.50}$$

Consider the $nG\times 1$ vector

$$a = M(r)^{-1'}\text{vec}\,E\,\Sigma^{-1}.$$

Then, from Proposition 6.3 of the same section,

$$J'(I_{nG}\otimes a) = \left(I_{pG}\otimes a^{\bar{\tau}'_n}\right)C,$$

and if we use the properties of the devec operator

$$a^{\bar{\tau}_n} = [M(r)^{-1'}]^{\bar{\tau}_n}(I_G\otimes\text{vec}\,E\,\Sigma^{-1}) = [M(r)^{-1}]^{\tau'_n}(I_G\otimes\text{vec}E\,\Sigma^{-1}), \tag{6.51}$$

so we can now write

$$\frac{\partial^2 l}{\partial\delta\partial r'} = -\,X^{*\prime}(\Sigma^{-1}\otimes I_n)M(r)^{-1}(I_G\otimes E_p)K_{G,pG} - X^{*\prime}C'\left\{I_{pG}\otimes[M(r)^{-1}]^{\tau'_n}(I_G\otimes\text{vec}\,E\,\Sigma^{-1})\right\}.$$

$\boldsymbol{\partial^2 l/\partial r\,\partial r'}$: Again we start with $\partial l/\partial r$. As before, we let $a(r) = M(r)^{-1'}(\Sigma^{-1}\otimes I_n)\varepsilon$ and $A(r) = I_G\otimes E'_p$. With this notation we can write

$$\frac{\partial l}{\partial r} = K_{pG,G}A(r)a(r)$$

and, by using the product rule of matrix calculus,

$$\frac{\partial^2 l}{\partial r\partial r'} = \left\{\frac{\partial\,\text{vec}\,A(r)}{\partial r}[a(r)\otimes I_{pG^2}] + \frac{\partial a(r)}{\partial r}A(r)'\right\}K_{G,pG}. \tag{6.52}$$

However, from Eq. (3.7),

$$\text{vec}\,A(r) = Q\,\text{vec}\,E'_p = Q\,K_{n,pG}\,\text{vec}\,E_p = Q\,K_{n,pG}\,C\varepsilon, \tag{6.53}$$

where $Q = K^{\tau_n}_{nG}\otimes I_{pG}$, so

$$\frac{\partial\,\text{vec}A(r)}{\partial r} = \frac{\partial\varepsilon}{\partial r}C'K_{pG,n}Q' = -J'(\varepsilon\otimes I_{nG})M(r)^{-1'}C'K_{pG,n}Q'. \tag{6.54}$$

Again by using the product rule, we can write

$$\frac{\partial a(r)}{\partial r} = \frac{\partial \operatorname{vec} M(r)^{-1'}}{\partial r}[(\Sigma^{-1} \otimes I_n)\varepsilon \otimes I_{nG}] + \frac{\partial(\Sigma^{-1} \otimes I_n)\varepsilon}{\partial r} M(r)^{-1} \tag{6.55}$$

and, from Eq. (6.45),

$$\frac{\partial \operatorname{vec} M(r)^{-1'}}{\partial r} = -J'[M(r)^{-1} \otimes M(r)^{-1'}]K_{nG,nG}.$$

This, together with Eq. (6.46) and the properties of the commutation matrix, allows us to write

$$\frac{\partial a(r)}{\partial r} = -J'[M(r)^{-1} \otimes a(r)] - J'(\varepsilon \otimes I_{nG})M(r)^{-1'}(\Sigma^{-1} \otimes I_n)M(r)^{-1}. \tag{6.56}$$

Substituting Eqs. (6.54) and (6.56) into Eq. (6.52) gives

$$\begin{aligned}\frac{\partial^2 l}{\partial r \partial r'} &= -J'(\varepsilon \otimes I_{nG})M(r)^{-1'}C'K_{pG,n}Q'[a(r) \otimes I_{pG^2}]K_{G,pG} \\ &\quad - J'[M(r)^{-1'} \otimes a(r)](I_G \otimes E_p)K_{G,pG} \\ &\quad - J'(\varepsilon \otimes I_{nG})M(r)^{-1'}(\Sigma^{-1} \otimes I_n)M(r)^{-1}(I_G \otimes E_p)K_{G,pG}.\end{aligned} \tag{6.57}$$

To write this derivative in terms of commutation matrices as we want to do, we use the properties of J and our theorems concerning $K_{nG}^{\bar{\tau}}$. To this end, we consider the first matrix on the right-hand side of Eq. (6.57). As $Q' = K_{Gn}^{\bar{\tau}_n} \otimes I_{pG}$, we write, by using Theorem 3.11,

$$Q'[a(r) \otimes I_{pG^2}] = \{K_{Gn}^{\bar{\tau}_n}[a(r) \otimes I_G]\} \otimes I_{pG} = a(r)^{\bar{\tau}_n} \otimes I_{pG}.$$

Then, recalling that $J'(\varepsilon \otimes I_{nG}) = K_{pG,G}(I_G \otimes E_p')$ and again using properties of the commutation matrix, we write this first matrix as

$$-K_{pG,G}(I_G \otimes E_p')M(r)^{-1'}C'\left[I_{pG} \otimes a(r)^{\bar{\tau}_n}\right]. \tag{6.58}$$

Next, the second matrix on the right-hand side of Eq. (6.57) can be written as

$$-J'[I_{nG} \otimes a(r)]M(r)^{-1'}(I_G \otimes E_p)K_{G,pG},$$

and from Proposition 6.3 of Subsection 6.3.3.1, we see that this second matrix is just the transpose of the first matrix. Thus, by using Eq. (6.14), we obtain our final expression for our derivative:

$$\frac{\partial^2 l}{\partial r \partial r'}$$
$$= -K_{pG,G}(I_G \otimes E'_p)M(r)^{-1'}C'\{I_{pG} \otimes [M(r)^{-1}]^{\tau'_n}(I_G \otimes \text{vec}\, E\,\Sigma^{-1})\}$$
$$- \{I_{pG} \otimes [I_G \otimes (\text{vec}\, E\,\Sigma^{-1})'][M(r)^{-1}]^{\tau_n}\}CM(r)^{-1}(I_G \otimes E_p)K_{G,pG}$$
$$- K_{pG,G}(I_G \otimes E'_p)M(r)^{-1'}(\Sigma^{-1} \otimes I_n)M(r)^{-1}(I_G \otimes E_p)K_{G,pG}.$$

6.4.6. The Information Matrix $I(\theta) = -p\lim \frac{1}{n}\partial^2 l/\partial\theta\partial\theta'$

The work required for evaluating some of the probability limits associated with this matrix is described in Appendix 6.A. By using the results of this appendix, we can write the information matrix as

$$I(\theta) = \begin{bmatrix} I_{\delta\delta} & I_{\delta r} & I_{\delta\nu} \\ I_{r\delta} & I_{rr} & I_{r\nu} \\ I_{\nu\delta} & I_{\nu r} & I_{\nu\nu} \end{bmatrix},$$

where

$$I_{\delta\delta} = p\lim \frac{1}{n}X^{*\prime}(\Sigma^{-1} \otimes \mathrm{I_n})X^*,$$
$$I_{\delta r} = p\lim \frac{1}{n}X^{*\prime}(\Sigma^{-1} \otimes I_n)M(r)^{-1}(I_G \otimes E_p)K_{G,pG} = (I_{r\delta})',$$
$$I_{\delta\nu} = O = (I_{\nu\delta})',$$
$$I_{r\nu} = O = (I_{\nu r})',$$
$$I_{rr} = p\lim \frac{1}{n}K_{pG,G}(I_G \otimes E'_p)M(r)^{-1'}(\Sigma^{-1} \otimes I_n)M(r)^{-1} \times (I_G \otimes E_p)K_{G,pG}, \quad (6.59)$$
$$I_{\nu\nu} = \frac{1}{2}D'(\Sigma^{-1} \otimes \Sigma^{-1})D. \quad (6.60)$$

In this appendix, it is also shown that, in order to ensure the existence of I_{rr}, we need to assume that $\lim M(r)^{-1'}M(r)^{-1}/n$ exists as n tends to infinity and we further evaluate I_{rr}. However, for the purposes of deriving statistical inference by using the information matrix, as we do in Subsection 6.4.7, it is sufficient to write I_{rr} as given by Eq. (6.59).

For the special case in which X contains no lagged dependent variables,

$$I_{\delta r} = O = (I_{r\delta})'.$$

6.4.7. The Cramer–Rao Lower Bound $I^{-1}(\theta)$

As $I(\theta)$ is block diagonal, inverting it presents little difficulty. Using the property of commutation matrices that $K_{pG,G}^{-1} = K'_{pG,G} = K_{G,pG}$, if we write

$$I^{-1}(\theta) = \begin{bmatrix} I^{\delta\delta} & I^{\delta r} & I^{\delta v} \\ I^{r\delta} & I^{rr} & I^{rv} \\ I^{v\delta} & I^{vr} & I^{vv} \end{bmatrix},$$

then

$$I^{\delta\delta} = p\lim n\{X^{*\prime}(\Sigma^{-1} \otimes I_n)X^* - X^{*\prime}\mathcal{F}[\mathcal{F}'(\Sigma \otimes I_n)\mathcal{F}]^{-1}\mathcal{F}'X^*\}^{-1}, \tag{6.61}$$

$$I^{\delta r} = (I^{r\delta})' = -I^{\delta\delta} p\lim X^{*\prime}\mathcal{F}[\mathcal{F}'(\Sigma \otimes I_n)\mathcal{F}]^{-1}K_{G,pG}, \tag{6.62}$$

$$I^{\delta v} = (I^{v\delta})' = O, \tag{6.63}$$

$$I^{rv} = (I^{rv})' = O, \tag{6.64}$$

$$I^{rr} = K_{pG,G}\, p\lim n\{\mathcal{F}'(\Sigma \otimes I_n)\mathcal{F} - \mathcal{F}'X^{*\prime} \times [X^{*\prime}(\Sigma^{-1} \otimes I_n)X^*]^{-1}X^{*\prime}\mathcal{F}\}^{-1}K_{G,pG}, \tag{6.65}$$

$$I^{vv} = 2LN(\Sigma \otimes \Sigma)NL', \tag{6.66}$$

where

$$\mathcal{F} = (\Sigma^{-1} \otimes I_n)M(r)^{-1}(I_G \otimes E_p).$$

The special case in which X is exogenous and contains no lagged dependant variables is simpler.

Here,

$$I^{-1}(\theta) = p\lim n \begin{bmatrix} [X^{*\prime}(\Sigma^{-1} \otimes I_n)X^*]^{-1} & O & O \\ O & K_{pG,G}[\mathcal{F}'(\Sigma \otimes I_n)\mathcal{F}]^{-1}K_{G,pG} & O \\ O & O & 2LN(\Sigma \otimes \Sigma)NL'/n \end{bmatrix}. \tag{6.67}$$

6.4.8. Statistical Inference from the Score Vector and the Information Matrix

Having used our work on the generalized vec and devec operators to assist us in the complicated matrix calculus needed to obtain the score vector and the information matrix, we can now avail ourselves of these latter concepts to derive statistical results for our model in much the same way as we have done for previous models.

6.4.8.1. Efficient Estimation of δ

1. CASE IN WHICH R IS KNOWN. Consider the equation

$$y^* = X^*\delta + \varepsilon, \tag{6.68}$$

where $y^* = M(r)^{-1}y$ and $X^* = M(r)^{-1}X$. Clearly this equation satisfies the assumption of the SURE model without vector moving-average disturbances.

With R known, we can form y^* and X^* and an asymptotically efficient estimator of δ would be the JGLS estimator obtained from Eq. (6.68), that is,

$$\tilde{\delta} = [X^{*\prime}(\hat{\Sigma}^{-1} \otimes I_n)X^*]^{-1}X^{*\prime}(\hat{\Sigma}^{-1} \otimes I_n)y^*, \tag{6.69}$$

where $\hat{\Sigma} = \hat{E}^{\prime}\hat{E}/n$, $\hat{E} = \text{devec}_n\, \hat{\varepsilon}$, and $\hat{\varepsilon}$ is the OLS residual vector. As $\tilde{\delta}$ is a BAN estimator we have

$$\sqrt{n}(\tilde{\delta} - \delta) \xrightarrow{d} N(O,\ V_1),$$

where V_1 is the Cramer–Rao lower bound referring to δ. With r known, our unknown parameters would be $(\delta'\ \nu')'$, and the information matrix for both the case in which X is exogenous and for the case in which X contains lagged dependent variables would be

$$I^*\begin{pmatrix}\delta\\ \nu\end{pmatrix} = p\lim \frac{1}{n}\begin{bmatrix} X^{*\prime}(\Sigma^{-1} \otimes I_n)X^* & O \\ O & \frac{n}{2}D'(\Sigma^{-1} \otimes \Sigma^{-1})D \end{bmatrix}.$$

The asymptotic covariance matrix of $\tilde{\delta}$ would then be

$$V_1 = [p\lim \mathrm{X}^{*\prime}(\Sigma^{-1} \otimes I_n)X^*/n]^{-1}.$$

2. Case in which R is unknown. The estimator $\tilde{\delta}$ is not available to us in the more realistic case in which R is unknown. However, once a consistent estimator $\hat{r}$ is obtained, we can form $\hat{X}^* = M(\hat{r})^{-1}X,\ \hat{y}^* = M(\hat{r})^{-1}y$, and

$$\tilde{\tilde{\delta}} = [\hat{X}^{*\prime}(\hat{\Sigma}^{-1} \otimes I_n)\hat{X}^*]^{-1}\hat{X}^{*\prime}(\hat{\Sigma}^{-1} \otimes I_n)\hat{y}^*. \tag{6.70}$$

As with the autoregressive case, the estimator $\tilde{\tilde{\delta}}$ is asymptotically efficient for both the case in which X is exogenous and for the case in which X contains lagged dependent variables, but the efficiency of the estimator differs for the two cases.

Consider the case in which X is exogenous. As $\tilde{\tilde{\delta}}$ is a BAN estimator,

$$\sqrt{n}(\tilde{\tilde{\delta}} - \delta) \xrightarrow{d} N(0, V_2),$$

where V_2 is the appropriate Cramer–Rao lower bound obtained from $I^{-1}(\theta)$ given by Eq. (6.67), that is,

$$V_2 \equiv V_1 = [p\lim \mathrm{X}^{*\prime}(\Sigma^{-1} \otimes I_n)X^*/n]^{-1}.$$

This means that the JGLS estimator $\tilde{\tilde{\delta}}$ with unknown R is as asymptotically efficient as the JGLS estimator $\tilde{\delta}$ with known R. Not knowing R costs us nothing in terms of asymptotic efficiency.

Next consider the case in which X contains lagged dependent variables. For this case $\underset{\sim}{I}^{-1}(\theta)$ is given by Eqs. (6.61)–(6.66), so the asymptotic covariance matrix of $\tilde{\tilde{\delta}}$ is now

$$V_2 = I^{\delta\delta} = p \lim n\{X^{*\prime}(\Sigma^{-1} \otimes I_n)X^* - X^{*\prime}\mathcal{F}[\mathcal{F}'(\Sigma \otimes I_n)\mathcal{F}]^{-1}\mathcal{F}'X^*\}^{-1}.$$

As with the autoregressive case it is easily seen that $V_2 - V_1$ is positive semidefinite so now $\tilde{\tilde{\delta}}$ is less efficient asymptotically than $\tilde{\delta}$. Not knowing R now costs us in terms of asymptotic efficiency.

6.4.8.2. Maximum-Likelihood Estimators as Iterative Joint-Generalized-Least-Squares Estimators?

Interestingly enough, a similar interpretation of the MLE of θ as obtained in the autoregressive case does not seem to be available to us for this case. Consider the score vector for this model. Solving $\partial l/\partial\delta = 0$ and $\partial l/\partial\nu = 0$ gives

$$\tilde{\delta} = [X^{*\prime}(\Sigma^{-1} \otimes I_n)X^*]^{-1}X^{*\prime}(\Sigma^{-1} \otimes I)y^*, \tag{6.71}$$

and

$$\hat{\Sigma} = E'E/n,$$

as expected, but problems arise when we attempt to extract r from the equation $\partial l/\partial r = 0$. Unlike the autoregressive case this equation highly nonlinear in r, involving as it does $M(r)^{-1}$. Notwithstanding this, Eq. (6.71) clearly points to the estimator $\tilde{\tilde{\delta}}$ given by Eq. (6.70).

6.4.8.3. Lagrangian Multiplier Test Statistic $H_0 : r = 0$

The analysis of Subsection 6.3.8.3 with respect to the null hypothesis $H_0 : \sigma_{ij} = 0, i \neq j$, can be carried over to this model with $X^* = M(r)^{-1}X$ and $y^* = M(r)^{-1}y$ in place of X^d and y^d, respectively. However, as noted in that section, a good diagnostic procedure would be to first test for $H_0 : r = 0$ and if under this test the null hypothesis is accepted to then to use the Breusch–Pagan LMT statistic to test for $H_0 : \sigma_{ij} = 0$, $i \neq j$. It is the former null hypothesis, $H_0 : r = 0$, that we turn our attention to now.

What we show is that the LMT statistic for the vector moving-average disturbance case before us is the same test statistic as that developed for the preceding vector autoregressive disturbances model. It follows then that the LMT statistic is incapable of distinguishing between the two disturbance systems.[3] We do this by noting that with $r = 0$, $M(r) = I_{nG}$, $X^* = X^d = X$, $U = E$, $u = e$, $U_p = E_p$, $p \lim E_p'E_p/n = p \lim U_p'U_p/n = I_p \otimes \Sigma$, and

[3] This result is a generalization of the result obtained by Godfrey (1978a) for the linear-regression model discussed in Subsection 5.3.5.3.

$\mathcal{F} = \Sigma^{-1} \otimes U_p$, so for both models

$$I^{rr}|_{r=0} = K_{pG,G}\{\Sigma^{-1} \otimes I_p \otimes \Sigma - (\Sigma^{-1} \otimes U_p')X \times [X'(\Sigma^{-1} \otimes I_n)X]^{-1}X'(\Sigma^{-1} \otimes U_p)\}^{-1}K_{G,pG},$$

$$\left.\frac{\partial l}{\partial r}\right|_{r=0} = \pm K_{pG,G}(\Sigma^{-1} \otimes U_p')u.$$

It follows then that the LMT statistic for $H_0 : r = 0$ is the same for both models, for both the case in which X is exogenous and for the case in which X contains lagged dependent variables.

APPENDIX 6.A. PROBABILITY LIMITS ASSOCIATED WITH THE INFORMATION MATRIX OF THE MODEL WITH MOVING-AVERAGE DISTURBANCES

$p \lim (1/n)\partial^2 l/\partial\delta\partial r'$: Recalling that $X^* = M(r)^{-1}X$ and writing $M(r)^{-1} = (M_1 \cdots M_G)$, where each submatrix M_i is $nG \times n$, we have

$$X^{*\prime}(\Sigma^{-1} \otimes I_n)M(r)^{-1}(I_G \otimes E_p) = \begin{bmatrix} X_1'M_1'(\Sigma^{-1} \otimes I_n)M_1E_p & \cdots & X_1'M_1'(\Sigma^{-1} \otimes I_n)M_GE_p \\ \vdots & & \vdots \\ X_G'M_G'(\Sigma^{-1} \otimes I_n)M_1E_p & \cdots & X_G'M_G'(\Sigma^{-1} \otimes I_n)M_GE_p \end{bmatrix}.$$

Clearly if each X_i is truly exogenous then $p \lim X_i'M_i'(\Sigma^{-1} \otimes I_n)M_jE_p/n = O$. However, if X_i contains lagged dependent variables this probability limit will not be the null matrix.

Consider now

$$X^{*\prime}C'\left(I_{pG} \otimes a^{\bar{\tau}_n}\right) = X^{*\prime}\left(I_G \otimes S_1'a^{\bar{\tau}_n} \cdots I_G \otimes S_p'a^{\bar{\tau}_n}\right). \tag{6.A.1}$$

We consider the first matrix on the right-hand side of Eq. (6.A.1) as typical, and we use the notation of Subsection 6.4.2 to write, say,

$$M(r)^{-1\prime} = \begin{bmatrix} \mathcal{M}_{11} & \cdots & \mathcal{M}_{1G} \\ \vdots & & \vdots \\ \mathcal{M}_{G1} & \cdots & \mathcal{M}_{GG} \end{bmatrix} = \begin{pmatrix} \mathcal{M}_1 \\ \vdots \\ \mathcal{M}_G \end{pmatrix}.$$

Then

$$X^{*\prime}\left(I_G \otimes S_1'\, a^{\bar{\tau}_n}\right) = \begin{bmatrix} X_1'\mathcal{M}_{11}S_1'a^{\bar{\tau}_n} & \cdots & X_1'\mathcal{M}_{1G}S_1'a^{\bar{\tau}_n} \\ \vdots & & \vdots \\ X_G'\mathcal{M}_{G1}S_1'a^{\bar{\tau}_n} & \cdots & X_G'\mathcal{M}_{GG}S_1'a^{\bar{\tau}_n} \end{bmatrix}. \tag{6.A.2}$$

Again, we take the matrix in the (1, 1) position of the right-hand side of Eq. (6.A.2) as typical. Now, under our notation

$$a^{\bar{\tau}_n} = (\mathcal{M}_1 \operatorname{vec} E\Sigma^{-1} \cdots \mathcal{M}_G \operatorname{vec} E\Sigma^{-1}), \tag{6.A.3}$$

so

$$X_1'\mathcal{M}_{11}S_1'a^{\bar{\tau}_n} = X_1'\mathcal{M}_{11}S_1'(\mathcal{M}_1 \text{ vec } E\Sigma^{-1} \cdots \mathcal{M}_G \text{ vec } E\Sigma^{-1}).$$

However,

$$\begin{aligned} X_1'\mathcal{M}_{11}S_1'\mathcal{M}_1 \text{ vec } E\Sigma^{-1} &= X_1'\mathcal{M}_{11}S_1'\mathcal{M}_1(\Sigma^{-1} \otimes I_n)\varepsilon \\ &= X_1'\mathcal{M}_{11}S_1'\left(\sum_{i=1}^{G}\sum_{j=1}^{G}\sigma^{ij}\mathcal{M}_{1i}\varepsilon_j\right), \end{aligned}$$

where $\Sigma^{-1} = \{\sigma^{ij}\}$. Therefore, in evaluating $p \lim\ X^{*\prime}C'(I_{pG} \otimes a^{\bar{\tau}_n})/n$, we are typically looking at $p \lim\ X_1'\mathcal{M}_{11}S_1'\mathcal{M}_{1i}\varepsilon_j/n$.

Now, in Subsection 6.4.2, we saw that $\mathcal{M}_{ii}$ is upper triangular and $\mathcal{M}_{ij}$, $i \neq j$, is strictly upper triangular so $S_1'\mathcal{M}_{ii}$ is strictly upper triangular. It follows that $A = \mathcal{M}_{11}S_1'\mathcal{M}_{1i}$ is strictly upper triangular and so $p \lim\ X_1'A\varepsilon_j/n$ is the null vector even if X_1 contains lagged dependent variables. We conclude that, regardless of whether X contains lagged dependent variables,

$$p \lim X^{*\prime}C'\left(I_{pG} \otimes a^{\bar{\tau}_n}\right)/n = O.$$

$\boldsymbol{p \lim (1/n)\partial^2 l/\partial r\, \partial r'}$

$\boldsymbol{p \lim (1/n) K_{pG,G}(I_G \otimes E_p')M(r)^{-1\prime}C'(I_{pG} \otimes a^{\bar{\tau}_n})}$: We wish to show that this probability limit is the null matrix. We do this by proving that the probability limit of a typical element of the matrix is zero. To this end, we consider

$$E_p' = (I_p \otimes E')S' = \begin{pmatrix} E'S_1' \\ \vdots \\ E'S_p' \end{pmatrix} = \begin{pmatrix} \varepsilon_1'S_1' \\ \vdots \\ \varepsilon_G'S_1' \\ \vdots \\ \varepsilon_1'S_p' \\ \vdots \\ \varepsilon_G'S_p' \end{pmatrix},$$

so, by the property of the commutation matrix given in Subsection 3.3.2,

$$K_{pG,G}(I_G \otimes E_p') = \begin{pmatrix} I_G \otimes \varepsilon_1'S_1' \\ \vdots \\ I_G \otimes \varepsilon_G'S_1' \\ \vdots \\ I_G \otimes \varepsilon_1'S_p' \\ \vdots \\ I_G \otimes \varepsilon_G'S_p' \end{pmatrix}.$$

It follows then that the submatrix in the (1, 1) position of the matrix we are considering is $p\lim (1/n)(I_G \otimes \varepsilon_1' S_1')M(r)^{-1'}(I_G \otimes S_1' a^{\bar{\tau}_n})$ and the row vector in the (1, 1) position is $p\lim (1/n)\varepsilon_1' S_1' \mathcal{M}_{11} S_1' a^{\bar{\tau}_n}$. Now by using Eq. (6.A.3), we find that the first element in this vector is

$$p\lim \frac{1}{n}\varepsilon_1' S_1' \mathcal{M}_{11} S_1' \mathcal{M}_1(\Sigma^{-1} \otimes I_n)\varepsilon = p\lim \frac{1}{n}\varepsilon_1' S_1' \mathcal{M}_1 S_1' \sum_{i=1}^{G}\sum_{j=1}^{G} \sigma^{ij} \mathcal{M}_{1i}\varepsilon_j.$$

The typical element of the matrix we have in hand is then $\sigma^{ij} p\lim \varepsilon_i' S_i' \mathcal{M}_{kl} S_r' \mathcal{M}_{sj}\varepsilon_j/n$. In Subsection 6.4.2, we saw that each $\mathcal{M}_{ii}$ is upper triangular and each $\mathcal{M}_{ij}$, $i \neq j$, is strictly upper triangular. It follows from the properties of shifting matrices that $S_k' \mathcal{M}_{ij}$ is strictly upper triangular for all k, i, j so the matrix is the quadratic form of our $p\lim$ being the product of strictly upper-triangular matrices is also strictly upper triangular. We conclude then that the probability limit of a typical element of our matrix is zero.

$p\lim (1/n)K_{pG,G}(I_G \otimes E_p')M(r)^{-1'}(\Sigma^{-1} \otimes I_n)M(r)^{-1}(I_G \otimes E_p)K_{G,pG}$: It is more convenient in this subsection to consider the limits of expectations rather than to work with probability limits. We have seen that we can write

$$(I_G \otimes E_p)K_{G,pG} = (I_G \otimes S_1\varepsilon_1 \cdots I_G \otimes S_1\varepsilon_G \cdots I_G \otimes S_p\varepsilon_1 \cdots I_G \otimes S_p\varepsilon_G),$$

so we need to consider the limit as n tends to infinity of the expectation of

$$\frac{1}{n}(I_G \otimes \varepsilon_i' S_l')M(r)^{-1'}(\Sigma^{-1} \otimes I_n)M(r)^{-1}(I_G \otimes S_k\varepsilon_j) \tag{6.A.4}$$

for $i, j = 1, \ldots, G$ and $l, k = 1, \ldots, p$.

The submatrix in the (rs) block position of expression (6.A.4) is

$$\frac{1}{n}\varepsilon_i' S_l' \mathcal{M}_r(\Sigma^{-1} \otimes I_n)\mathcal{M}_s' S_k\varepsilon_j = \frac{1}{n}\sum_{x=1}^{G}\sum_{y=1}^{G} \sigma^{xy}\varepsilon_i' S_l' \mathcal{M}_{rx}\mathcal{M}'_{sy} S_k\varepsilon_j$$

for $r, s = 1, \ldots, G$, so typically we are looking at

$$\lim \frac{1}{n}\mathcal{E}(\varepsilon_i' S_l \mathcal{M}_{rx}\mathcal{M}'_{sy} S_k\varepsilon_j) = \sigma_{ij} \lim \frac{1}{n}\text{tr}\, S_l' \mathcal{M}_{rx}\mathcal{M}'_{sy} S_k.$$

We need to assume that such limits exist so it will pay us to look at the nature of these traces. Recall from Subsection 3.7.4.5 that if

$$l = k,$$

$\text{tr}\, S_l' \mathcal{M}_{rx}\mathcal{M}'_{sy} S_k = \text{tr}\mathcal{M}_{rx}\mathcal{M}'_{sy}$ minus the sum of the first l elements in the main diagonal of $\mathcal{M}_{rx}\mathcal{M}'_{sy}$; if

$$l < k,$$

$\text{tr}\, S_l' \mathcal{M}_{rx}\mathcal{M}'_{sy} S_k$ is the sum of the elements of the $k-1$ diagonal above the main diagonal of $\mathcal{M}_{rx}\mathcal{M}'_{sy}$ minus the sum of the first l elements of this diagonal;

and if

$$l > k,$$

$\mathrm{tr}S_l'\mathcal{M}_{rx}\mathcal{M}_{sy}'S_k$ is the sum of the elements of the $l-1$ diagonal below the main diagonal of $\mathcal{M}_{rx}\mathcal{M}'_{sy}$ minus the sum of the first k elements of this diagonal.

It remains for us to consider the nature of the matrix $\mathcal{M}_{rx}$. Recall from Subsection 6.4.2 that $\mathcal{M}_{rx}$ is of the form

$$I_n + a_1 S_1' + \cdots + a_{n-1}S_{n-1}' \quad \text{for } r = x,$$

or

$$b_1 S_1' + \cdots + b_{n-1}S_{n-1}' \quad \text{for } r \neq x$$

for suitable a_is and b_is.

We now have some insight into the nature of the limits whose existence we need to assume. Suppose we make the initial assumption that

$$\lim_{n\to\infty} M(r)^{-1'}M(r)^{-1}/n$$

exists. Then this implies that

$$\lim_{n\to\infty} \mathcal{M}_{rx}\mathcal{M}'_{sy}/n$$

exists and hence

$$\lim_{n\to\infty} \mathrm{tr}S_l'\mathcal{M}_{rx}\mathcal{M}'_{sy}S_k/n$$

exists. Making this initial assumption, then we let

$$C_{lk} = \lim \frac{1}{n}\begin{bmatrix} \mathrm{tr}S_l'\mathcal{M}_1(\Sigma^{-1}\otimes I_n)\mathcal{M}'_1 S_k & \cdots & \mathrm{tr}S_l'\mathcal{M}_1(\Sigma^{-1}\otimes I_n)\mathcal{M}'_G S_k \\ \vdots & & \vdots \\ \mathrm{tr}S_l'\mathcal{M}_G(\Sigma^{-1}\otimes I_n)\mathcal{M}'_1 S_k & \cdots & \mathrm{tr}S_l'\mathcal{M}_G(\Sigma^{-1}\otimes I_n)\mathcal{M}'_G S_k \end{bmatrix}$$
$$= C_{kl}$$

for $l, k = 1, \ldots, p$. Then we can write

$$I_{rr} = \begin{bmatrix} \Sigma\otimes C_{11} & \cdots & \Sigma\otimes C_{1p} \\ \vdots & & \vdots \\ \Sigma\otimes C_{p1} & \cdots & \Sigma\otimes C_{pp} \end{bmatrix}.$$

7 Linear Simultaneous Equations Models

7.1. INTRODUCTION

The most complicated statistical models we consider are variations of the linear simultaneous equations (LSE) model, the statistical model that lies behind linear economic models. The complication that the standard LSE model adds to the standard SURE model is that, in the former model, current values of some of the right-hand variables of our equations must be regarded as random variables correlated to the current value of the disturbance term. Suppose we write the ith equation of the standard LSE model as

$$y_j = H_j\delta_j + u_j, \quad j = 1, \ldots, G,$$

where y_j and u_j are $n \times 1$ random vectors and H_j is the matrix of observations on the right-hand variables of this equation. We partition H_j as follows:

$$H_j = (Y_j X_j).$$

The variables in X_j are statistically the equivalent of the X_js on the right-hand sides of the equations in the SURE model. The variables in Y_j are those contemporaneously correlated with the disturbance term, so the elements in the tth row of Y_j are correlated to u_{tj}, the tth element of u_j. Now, even if we regard the elements of the disturbance vector u_j as being statistically independent random variables, we still have $\mathcal{E}(Y_j' u_j) \neq 0$ and asymptotically $p \lim H_j' u_j / n \neq 0$.

Econometricians have traditionally solved the problem of right-hand variables that are contemporaneously correlated with the disturbance term by forming instrumental variable estimators (IVEs). As we shall have quite a lot to do with such estimators in this chapter, it will pay us to examine briefly two generic types of IVEs developed by Bowden and Turkington (1984).

We consider a statistical model that is broad enough to encompass the LSE model and variations of this model. We write an equation system as

$$y = H\delta + u, \tag{7.1}$$

where y and u are $nG \times 1$ random vectors and u has an expectation equal to the null vector, and we suppose some of the variables forming the $nG \times l$ data matrix H are correlated with the disturbance vector in the sense that $p \lim H'u/n \neq 0$. Suppose we further assume that the covariance matrix of u is a positive-definite nonscalar $nG \times nG$ matrix $\mathcal{V}$ and that there exists an $nG \times q$ matrix Z, with $q > l$ but not dependent on n, available to form instrumental variables for H. The following requirements are the essential asymptotic requirements for Z:

1. $p \lim Z'H/n$ exists but is not equal to the null matrix,
2. $p \lim Zu/n = 0$.

Bowden and Turkington (1984) proposed two generic IVEs for δ that may be motivated as follows.

THE IV-GLS ESTIMATOR. Equation system (7.1) has two statistical problems associated with it, namely the nonscalar covariance matrix $\mathcal{V}$ of the disturbance term and the correlation of right-hand variables with this disturbance term. Suppose we deal with the former problem first by premultiplying Eq. (7.1) by the nonsingular matrix $\mathcal{P}$, where $\mathcal{P}'\mathcal{P} = \mathcal{V}^{-1}$, to obtain

$$\mathcal{P}y = \mathcal{P}H\delta + \mathcal{P}u. \tag{7.2}$$

The disturbance term of this transformed equation has a scalar covariance matrix, but we are still left with the problem of right-hand variables correlated with this disturbance vector. Suppose now we form an IV for $\mathcal{P}H$ in this equation by regressing $\mathcal{P}H$ on $\mathcal{P}Z$ to get

$$\hat{\mathcal{P}H} = \mathcal{P}Z(Z'\mathcal{V}^{-1}Z)^{-1}Z'\mathcal{V}^{-1}H.$$

Using $\hat{\mathcal{P}H}$ as an IV for $\mathcal{P}H$ in Eq. (7.2) gives the estimator

$$\delta_1^* = [H'\mathcal{V}^{-1}Z(Z'\mathcal{V}^{-1}Z)^{-1}Z'\mathcal{V}^{-1}H]^{-1}H'\mathcal{V}^{-1}Z(Z'\mathcal{V}^{-1}Z)^{-1}Z'\mathcal{V}^{-1}y.$$

Usually $\mathcal{V}$ is unknown so δ_1^* is not available to us. However, suppose the elements of $\mathcal{V}$ are functions of the elements of an $r \times 1$ vector ρ so we write $\mathcal{V} = \mathcal{V}(\rho)$, where r is not a function of n. Suppose further that it is possible to obtain a consistent estimator $\hat{\rho}$ of ρ and let $\hat{\mathcal{V}} = \mathcal{V}(\hat{\rho})$. Then the IV-GLS estimator is

$$\tilde{\delta}_1 = [H'\hat{\mathcal{V}}^{-1}Z(Z'\hat{\mathcal{V}}^{-1}Z)^{-1}Z'\hat{\mathcal{V}}^{-1}H]^{-1}H'\hat{\mathcal{V}}^{-1}Z(Z'\hat{\mathcal{V}}^{-1}Z)^{-1}Z'\hat{\mathcal{V}}^{-1}y. \tag{7.3}$$

Such an estimator has also been proposed by White (1984).

THE IV-OLS ESTIMATOR. Suppose that in Eq. (7.1) we deal with the second econometric problem first and attempt to break the correlation of right-hand variables with the disturbance vector by premultiplying Eq. (7.1) by Z', obtaining

$$Z'y = Z'H\delta + Z'u. \tag{7.4}$$

Equation (7.4) still has a disturbance vector whose covariance matrix is non-scalar but we can deal with this by applying a GLS estimator to the equation. Replacing the unknown $\mathcal{V}$ in this GLS estimator by $\hat{\mathcal{V}}$ gives the IV-OLS estimator

$$\tilde{\delta}_2 = [H'Z(Z'\hat{\mathcal{V}}Z)^{-1}Z'H]^{-1}H'Z(Z'\hat{\mathcal{V}}Z)^{-1}Z'y. \tag{7.5}$$

Such estimators are used throughout this chapter.

As in Chap. 6 on the SURE model, in this chapter we consider three LSE models: First we consider the basic LSE model, then the LSE model in which we assume the disturbances are subject to vector autoregressive disturbances, and finally the LSE model in which the disturbances are subject to a vector moving-average system. For each version of the model, we apply classical statistical procedures, drawing heavily, as always, on our rules of matrix calculus to do this. Because readers may not be as familiar with these models as they are with the previous models considered, I have broken our tradition and have largely reinstated the asymptotic analysis to the main text.

7.2. THE STANDARD LINEAR SIMULTANEOUS EQUATIONS MODEL

7.2.1. The Model and Its Assumptions

We consider a complete system of G linear stochastic structural equations in G jointly dependent current endogenous variables and k predetermined variables.

The ith equation is written as

$$y_i = Y_i\beta_i + X_i\gamma_i + u_i = H_i\delta_i + u_i, i = 1, \dots, G,$$

where y_i is an $n \times 1$ vector of sample observations on one of the current endogenous variables, Y_i is an $n \times G_i$ matrix of observations on the other G_i current endogenous variables in the ith equation, X_i is an $n \times k_i$ matrix on the k_i predetermined variables in the equation, u_i is an $n \times 1$ vector of random disturbances, H_i is the $n \times (G_i + k_i)$ matrix $(Y_i \; X_i)$, and δ_i is the $(G_i + k_i) \times 1$ vector $(\beta_i' \; \gamma_i')'$. The usual statistical assumptions are placed on the random disturbances. The expectation of u_i is the null vector, and it is assumed that disturbances are contemporaneously correlated so that

$$\begin{aligned}
\mathcal{E}(u_{si}u_{tj}) &= 0 \text{ for periods } s \neq t,\\
\mathcal{E}(u_{si}u_{tj}) &= \sigma_{ij} \text{ for } s = t; i, j = 1, \dots, G,\\
\mathcal{E}(u_i u_j') &= \sigma_{ij} I_n.
\end{aligned}$$

We write our model and assumptions more succinctly as

$$y = H\delta + u, \tag{7.6}$$

$$\mathcal{E}(u) = 0, \quad \mathcal{V}(u) = \Sigma \otimes I_n, \quad u \sim N(0, \Sigma \otimes I_n),$$

where

$$y = (y_1' \cdots y_G')', \quad u = (u_1' \cdots u_G')', \quad \delta = (\delta_1' \cdots \delta_G')',$$

H is the block diagonal matrix

$$\begin{bmatrix} H_1 & & O \\ & \ddots & \\ O & & H_G \end{bmatrix},$$

and Σ is the symmetric matrix, assumed to be positive definite so that Σ^{-1} exists, whose (i, j)th element is σ_{ij}. We assume that each equation in the model is identifiable by a priori restrictions, that the $n \times k$ matrix X of all predetermined variables has rank k, and that $p \lim(X'u_i/n) = 0$ for all i. Finally, we assume that H_i has full column rank and that $p \lim H_i' H_j/n$ exists for all i and j.

A different way of writing our model is

$$YB + X\Gamma = U, \tag{7.7}$$

where Y is the $n \times G$ matrix of observations on the G current endogenous variables, X is the $n \times k$ matrix on the k predetermined variables, B is the $G \times G$ matrix of coefficients of the endogenous variables in our equations, Γ is the $k \times G$ matrix of coefficients of the exogenous variables in our equations, and U is the $n \times G$ matrix $(u_1 \cdots u_G)$. It follows that some of the elements of B are known a priori to be equal to one or zero as y_i has a coefficient of one in the ith equation and some endogenous variables are excluded from certain equations. Similarly, some of the elements of Γ are known a priori to be zero as certain predetermined variables are excluded from each equation. We assume that B is nonsingular. Note that $y = \text{vec}\, Y$ and $u = \text{vec}\, U$.

Equation (7.6) or Eq. (7.7) is often called the structural form of the model. We obtain the reduced form of the model from Eq. (7.7) by solving for Y to get

$$Y = -X\Gamma B^{-1} + UB^{-1} = X\Pi + V, \tag{7.8}$$

where $\Pi = -\Gamma B^{-1}$ is the matrix of reduced-form parameters and $V = UB^{-1}$ is the matrix of reduced-form disturbances. Taking the vecs of both sides of Eq. (7.8), we obtain

$$y = (I_G \otimes X)\pi + v, \tag{7.9}$$

where $\pi = \text{vec}\, \Pi$ and $v = \text{vec}\, V = (B^{-1'} \otimes I_n)u$. Note that the covariance matrix of the reduced-form disturbances is

$$\mathcal{V}(v) = B^{-1'}\Sigma B^{-1} \otimes I_n.$$

7.2.2. Parameters of the Model and the Log-Likelihood Function

The unknown parameters of our model are $\theta = (\delta' v')'$ where $\nu = \text{vech}\, \Sigma$. Here the log-likelihood function takes a little more work to obtain than that of the previous models we have looked at.

Our sample point is the vector y, and thus the likelihood function is the joint probability density function of y. We obtain this function by starting with the joint probability density of u. We have assumed that $u \sim N(0, \Sigma \otimes I_n)$ so the joint probability density function of y is

$$f(y) = |\mathcal{J}| \frac{1}{(2\pi)^{\frac{n}{2}} (\det \Sigma \otimes I_n)^{\frac{1}{2}}} \exp\left[-\frac{1}{2} u'(\Sigma^{-1} \otimes I)u\right],$$

with u set equal to $y - H\delta$ and where $|\mathcal{J}|$ is the absolute value of the Jacobian

$$\mathcal{J} = \det \frac{\partial u}{\partial y}.$$

Our first application of matrix calculus to this model involves working out this Jacobian. Taking the vec of both sides of $U = YB + X\Gamma$, we have

$$u = (B' \otimes I_n)y + (\Gamma' \otimes I)x,$$

where $u = \text{vec}\, U$, $y = \text{vec}\, Y$, and $x = \text{vec}\, X$. It follows that

$$\frac{\partial u}{\partial y} = (B \otimes I_n),$$

$$f(y) = \frac{|\det(B \otimes I_n)|}{(2\pi)^{\frac{n}{2}} (\det \Sigma \otimes I_n)^{\frac{1}{2}}} \exp\left[-\frac{1}{2} u'(\Sigma^{-1} \otimes I_n)u\right].$$

However, from the properties of the determinant of a Kronecker product we have $\det(\Sigma \otimes I_n) = (\det \Sigma)^n$,
so

$$f(y) = \frac{|(\det B)^n|}{(2\pi)^{\frac{n}{2}} (\det \Sigma)^{\frac{n}{2}}} \exp\left[-\frac{1}{2} u'(\Sigma^{-1} \otimes I_n)u\right],$$

with u set equal to $y - H\delta$ in this expression. This is the likelihood function $L(\theta)$. The log-likelihood function, apart from a constant, is

$$l(\theta) = n \log|\det B| - \frac{n}{2} \log \det \Sigma - \frac{1}{2} u'(\Sigma^{-1} \otimes I)u,$$

with u set equal to $y - H\delta$.

An alternative way of writing this function is

$$l(\theta) = n \log|\det B| - \frac{n}{2} \log \det \Sigma - \frac{1}{2} \text{tr}\, \Sigma^{-1} U'U, \tag{7.10}$$

where U is set equal to $YB + X\Gamma$.

Comparing Eq. (7.10) with the log-likelihood function of the standard SURE model given by Eq. (6.2) in Subsection 6.2.1 we see we now have an additional component, namely $n \log|\det B|$, and it is this additional component that makes the classical statistical analysis of the LSE model that much more difficult than that for the SURE model. This extra term is of course a function of δ but not of ν. It follows then that our derivatives of the log-likelihood function with respect to ν will be the same as these derived for the basic SURE model in Section 6.2. What changes are the derivatives of $l(\theta)$ with respect to δ. This being the case, we find that the concentrated log likelihood $l^*(\delta)$ obtained when δ is the vector of parameters of primary interest is given by substituting $\tilde{\Sigma} = U'U/n$ into the log-likelihood function as we did in Subsection 6.2.1. From Equation (7.10) we get, apart from a constant,

$$l^*(\delta) = n \log|\det B| - \frac{n}{2} \log \det \tilde{\Sigma},$$

where $\tilde{\Sigma}$ is set equal to $U'U/n$. Comparing this with the corresponding concentrated function of the SURE given by Eq. (6.4) we see again that we have the additional component $n \log|\det B|$.

7.2.3. The Derivative $\partial \log|\det B|/\partial\delta$

The extra term in the log-likelihood functions gives rise to a new derivative that must be considered, namely $\partial \log|\det B|/\partial\delta$, and this derivative is obtained in this subsection. Our first task is to express matrix B of Eq. (7.7) in terms of δ of Eq. (7.6). To this end, we write the ith equation of our model as

$$y_i = Y\bar{W}_i\beta_i + X\bar{T}_i\gamma_i + u_i,$$

where $\bar{W}_i$ and $\bar{T}_i$ are $G \times G_i$ and $k \times k_i$ selection matrices, respectively, with the properties that

$$Y\bar{W}_i = Y_i, X\bar{T}_i = X_i.$$

Alternatively we can write

$$y_i = YW_i\delta_i + XT_i\delta_i + u_i,$$

where W_i and T_i are the $G \times (G_i + k_i)$ and $k \times (G_i + k_i)$ selection matrices given by $W_i = (\bar{W}_i\ O)$ and $T_i = (O\ \bar{T}_i)$, respectively.

Under this notation, we can write

$$Y = (y_1 \cdots y_G) = Y(W_1\delta_1 \cdots W_G\delta_G) + X(T_1\delta_1 \cdots T_G\delta_G) + U.$$

It follows then that

$$\begin{aligned} B &= I_G - (W_1\delta_1 \cdots W_G\delta_G), \qquad (7.11)\\ \Gamma &= -(T_1\delta_1 \cdots T_G\delta_G). \end{aligned}$$

Moreover,

$$\operatorname{vec} B = \operatorname{vec} I_G - W\delta, \qquad (7.12)$$

where W is the block diagonal matrix

$$W = \begin{bmatrix} W_1 & & O \\ & \ddots & \\ O & & W_G \end{bmatrix}.$$

Returning to our derivative now, clearly from

$$\frac{\partial \operatorname{vec} B}{\partial \delta} = -W', \tag{7.13}$$

and as

$$\frac{\partial \log|\det B|}{\partial \delta} = \frac{\partial \operatorname{vec} B}{\partial \delta}\frac{\partial \log|\det B|}{\partial \operatorname{vec} B},$$

we obtain

$$\frac{\partial \log|\det B|}{\partial \delta} = -W'\operatorname{vec}(B^{-1'}) \tag{7.14}$$

7.2.4. The Score Vector $\partial l/\partial \theta$

With this derivative in hand, we easily obtain the score vector, where first component is

$$\begin{aligned}\frac{\partial l}{\partial \delta} &= n\frac{\partial \log|\det B|}{\partial \delta} - \frac{1}{2}\frac{\partial}{\partial \delta}u'(\Sigma^{-1} \otimes I_n)u \\ &= -nW'\operatorname{vec}(B^{-1'}) + H'(\Sigma^{-1} \otimes I_n)u. \end{aligned} \tag{7.15}$$

Comparing this with the corresponding component of the score vector for the SURE model, Eq. (6.5), we see that we now have an additional term, namely $-nW'\operatorname{vec}(B^{-1'})$.

The second component of the score vector, as noted above, is the same as that component for the SURE model, namely

$$\frac{\partial l}{\partial \nu} = \frac{D'}{2}(\operatorname{vec}\Sigma^{-1}U'U\Sigma^{-1} - n\operatorname{vec}\Sigma^{-1}). \tag{7.16}$$

7.2.5. The Hessian Matrix $\partial^2 l/\partial \theta \partial \theta'$

Two components of this matrix are the same as those of the SURE model with the proviso that we put H in place of X. They are repeated here for convenience:

$$\begin{aligned}\frac{\partial^2 l}{\partial \nu \partial \nu'} &= D'(\Sigma^{-1} \otimes \Sigma^{-1})\left[\frac{n}{2}I_{G^2} - (I_G \otimes U'U\Sigma^{-1})\right]D, \\ \frac{\partial^2 l}{\partial \delta \partial \nu'} &= -H'(\Sigma^{-1} \otimes U\Sigma^{-1})D = \left(\frac{\partial^2 l}{\partial \nu \partial \delta'}\right)'.\end{aligned}$$

From $\partial l/\partial\delta$ given by Eq. (7.15), the final component may be written as

$$\frac{\partial l}{\partial\delta\partial\delta'} = -n\frac{\partial \operatorname{vec}(B^{-1'})}{\partial\delta}W + \frac{\partial u}{\partial\delta}(\Sigma^{-1}\otimes I_n)H. \tag{7.17}$$

Now,

$$\frac{\partial \operatorname{vec}(B^{-1'})}{\partial\delta} = \frac{\partial \operatorname{vec} B}{\partial\delta}\frac{\partial \operatorname{vec} B'}{\partial \operatorname{vec} B}\frac{\partial \operatorname{vec} B^{-1'}}{\partial \operatorname{vec} B'},$$

and by using our rules of matrix calculus and Eq. (7.13), we can write this as

$$\frac{\partial \operatorname{vec}(B^{-1'})}{\partial\delta} = W' K_{GG}(B^{-1'}\otimes B^{-1}). \tag{7.18}$$

Substituting Eq. (7.18) into Eq. (7.17) gives

$$\frac{\partial^2 l}{\partial\delta\partial\delta'} = -nW'K_{GG}(B^{-1'}\otimes B^{-1})W - H'(\Sigma^{-1}\otimes I_n)H.$$

7.2.6. The Information Matrix $I(\theta) = -p\lim\frac{1}{n}\frac{\partial^2 l}{\partial\theta\partial\theta'}$

Under our assumptions, $p\lim U'U/n = \Sigma$ and

$$\begin{aligned} p\lim H_i'U/n &= p\lim\frac{1}{n}(U'Y_i\;U'X_i)' \\ &= p\lim\frac{1}{n}(U'Y\bar{W}_i\;O)' = W_i'B^{-1'}\Sigma, \end{aligned}$$

so

$$p\lim H'(I_G\otimes U)/n = W'(I_G\otimes B^{-1'}\Sigma).$$

Thus, we can write

$$I(\theta) = \begin{bmatrix} p\lim H'(\Sigma^{-1}\otimes I_n)H/n & W'(\Sigma^{-1}\otimes B^{-1'})D \\ +W'K_{GG}(B^{-1'}\otimes B^{-1})W & \\ D'(\Sigma^{-1}\otimes B^{-1})W & \frac{1}{2}D'(\Sigma^{-1}\otimes\Sigma^{-1})D \end{bmatrix}.$$

It is instructive to compare this information matrix with the corresponding information matrix of the SURE given by Eq. (6.7) of Subsection 6.2.4. We see that the information matrix in hand is more complex on two counts. First, the matrix in the block $(1, 1)$ position has an extra term in it, namely $W'K_{GG}(B^{-1'}\otimes B^{-1})W$. Second, the matrix in the block $(1, 2)$ position is now nonnull.

7.2.7. The Cramer–Rao Lower Bound $I^{-1}(\theta)$

Inverting the information matrix to give the asymptotic Cramer–Rao lower bound presents no difficulty. We write

$$I^{-1}(\theta) = \begin{bmatrix} I^{\delta\delta} & I^{\delta\nu} \\ I^{\nu\delta} & I^{\nu\nu} \end{bmatrix}.$$

Then

$$\begin{aligned} I^{\delta\delta} = \{ & p\lim H'(\Sigma^{-1} \otimes I_n)H/n + W'K_{GG}(B^{-1'} \otimes B^{-1})W \\ & - 2W'(\Sigma^{-1} \otimes B^{-1'})D[D'(\Sigma^{-1} \otimes \Sigma^{-1})D]^{-1} \\ & \times D'(\Sigma^{-1} \otimes B^{-1})W\}^{-1}. \end{aligned}$$

However, from the properties of the duplication matrix (see Section 3.5) $[D'(\Sigma^{-1} \otimes \Sigma^{-1})D]^{-1} = LN(\Sigma \otimes \Sigma)NL'$, where $N = (1/2)(I_{G^2} + K_{GG})$, $DLN = N$, and $N(\Sigma \otimes \Sigma)N = N(\Sigma \otimes \Sigma)$, so the third matrix in the inverse can be written as $-2W'(\Sigma^{-1} \otimes B^{-1'})N(I_G \otimes \Sigma B^{-1})W = -W'(\Sigma^{-1} \otimes B^{-1'} \Sigma B^{-1})W - W'K_{GG}(B^{-1'} \otimes B^{-1})W$.

Using standard asymptotic theory, we note that $p\lim H'(\Sigma^{-1} \otimes M)H/n = W'(\Sigma^{-1} \otimes B^{-1'}\Sigma B^{-1})W$, where M is the projection matrix $M = I_n - P_x$, with $P_x = X(X'X)^{-1}X'$. It follows that

$$I^{\delta\delta} = [p\lim H'(\Sigma^{-1} \otimes P_x)H/n]^{-1}.$$

By a similar analysis,

$$I^{\delta\nu} = -2[p\lim H'(\Sigma^{-1} \otimes P_x)H/n]^{-1} W'(I_G \otimes B^{-1'}\Sigma)NL',$$

and

$$\begin{aligned} I^{\nu\nu} = 2LN\{ & (\Sigma \otimes \Sigma) + 2(I_G \otimes \Sigma B^{-1})W \\ & \times [p\lim H'(\Sigma^{-1} \otimes P_x)H/n]^{-1} W'(I_G \otimes B^{-1'}\Sigma)\}NL'. \end{aligned} \tag{7.19}$$

7.2.8. Statistical Inference from the Score Vector and the Information Matrix

7.2.8.1. Full-Information Maximum-Likelihood Estimator as Iterative Instrumental Variable Estimator

In the introduction to this chapter, we considered a general statistical model that is broad enough to encompass variations of the LSE model that we consider. Associated with this general model is a matrix of instrumental variables Z and two generic IV estimators: the IV-OLS estimator and the IV-GLS estimator given by Eqs. (7.3) and (7.5), respectively. The basic LSE model studied in this section is a special example of this framework in which $\mathcal{V} = \Sigma \otimes I_n$ and the instrumental variables are obtainable from the reduced form. Considering the reduced form written as Eq. (7.9), we see that $(I_G \otimes X)$ qualifies as instrumental variables for y, and as it is the ys in H that cause the asymptotic correlation between H and u, this means that $(I_G \otimes X)$ qualifies as instrumental variables for H as well. Therefore for the model before us in the generic IVEs $\tilde{\delta}_1$ and $\tilde{\delta}_2$ given by Eqs. (7.3) and (7.5), respectively, we set $\mathcal{V} = \Sigma \otimes I_n$ and $Z = I_G \otimes X$. Doing this we see that both estimators collapse to the same estimator, namely

$$\hat{\delta} = [H'(\Sigma^{-1} \otimes P_x)H]^{-1}H'(\Sigma^{-1} \otimes P_x)y.$$

This is the three-stage least-squares (3SLS) estimator with known Σ.

For the more realistic case in which Σ is unknown, we first obtain a consistent estimator for Σ by using the two-stage least-squares (2SLS) residual vectors $\hat{u}_i$. We let $\hat{\sigma}_{ij} = \hat{u}'\hat{u}_j/n$ and use $\hat{\Sigma} = \{\hat{\sigma}_{ij}\}$. The 3SLS estimator is then

$$\hat{\hat{\delta}} = [H'(\hat{\Sigma}^{-1} \otimes P_x)H]^{-1}H'(\hat{\Sigma}^{-1} \otimes P_x)y,$$

or

$$\hat{\hat{\delta}} = [\hat{H}'(\hat{\Sigma}^{-1} \otimes I_n)H]^{-1}\hat{H}'(\hat{\Sigma}^{-1} \otimes I_n)y, \tag{7.20}$$

where $\hat{H} = (I_G \otimes P_x)H$ is the predicted value for H from the regression of H on $(I_G \otimes X)$.

This estimator was first developed by Zellner and Thiel (1962). It is well known that it is a BAN estimator [see, for example, Rothenberg (1964)] so its asymptotic covariance matrix is given by

$$I^{\delta\delta} = [p \lim H'(\Sigma^{-1} \otimes P_x)H/n]^{-1}.$$

We now show that the MLE [usually referred to in this context as the full-information maximum-likelihood (FIML) estimator] has a similar IVE interpretation except this interpretation is iterative. This result was first obtained by Durbin in an unpublished paper [see Durbin (1988)] and again demonstrated by Hausman (1975).

To this end, consider the score vector that is reproduced here for convenience:

$$\frac{\partial l}{\partial \delta} = -nW' \operatorname{vec}(B^{-1'}) + H'(\Sigma^{-1} \otimes I_n)u, \tag{7.21}$$

$$\frac{\partial l}{\partial v} = \frac{D'}{2}(\operatorname{vec}\Sigma^{-1}U'U\Sigma^{-1} - n \operatorname{vec}\Sigma^{-1}).$$

Setting $\partial l/\partial v$ to the null vector gives $\tilde{\Sigma} = U'U/n$. Now, we write

$$W' \operatorname{vec}(B^{-1'}) = W'(\tilde{\Sigma}^{-1} \otimes I_G)\operatorname{vec} B^{-1'}\tilde{\Sigma}$$

and note that $B^{-1'}\tilde{\Sigma} = B^{-1}U'U/n = V'U/n$, where V is the disturbance matrix of reduced-form equation (7.8). So we write

$$W' \operatorname{vec}(B^{-1'}) = \frac{1}{n} W'(\tilde{\Sigma}^{-1} \otimes I_G)(I_G \otimes V')u$$
$$= \frac{1}{n} W'(I_G \otimes V')(\tilde{\Sigma}^{-1} \otimes I_n)u$$

and substituting this expression into Eq. (7.21) gives

$$\frac{\partial l}{\partial \delta} = [H' - W'(I_G \otimes V')](\tilde{\Sigma}^{-1} \otimes I_n)u.$$

To evaluate this derivative further, we consider

$$H - (I_G \otimes V)W = \begin{bmatrix} H_1 - VW_1 & & O \\ & \ddots & \\ O & & H_G - VW_G \end{bmatrix},$$

where $H_i - VW_i = (Y_i \; X_i) - V(\bar{W}_i \; O)$. If we write the reduced form of the endogenous variables on the right-hand side of this ith equation of our model as

$$Y_i = X\Pi_i + V_i,$$

then, as $Y\bar{W}_i = Y_i$, it follows that $V\bar{W}_i = V_i$ and $H_i - VW_i = (X\Pi_i \; X_i)$. Let $\bar{H}_i = (X\Pi_i \; X_i)$ and let $\bar{H}$ be the block diagonal matrix with $\bar{H}_i$ in the ith block diagonal position. Then we can write

$$\frac{\partial l}{\partial \delta} = \bar{H}'(\tilde{\Sigma}^{-1} \otimes I_n)u.$$

Setting this derivative to the null vector and replacing the remaining parameters with their MLEs gives

$$\tilde{\bar{H}}'(\tilde{\Sigma}^{-1} \otimes I_n)(y - H\tilde{\delta}) = 0, \tag{7.22}$$

where $\tilde{\delta}$ is the FIML estimator of δ and $\tilde{\bar{H}}$ is the MLE of $\bar{H}$ given by the block diagonal matrix with $\tilde{\bar{H}}_i = (X\tilde{\Pi}_i \; X_i)$ in the ith block diagonal position, $\tilde{\Pi}_i$ being the MLE of Π_i. Solving Eq. (7.22) for δ gives

$$\tilde{\delta} = [\tilde{\bar{H}}'(\tilde{\Sigma}^{-1} \otimes I_n)H]^{-1}\tilde{\bar{H}}'(\tilde{\Sigma}^{-1} \otimes I_n)y.$$

A few points should be noted about this interpretation of the FIML estimator. First, it is clearly an iterative interpretation as we have not solved explicitly for $\tilde{\delta}$, with the matrices $\tilde{\Pi}_i$ and $\tilde{\Sigma}$ still depending on $\tilde{\delta}$. Second, this IVE is similar to the 3SLS estimator of Eq. (7.20). The 3SLS estimator uses $\hat{Y}_i = X\hat{\Pi}_i$ as instrumental variables for Y_i where $\hat{\Pi}_i$ is the OLS estimator of Π_i, i.e., $\hat{\Pi}_i = (X'X)^{-1}X'Y_i$. The FIML estimator uses $\tilde{Y}_i = X\tilde{\Pi}_i$ as instrumental variables for Y_i, where $\tilde{\Pi}_i$ is the MLE of Π_i.

7.2.8.2. The Lagrangian Multiplier Test Statistic for $H_0 : \sigma_{ij} = 0, i \neq j$

If the disturbances are not contemporaneously correlated there is nothing to link the equations together. Single-equation estimators such as 2SLS estimators or limited-information maximum-likelihood (LIML) estimators would then be as efficient asymptotically as the system estimators such as 3SLS and FIML estimators. Needless to say, the former estimators require a lot less computational effort than the latter estimators. The null hypothesis that interests us then is

$$H_0 : \sigma_{ij} = 0, \quad i \neq j,$$

the alternative being

$$H_A : \sigma_{ij} \neq 0.$$

The LMT procedure has appeal for testing the null hypothesis as we need compute only LIML estimators in forming the test statistic.If we then accept the null hypothesis then on the grounds of asymptotic efficiency these estimators suffice. There is no need to move to the more computationally difficult estimators.

With the score vector and the asymptotic Cramer–Rao lower bound in hand, it is a relatively simple matter to form the required test statistic. We proceed as we did for LMT statistic for the equivalent hypothesis in the SURE model, which gave rise to the Breusch–Pagan test statistic discussed in Subsection 6.2.4.2. Let $\bar{v} = \bar{v}(\Sigma)$. Then we can write

$$H_0 : \bar{v} = 0 \text{ against } H_A : \bar{v} \neq 0,$$

and the LMT statistic is

$$T_1 = \frac{1}{n} \frac{\partial l'}{\partial \bar{v}}\bigg|_{\hat{\theta}} I^{\bar{v}\bar{v}}(\hat{\theta}) \frac{\partial l}{\partial \bar{v}}\bigg|_{\hat{\theta}}$$

where $I^{\bar{v}\bar{v}}$ refers to that part of the Cramer–Rao lower bound corresponding to the parameters $\bar{v}$ and $\hat{\theta}$ sets $\bar{v}$ equal to the null vector and evaluates all other parameters at the unconstrained MLE, that is, at the LIML estimators. Under H_0, T_1 tends to a χ^2 random variable with $(1/2)G(G-1)$ degrees of freedom so the upper tail of this distribution is used to find the appropriate critical region.

In forming T_1, we follow the procedure adopted for the SURE model and obtain $\partial l/\partial \bar{v}$ and $I^{\bar{v}\bar{v}}$ from $\partial l/\partial v$ and I^{vv}, which we have in hand by using the selection matrix S defined by $\bar{v} = Sv$. Recall that S has the property $SL = \bar{L}$, where L and $\bar{L}$ are the $(1/2)G(G+1) \times G^2$ and $(1/2)G(G-1) \times G^2$ elimination matrices defined in Section 3.4. Moreover, as $\partial l/\partial v$ for the model before us is the same as that for the SURE model, we have

$$\frac{\partial l}{\partial \bar{v}} = \bar{v}(A) = \bar{L} \operatorname{vec} A,$$

where $A = \Sigma^{-1}U'U\Sigma^{-1}$, and, under H_0,

$$A = \begin{bmatrix} \rho_{11} & \dots & \rho_{1G} \\ \vdots & & \vdots \\ \rho_{G1} & \dots & \rho_{GG} \end{bmatrix} \quad \text{with } \rho_{ij} = \frac{u_i' u_j}{\sigma_{ii}\sigma_{jj}}.$$

Again, as in the SURE model,

$$I^{\bar{v}\bar{v}} = \mathcal{S} I^{vv} \mathcal{S}'.$$

However, now I^{vv} is far more complicated, being given by Eq. (7.19) rather than by $2LN(\Sigma \otimes \Sigma)NL'$, as in the SURE model. Using Eq. (7.19) and the fact that $\mathcal{S}L = \bar{L}$, we can write

$$T_1 = \frac{1}{n}(\operatorname{vec} A)'\bar{L}'\bar{L}NV(\theta)N\bar{L}'\bar{L}\operatorname{vec} A|_{\hat{\theta}},$$

where

$$V(\theta) = 2\{(\Sigma \otimes \Sigma) + 2(I_G \otimes \Sigma B^{-1}) \\ \times W[p\lim H'(\Sigma^{-1} \otimes P_x)H/n]^{-1}W'(I_G \otimes B^{-1'}\Sigma)\}.$$

However, from Section 3.6,

$$\bar{L}'\bar{L}\operatorname{vec} A = \operatorname{vec} \bar{A},$$

where

$$\bar{A} = \begin{bmatrix} 0 & & & & \\ \rho_{21} & 0 & & O & \\ \rho_{31} & \rho_{32} & 0 & & \\ \vdots & \vdots & \ddots & \ddots & \\ \rho_{G1} & \rho_{G2} & \cdots & \rho_{GG-1} & 0 \end{bmatrix},$$

so we write

$$T_1 = \frac{1}{n}(\operatorname{vec} \bar{A})'NV(\theta)N\operatorname{vec} \bar{A}, \tag{7.23}$$

which is a quadratic form in $N \operatorname{vec} \bar{A}$, with $V(\theta)/n$ as the matrix in this quadratic form.

We consider first the vector in this quadratic form. By definition,

$$N \operatorname{vec} \bar{A} = \frac{1}{2}\operatorname{vec}(\bar{A} + \bar{A}'),$$

$$\bar{A}' = \begin{bmatrix} 0 & \rho_{21} & \rho_{31} & \cdots & \rho_{G1} \\ & 0 & \rho_{32} & \cdots & \rho_{G2} \\ & & \ddots & & \vdots \\ & O & & \ddots & \rho_{GG-1} \\ & & & & 0 \end{bmatrix} = \begin{bmatrix} 0 & \rho_{12} & \rho_{13} & \cdots & \rho_{1G} \\ & 0 & \rho_{23} & \cdots & \rho_{2G} \\ & & \ddots & & \vdots \\ & O & & \ddots & \rho_{G-1G} \\ & & & & 0 \end{bmatrix}$$

as $\rho_{ij} = \rho_{ji}$. Therefore,

$$\bar{A} + \bar{A}' = \begin{bmatrix} 0 & \rho_{12} & \rho_{13} & \cdots & \rho_{1G} \\ \rho_{21} & 0 & \rho_{23} & \cdots & \rho_{2G} \\ \rho_{31} & \rho_{32} & 0 & & \rho_{3G} \\ \vdots & \vdots & & \ddots & \vdots \\ & & & & \rho_{G-1\,G} \\ \rho_{G1} & \rho_{G2} & \cdots & \rho_{G\,G-1} & 0 \end{bmatrix} = (\dot{r}_1, \dot{r}_2 \cdots \dot{r}_G),$$

where

$$\dot{r}_1 = \begin{pmatrix} 0 \\ \rho_{21} \\ \vdots \\ \rho_{G1} \end{pmatrix}, \quad \dot{r}_2 = \begin{pmatrix} \rho_{12} \\ 0 \\ \rho_{32} \\ \vdots \\ \rho_{G2} \end{pmatrix} \cdots \dot{r}_G = \begin{pmatrix} \rho_{1G} \\ \vdots \\ \rho_{G-1G} \\ 0 \end{pmatrix}.$$

Thus, we can write

$$N \operatorname{vec} \bar{A} = \frac{1}{2}\begin{pmatrix} \dot{r}_1 \\ \vdots \\ \dot{r}_G \end{pmatrix}. \tag{7.24}$$

Next, we consider the matrix $V(\theta)/n$ of the quadratic form. The first part of $V(\theta)$ in this matrix, namely $2(\Sigma \otimes \Sigma)$, under H_0 is given by

$$2(\Sigma \otimes \Sigma) = 2\begin{bmatrix} \sigma_{11}\Sigma_0 & & O \\ & \ddots & \\ O & & \sigma_{GG}\Sigma_0 \end{bmatrix} \text{ with } \Sigma_0 = \begin{bmatrix} \sigma_{11} & & O \\ & \ddots & \\ O & & \sigma_{GG} \end{bmatrix}.$$

The second part of $V(\theta)$ under H_0 requires a little more work. Under H_0

$$[H'(\Sigma^{-1} \otimes P_x)H]^{-1} = \begin{bmatrix} \sigma_{11}(H_1' P_x H_1)^{-1} & & O \\ & \ddots & \\ O & & \sigma_{GG}(H_G' P_x H_G)^{-1} \end{bmatrix},$$

so this second part, if we ignore the p lim and the 2, is the diagonal matrix

$$\begin{bmatrix} \sigma_{11}\Sigma_0 B^{-1} W_1 (H_1' P_x H_1/n)^{-1} W_1' B^{-1'} \Sigma_0 & & O \\ & \ddots & \\ O & & \sigma_{GG}\Sigma_0 B^{-1} W_G (H_G' P_x H_G/n)^{-1} W_G' B^{-1'} \Sigma_0 \end{bmatrix}.$$

We can further simplify this part by noting that $W_i(H_i' P_x H_i)^{-1} W_i' = \bar{W}_i[Y_i'(P_x - P_{x_i})Y_i]^{-1}\bar{W}_i'$, where $P_{x_i} = X_i(X_i'X_i)^{-1}X_i'$. Putting the two parts together we have, still ignoring the p lim, that

$$V(\theta) = 2\begin{bmatrix} \sigma_{11}\{\Sigma_0 + 2\Sigma_0 B^{-1}\bar{W}_1[Y_1'(P_x - P_{x_1})Y_1/n]^{-1}\bar{W}_1' B^{-1'}\Sigma_0\} & & O \\ & \ddots & \\ O & & \sigma_{GG}\{\Sigma_0 + 2\Sigma_0 B^{-1}\bar{W}_G[Y_G'(P_x - P_{x_G})Y_G/n]^{-1}\bar{W}_G' B^{-1'}\Sigma_0\} \end{bmatrix}. \tag{7.25}$$

Equations (7.23)–(7.25) taken together led to the following procedure for forming the LMT statistic:

1. Apply the LIML estimator to each equation $y_i = H_i\delta_i + u_i$ to get the estimations, $\hat{\delta}_i$ say. Form the residual vectors $\hat{u}_i = y_i - H_i\hat{\delta}_i$ for $i = 1, \dots, G$.
2. Using $\hat{\delta}_i$ and $\hat{u}_i$, form $\hat{\sigma}_{ij} = \hat{u}_i'\hat{u}_j/n$, $\hat{\rho}_{ij} = \dfrac{n\hat{\sigma}_{ij}}{\hat{\sigma}_{ii}\hat{\sigma}_{jj}}$, for $i, j = 1, \dots, G$, and $\hat{B}$.
3. Form

$$\hat{r}_i = \begin{pmatrix} \hat{\rho}_{1i} \\ \vdots \\ \hat{\rho}_{i-1i} \\ 0 \\ \hat{\rho}_{i+1i} \\ \vdots \\ \hat{\rho}_{Gi} \end{pmatrix},$$

$$\hat{\Sigma}_0 = \begin{bmatrix} \hat{\sigma}_{11} & & O \\ & \ddots & \\ O & & \hat{\sigma}_{GG} \end{bmatrix},$$

$$A_i = \frac{1}{2}\hat{\sigma}_{ii}\{\hat{\Sigma}_0 + 2\hat{\Sigma}_0\hat{B}^{-1}\bar{W}_i[Y_i'(P_x - P_{x_i})Y_i/n]^{-1}\bar{W}_i'\hat{B}^{-1'}\hat{\Sigma}_0\}$$

for $i = 1, \dots, G$.

4. Form

$$T_1 = \frac{1}{n}\sum_{i=1}^{G}\hat{r}_i' A_i \hat{r}_i.$$

In forming this test statistic, we may make use of the 2SLS estimator instead of the LIML estimator. The 2SLS estimator of δ_i, $\hat{\delta}_i^{2S}$ say, is asymptotically equivalent to the LIML estimator $\hat{\delta}_i$. Moreover, an estimator of σ_{ij} that uses the 2SLS residual vector is asymptotically equivalent to the one that uses the LIML residual vector. Hence, an asymptotically equivalent version of the LMT statistic would use a 2SLS estimator in place of the LIML estimator in the preceding procedure.

The test statistic T_1 was first obtained by Turkington (1989) and may be viewed as a generalization of the Breusch–Pagan test statistic discussed in Subsection 6.2.4.2. Indeed, comparing the two test statistics, we see we can write the Turkington test statistic as

$$T_1 = T_1' + \sum_{i=1}^{G} \eta_i' [\hat{\sigma}_{ii} Y_i'(P_x - P_{x_i})Y_i]^{-1} \eta_i,$$

where T_1' is the Breusch–Pagan test statistic and $\eta_i = \hat{\sigma}_{ii} \bar{W}_i' \hat{B}^{-1'} \hat{\Sigma}_0 \hat{r}_i$. Therefore the Breusch–Pagan test statistic is modified by the addition of the quadratic forms $\eta_i' [\hat{\sigma}_{ii} Y_i'(P_x - P_{x_i})Y_i]^{-1} \eta_i$. It is instructive to investigate what is being measured by these quadratic forms. To do this, we first note that as $Y\bar{W}_i = Y_i$ it follows that $V_i = V\bar{W}_i = UB^{-1}\bar{W}_i$. We consider now

$$\hat{\sigma}_{ii} \hat{\Sigma}_0 \hat{r}_i = \hat{\sigma}_{ii} \begin{pmatrix} \hat{\sigma}_{11}\hat{\rho}_{1i} \\ \vdots \\ \hat{\sigma}_{i-1\,i-1}\hat{\rho}_{i-1i} \\ 0 \\ \hat{\sigma}_{i+1\,i+1}\hat{\rho}_{i+1i} \\ \vdots \\ \hat{\sigma}_{GG}\hat{\rho}_{Gi} \end{pmatrix} = \begin{pmatrix} \hat{u}_1'\hat{u}_i \\ \vdots \\ \hat{u}_{i-1}'\hat{u}_i \\ 0 \\ \hat{u}_{i+1}'\hat{u}_i \\ \vdots \\ \hat{u}_G'\hat{u}_i \end{pmatrix} = \hat{\mathring{U}}_i'\hat{u}_i$$

where $\hat{\mathring{U}}_i = (\hat{u}_1 \cdots \hat{u}_{i-1} 0\, \hat{u}_{i+1} \cdots \hat{u}_G)$, so $\eta_i = \bar{W}_i' \hat{B}^{-1'} \hat{\mathring{U}}_i' \hat{u}_i = \hat{\mathring{V}}_i' \hat{u}_i$, where $\hat{\mathring{V}}_i = \hat{\mathring{U}}_i \hat{B}^{-1} \bar{W}_i$. It follows then that the quadratic form $\eta_i' [\hat{\sigma}_{ii} Y_i'(P_X - P_{x_i})Y_i]^{-1} \eta_i$ measures the distance the vector $\mathring{V}_i' \hat{u}_i$ is from the null vector; that is, it concerns itself with the correlations between u_i and V_i, excluding the part of V_i that depends directly on u_i.

7.3. THE LINEAR SIMULTANEOUS EQUATIONS MODEL WITH VECTOR AUTOREGRESSIVE DISTURBANCES

7.3.1. The Model and Its Assumptions

In this section, we extended the LSE model by allowing the disturbances to be subject to a vector autoregressive system of the order of p. We use the same notation for this system as that of Subsection 6.3.1. Replacing presample values with zero, we can write our model as

$$y = H\delta + u,$$
$$M(r)u = \varepsilon,$$
$$\varepsilon \sim N(0, \Sigma \otimes I_n),$$

where, as in Subsection 6.3.1 $M(r)$ is the $nG \times nG$ matrix given by

$$M(r) = I_{Gn} + N(r) = I_{Gn} + (R \otimes I_n)C,$$

C is the $Gnp \times Gn$ matrix given by

$$C = \begin{pmatrix} I_G \otimes S_1 \\ \vdots \\ I_G \otimes S_p \end{pmatrix}, \tag{7.26}$$

and $S_1 \cdots S_p$ are shifting matrices. Alternatively, we can write this model as

$$YB + X\Gamma = U, \tag{7.27}$$
$$U = -U_p R' + E, \tag{7.28}$$

where the rows of the random matrix E are assumed to be independently, identically normally distributed random vectors with null vectors as means and covariance matrix Σ. Recall that U_p is the $n \times Gp$ matrix $(U_{-1} \cdots U_{-p})$, and if we replace presample values with zeros we can write

$$U_p = S(I_p \otimes U),$$

where S is the $n \times np$ matrix

$$S = (S_1 \cdots S_p).$$

As in Subsection 6.3.1, we assume that there are no unit root problems. From Eq. (7.28) we can write

$$\begin{aligned} U_p &= (Y_{-1}B + X_{-1}\Gamma \cdots Y_{-p}B + X_{-p}\Gamma) \\ &= (Y_{-1}B \cdots Y_{-p}B) + (X_{-1}\Gamma \cdots X_{-p}\Gamma) \\ &= Y_p(I_p \otimes B) + X_p(I_p \otimes \Gamma), \end{aligned} \tag{7.29}$$

where $Y_p = (Y_{-1} \cdots Y_{-p})$ and $X_p = (X_{-1} \cdots X_{-p})$.

Using Eq. (7.29) for U_p and Eq. (7.28), we can write the reduced form as

$$Y = X\Pi_1 + UB^{-1} = X\Pi_1 + X_p\Pi_2 + Y_p\Pi_3 + EB^{-1}, \tag{7.30}$$

where

$$\Pi_1 = -\Gamma B^{-1}, \quad \Pi_2 = -(I_p \otimes \Gamma)R'B^{-1}, \quad \Pi_3 = -(I_p \otimes B)R'B^{-1}.$$

The predetermined variables in the model are given by $Z = (X \; X_p \; Y_p)$. For our asymptotic theory we make the usual assumptions, namely that $p \lim(I_G \otimes Z') \times \varepsilon/n = 0$, $p \lim Z'Z/n$ exists, and this $p \lim$ is nonsingular. Further assumptions about asymptotic behavior will be given when needed in future sections.

7.3.2. The Parameters of the Model, the Log-Likelihood Function, the Score Vector, and the Hessian Matrix

The parameters of the model are given by the vector $\theta = (\delta' r' \nu')'$, and an analysis similar to that conducted in Subsection 7.2.2 above gives the log-likelihood function that, apart from a constant, is

$$l(\theta) = n \log|\det B| - \frac{n}{2} \log \det \Sigma - \frac{1}{2} \varepsilon'(\Sigma^{-1} \otimes I_n)\varepsilon,$$

where in this function we set ε equal to $M(r)(y - H\delta)$. Note that we can write $\varepsilon = y^d - H^d \delta$, where $y^d = M(r)y$ and $H^d = M(r)H$.

When we compare this log-likelihood function with that obtained for the SURE model with vector autoregressive disturbances, given by Eq. (7.17) of Subsection 6.3.4, we see that again we have an additional term, namely $n \log|\det B|$. Moreover, as this term is a function of δ but not of r or ν, it follows that the derivatives with respect to r and ν that we need for both the score vector and for the Hessian matrix are the same as those derived in Subsections 6.3.4 and 6.3.5 with the proviso that we replace X^d with H^d. Similarly the derivatives involving δ but not r can be derived from those obtained in Subsections 7.2.4 and 7.2.5 above with the proviso that H is now replaced with H^d, u with ε, and U with E. Finally, we obtain $\partial^2 l / \partial\delta\partial r'$ from Eq. (6.25) of Subsection 6.3.5 by replacing X and X^d in this equation with H and H^d, respectively. Thus, we obtain the score vector and the Hessian matrix.

SCORE VECTOR

$$\begin{aligned}
\frac{\partial l}{\partial \delta} &= -nW' \operatorname{vec}(B^{-1'}) + H^{d'}(\Sigma^{-1} \otimes I_n)\varepsilon, \\
\frac{\partial l}{\partial r} &= -K_{pG,G}(\Sigma^{-1} \otimes U_p')\varepsilon, \qquad (7.31) \\
\frac{\partial l}{\partial \nu} &= \frac{D'}{2}(\operatorname{vec} \Sigma^{-1} E'E\Sigma^{-1} - n \operatorname{vec} \Sigma^{-1}).
\end{aligned}$$

HESSIAN MATRIX

$$\begin{aligned}
\frac{\partial^2 l}{\partial\delta\partial\delta'} &= -nW'K_{GG}(B^{-1'} \otimes B^{-1})W - H^{d'}(\Sigma^{-1} \otimes I_n)H^d, \\
\frac{\partial^2 l}{\partial\delta\partial r'} &= H'C'(I_{pG} \otimes E\Sigma^{-1}) + H^{d'}(\Sigma^{-1} \otimes U_p)K_{G,pG}, \\
\frac{\partial^2 l}{\partial\delta\partial\nu'} &= -H^{d'}(\Sigma^{-1} \otimes E\Sigma^{-1})D, \\
\frac{\partial^2 l}{\partial r\partial r'} &= -(U_p'U_p \otimes \Sigma^{-1}), \\
\frac{\partial^2 l}{\partial r\partial\nu'} &= K_{pG,G}(\Sigma^{-1} \otimes U_p'E\Sigma^{-1})D', \\
\frac{\partial^2 l}{\partial\nu\partial\nu'} &= \frac{n}{2}D'(\Sigma^{-1} \otimes \Sigma^{-1})D - D'(\Sigma^{-1} \otimes \Sigma^{-1}E'E\Sigma^{-1})D.
\end{aligned}$$

7.3.3. The Information Matrix $I(\theta) = -p\lim \frac{1}{n}\frac{\partial^2 l}{\partial\theta\partial\theta'}$

To obtain the information matrix, we need to evaluate some new probability limits. Under our assumption, $p\lim E'E/n = \Sigma$, $p\lim U_p'E/n = O$, and $p\lim X'E/n = O$. We assume further that $p\lim U_p'U_p/n$ exists and is equal to a positive-definite matrix, Ω say.

Let $H_p = (H_{-1} \cdots H_{-p})$, where

$$H_{-j} = \begin{bmatrix} H_{1,-j} & & O \\ & \ddots & \\ O & & H_{G,-j} \end{bmatrix}$$

and $H_{i,-j}$ denotes the matrix formed when we lag the values in H_i j periods, where $i = 1, \dots, G$, and $j = 1, \dots, p$. If we replace the presample values with zeros, then we can write

$$H_p = [(I_G \otimes S_1)H \cdots (I_G \otimes S_p)H],$$

where $S_1 \cdots S_p$ are shifting matrices, and then

$$CH = H_p^{\tau_l} = \begin{pmatrix} H_{-1} \\ \vdots \\ H_{-p} \end{pmatrix},$$

where $l = \sum_i (K_i + G_i)$. Clearly, regardless of whether X contains lagged endogenous variables,

$$p\lim H'C'(I_{pG} \otimes E)/n = p\lim H_p^{\tau_l'}(I \otimes E)/n = O.$$

Now, under our new notation,

$$H^d = M(r)H = H + (R \otimes I_n)CH = H + (R \otimes I_n)H_p^{\tau_l}, \tag{7.32}$$

so

$$\begin{aligned} p\lim H^{d'}(I_G \otimes E)/n &= p\lim H'(I \otimes E)/n \\ &= \operatorname{diag}\{p\lim H_i'E/n\} \\ &= \operatorname{diag}\begin{Bmatrix} p\lim Y_i'E/n \\ p\lim X_i'E/n \end{Bmatrix}. \end{aligned}$$

Now, as $p\lim X'E/n = O$, $p\lim X_i'E/n = O$, and from the reduced form, $Y = X\Pi_1 + UB^{-1} = X\Pi_1 - U_pR'B^{-1} + EB^{-1}$, $p\lim Y'E/n = B^{-1'}$, $p\lim E'E/n = B^{-1'}\Sigma$, and $p\lim Y_i'E/n = \bar{W}_i'B^{-1'}\Sigma$. We can then write

$$\begin{aligned} p\lim H^{d'}(I_G \otimes E)/n &= \operatorname{diag}\begin{Bmatrix} \bar{W}_i'B^{-1'}\Sigma \\ O \end{Bmatrix} = \operatorname{diag}\{W_i'B^{-1'}\Sigma\} \\ &= W'(I_G \otimes B^{-1'}\Sigma). \end{aligned} \tag{7.33}$$

With these probability limits in hand and using the probability limits already derived in the SURE model with vector autoregressive disturbances, we can write the information model as

$$I(\theta) = p\lim \frac{1}{n} \begin{bmatrix} nW'K_{GG}(B^{-1'} \otimes B^{-1})W \\ +H^{d'}(\Sigma^{-1} \otimes I_n)H^d & -H^{d'}(\Sigma^{-1} \otimes U_p)K_{G,pG} & nW'(\Sigma^{-1} \otimes B^{-1'})D \\ -K_{pG,G}(\Sigma^{-1} \otimes U_p')H^d & n(\Omega \otimes \Sigma^{-1}) & O \\ nD'(\Sigma^{-1} \otimes B^{-1})W & O & \frac{n}{2}D'(\Sigma^{-1} \otimes \Sigma^{-1})D \end{bmatrix}. \tag{7.34}$$

It is instructive to compare this information matrix with the corresponding information matrix of the SURE model with vector autoregressive disturbances given by Eq. (6.26) in Subsection 6.3.6. We note that the matrix in the block (1, 1) position has an extra term, namely $nW'K_{GG}(B^{-1'} \otimes B^{-1})W$. Also, the matrix in the block (1, 3) position is now nonnull. The information matrix for the LSE model is then considerably more complex than that for the SURE model.

For the case in which X is strictly exogenous and contains no lagged endogenous variables, the information matrix can be further evaluated. If X is exogenous, Eq. (7.30), as well as being the reduced form of the model, is also the final form. Also it allows us to write $p\lim(I_G \otimes X')u/n = 0$, and this simplifies the asymptotics in the evaluation of $p\lim H^{d'}(I_G \otimes U_p)/n$. We have seen that

$$H^{d'}(I_G \otimes U_p) = H'(I_G \otimes U_p) + H_p^{\tau_i'}(I_{pG} \otimes U_p)(R' \otimes I_{pG}), \tag{7.35}$$

and we deal with each part of the right-hand side of Eq. (7.35) in turn. First,

$$H'(I_G \otimes U_p) = \text{diag}\{H_i'U_p\} = \text{diag}\begin{Bmatrix} Y_i'U_p \\ X_i'U_p \end{Bmatrix}.$$

With X strictly exogenous, $p\lim X'U_p/n = O$, so $p\lim X_i'U_p/n = O$. Moreover, from reduced-form equation (7.30) and Eq. (7.28), we have $p\lim Y_i'U_p/n = -\bar{W}_i'B^{-1'}R\Omega$, so

$$\begin{aligned} p\lim H'(I_G \otimes U_p)/n &= -\text{diag}\begin{Bmatrix} \bar{W}_i'B^{-1'}R\Omega \\ O \end{Bmatrix} \\ &= -\text{diag}\{W_i'B^{-1'}R\Omega\} \\ &= -W'(I_G \otimes B^{-1'}R\Omega). \end{aligned} \tag{7.36}$$

Next,

$$H_p^{\tau_i'}(I_{pG} \otimes U_p) = [H_{-1}'(I_G \otimes U_p) \cdots H_{-p}'(I_G \otimes U_p)], \tag{7.37}$$

so we consider the matrix in the jth block position:

$$H'_{-j}(I_G \otimes U_p) = \text{diag}\left\{\begin{matrix} Y'_{i,-j}U_p \\ X'_{i,-j}U_p \end{matrix}\right\}.$$

With X exogenous, $p\lim X'_{i,-j}U_p/n = O$ and $p\lim Y'_{i,-j}U_p/n = \bar{W}'_i Y'_{-j}U_p/n = \bar{W}'_i B^{-1'}\Omega_j$, where $\Omega_j = p\lim U'_{-j}U_p/n$, a $G \times pG$ matrix and

$$\Omega = \begin{pmatrix} \Omega_1 \\ \vdots \\ \Omega_p \end{pmatrix}. \tag{7.38}$$

It follows then that

$$\begin{aligned} p\lim H'_{-j}(I_G \otimes U_p)/n &= \text{diag}\left\{\begin{matrix} \bar{W}_i B^{-1'}\Omega_j \\ O \end{matrix}\right\} = \text{diag}\{W_i B^{-1'}\Omega_j\} \\ &= W'(I_G \otimes B^{-1'}\Omega_j). \end{aligned}$$

Returning to Eq. (7.37), we see that

$$p\lim H_p^{\tau'_i}(I_{pG} \otimes U_p)/n = W'(I_G \otimes B^{-1'})(I_G \otimes \Omega_1 \cdots I_G \otimes \Omega_p).$$

We can simplify this expression by using selection matrices. Let $\mathcal{S}_j$ be the $G \times pG$ selection matrix given by

$$\mathcal{S}_j = (O \cdots I_G \cdots O), \tag{7.39}$$

where each null matrix is $G \times G$ and I_G is in the jth block position. Then, from Eq. (7.38),

$$\Omega_j = \mathcal{S}_j \Omega,$$

and

$$p\lim H_p^{\tau'_i}(I_{pG} \otimes U_p)/n = W'(I_G \otimes B^{-1'})\mathcal{S}(I_{pG} \otimes \Omega), \tag{7.40}$$

where

$$\mathcal{S} = (I_G \otimes \mathcal{S}_1 \cdots I_G \otimes \mathrm{S}_p). \tag{7.41}$$

Finally, it follows from Eqs. (7.35), (7.36), and (7.40) that, for the case before us,

$$\begin{aligned} p\lim H^{d'}(I_G \otimes U_p)/n = &-W'(I_G \otimes B^{-1'}R\Omega) \\ &+ W'(I_G \otimes B^{-1'})\mathcal{S}(R' \otimes \Omega), \end{aligned} \tag{7.42}$$

and by using this probability limit we can write the information matrix for the special case in which X is strictly exogenous as

$$I(\theta)=\begin{bmatrix} \begin{matrix} W'K_{GG}(B^{-1'}\otimes B^{-1})W \\ +p\lim H^{d'}(\Sigma^{-1}\otimes I_n)H^d/n \end{matrix} & \begin{matrix} W'(\Sigma^{-1}\otimes B^{-1'}R\Omega)K_{G,pG} \\ -W'(I_G\otimes B^{-1'})S(R'\Sigma^{-1}\otimes\Omega)K_{G,pG} \end{matrix} & W'(\Sigma^{-1}\otimes B^{-1'})D \\ \begin{matrix} K_{pG,G}(\Sigma^{-1}\otimes\Omega R'B^{-1})W \\ -K_{pG,G}(\Sigma^{-1}R\otimes\Omega)S'(I_G\otimes B^{-1})W \end{matrix} & \Omega\otimes\Sigma^{-1} & O \\ D'(\Sigma^{-1}\otimes B^{-1})W & O & \frac{1}{2}D'(\Sigma^{-1}\otimes\Sigma^{-1})D \end{bmatrix}.$$

7.3.4. The Cramer–Rao Lower Bound $I^{-1}(\theta)$

Inverting the information matrix to obtain the Cramer–Rao lower bound requires a little work. We let

$$I^{-1}(\theta)=\begin{bmatrix} I^{\delta\delta} & I^{\delta r} & I^{\delta\nu} \\ I^{r\delta} & I^{rr} & I^{r\nu} \\ I^{\nu\delta} & I^{\nu r} & I^{\nu\nu} \end{bmatrix}.$$

Then, for the general case,

$$\begin{aligned} I^{\delta\delta} = \{ & W'K_{GG}(B^{-1'}\otimes B^{-1})W + p\lim H^{d'}(\Sigma^{-1}\otimes I_n)H^d/n \\ & - p\lim H^{d'}(\Sigma^{-1}\otimes U_p)K_{G,pG} \\ & \times [(U_p'U_p)^{-1}\otimes\Sigma]K_{G,pG}(\Sigma^{-1}\otimes U_p')H^d/n \\ & - 2W'(\Sigma^{-1}\otimes B^{-1'})DL\,N(\Sigma\otimes\Sigma)N\,L'D'(\Sigma^{-1}\otimes B^{-1})W\}^{-1}. \end{aligned}$$

Before we obtain the other components of $I^{-1}(\theta)$, it will pay us to evaluate $I^{\delta\delta}$ further. Using the results $DLN = N$ and the properties of N and K_{GG}, we can write the third matrix in this inverse as

$$-W'(\Sigma^{-1}\otimes B^{-1'}\Sigma B^{-1})W - W'K_{GG}(B^{-1'}\otimes B^{-1})W.$$

We have seen already from Eq. (7.33) that $p\lim H^{d'}(I_G\otimes E)/n = W'(I_G\otimes B^{-1'}\Sigma)$ and so, as $p\lim E'E/n=\Sigma$, we have,

$$p\lim H^{d'}(\Sigma^{-1}\otimes P_E)H^d/n = W'(\Sigma^{-1}\otimes B^{-1'}\Sigma B^{-1})W,$$

where P_E is the projection matrix $P_E = E(E'E)^{-1}E'$.

One way of writing $I^{\delta\delta}$ would then be

$$I^{\delta\delta} = [p\lim H^{d'}(\Sigma^{-1}\otimes M_E)H^d/n - \mathcal{T}]^{-1} \tag{7.43}$$

where $\mathcal{T} = p\lim H^{d'}[\Sigma^{-1}\otimes U_p(U_p'U_p)^{-1}U_p']H^d/n$ and M_E is the projection matrix, $M_E = I_n - P_E$.

However, we can obtain a more convenient way of writing $I^{\delta\delta}$ by showing that

$$p\lim H^{d'}(\Sigma^{-1}\otimes M_z)H^d/n = W'(\Sigma^{-1}\otimes B^{-1'}\Sigma B^{-1})W$$

as well, where $M_z = I_n - Z(Z'Z)^{-1}Z'$ and Z is the matrix of predetermined variables, $Z = (X\ Y_p\ Y)$.

To do this, note that

$$H^{d'}(I_G \otimes M_z) = H'(I_G \otimes M_z) + H_p^{\tau_i'}(I_{pG} \otimes M_z)(R'\Sigma^{-1} \otimes I_n)$$

and, as H_p involves the variables in X_p and Y_p,

$$H_p^{\tau_i'}(I_G \otimes M_z) = O,$$

so

$$H^{d'}(\Sigma^{-1} \otimes M_z)H^d = H'(\Sigma^{-1} \otimes M_z)H = \{\sigma^{ij} H_i' M_z H_j\},$$

where $\Sigma^{-1} = \{\sigma^{ij}\}$. Moreover, as $X'M_z = O$,

$$H_i' M_z H_j = \begin{bmatrix} Y_i' M_z Y_j & O \\ O & O \end{bmatrix},$$

and, from reduced-form equation (7.30),

$$\begin{aligned} p\lim Y_i' M_z Y_j/n &= \bar{W}_i' B^{-1'}(p\lim E' M_z E/n)B^{-1}\bar{W}_j \\ &= \bar{W}_i' B^{-1'}\Sigma B^{-1}\bar{W}_j, \end{aligned}$$

so

$$\begin{aligned} &p\lim H_i' M_z H_j/n = W_i' B^{-1'}\Sigma B^{-1} W_j, \\ &p\lim H^{d'}(\Sigma^{-1} \otimes M_z)H^d/n = W'(\Sigma^{-1} \otimes B^{-1'}\Sigma B^{-1})W, \end{aligned}$$

as required. It follows then that we can write

$$I^{\delta\delta} = [p\lim H^{d'}(\Sigma^{-1} \otimes P_z)H^d/n - \mathcal{T}]^{-1}, \tag{7.44}$$

where $P_z = Z(Z'Z)^{-1}Z'$.

The other components of $I^{-1}(\theta)$ are

$$\begin{aligned} I^{\delta r} &= I^{\delta\delta} p\lim H^{d'}[I_G \otimes U_p(U_p'U_p)^{-1}]K_{pG,G} = (I^{\delta r})', \\ I^{\delta v} &= -2I^{\delta\delta}W'(I_G \otimes B^{-1'}\Sigma)NL' = (I^{v\delta})', \\ I^{rr} &= (\Omega^{-1} \otimes \Sigma) + K_{pG,G}\{p\lim[I_G \otimes (U_p'U_p)^{-1}U_p']H^d I^{\delta\delta} \\ &\quad \times H^{d'}[I_G \otimes U_p(U_p'U_p)^{-1}]\}K_{G,pG}, \qquad (7.45) \\ I^{rv} &= -2K_{pG,G}p\lim[I_G \otimes (U_p'U_p)^{-1}U_p']H^d I^{\delta\delta}W'(I_G \otimes B^{-1'}\Sigma) \\ &\quad \times NL' = (I^{vr})', \\ I^{vv} &= 2LN[(\Sigma \otimes \Sigma) + 2(I_G \otimes \Sigma B^{-1})WI^{\delta\delta}W'(I_G \otimes B^{-1'}\Sigma)]NL'. \end{aligned}$$

For the special case in which X is exogenous and contains no lagged endogenous values, we know that $p\lim H^{d'}(I_G \otimes U_p)/n$ is given by Eq. (7.42) so we can evaluate our probability limits further to obtain

$$\mathcal{T} = W'[(I_G \otimes B^{-1'} R\Omega) - (I_G \otimes B^{-1'})\mathcal{S}(R' \otimes \Omega)](\Sigma^{-1} \otimes \Omega^{-1}) \times [(I_G \otimes \Omega R' B^{-1}) - (R \otimes \Omega)\mathcal{S}'(I_G \otimes B^{-1})]W, \tag{7.46}$$

$$I^{\delta r} = -I^{\delta\delta} W'[(I_G \otimes B^{-1'} R) - (I_G \otimes B^{-1'})\mathcal{S}(R' \otimes I_{pG})]K_{G,pG},$$

$$I^{rr} = (\Omega^{-1} \otimes \Sigma) + K_{pG,G}[(I_G \otimes R' B^{-1}) - (R \otimes I_{pG})\mathcal{S}' \times (I_G \otimes B^{-1})]W I^{\delta\delta} W'[(I_G \otimes B^{-1'} R) - (I_G \otimes B^{-1'}) \times \mathcal{S}(R' \otimes I_{pG})]K_{G,pG}. \tag{7.47}$$

We now wish to show that for the case under consideration, in which X contains no lagged endogenous variables, we can write

$$I^{\delta\delta} = [A'(I_G \otimes F')p\lim X^{d'}\Phi^{-1}X^d/n(I_G \otimes F)A]^{-1}$$

where[1] $\Phi = \Sigma \otimes I_n$, A is the $G(G+k) \times l$ diagonal matrix given by $A = \text{diag}\{A_i\}$, and A_i is the $(G+k) \times (G_i + k_i)$ selection matrix given by $A_i = (W_i' \; T_i')'$, F is the $k \times (G+k)$ matrix given by $F = (\Pi_1 \; I_K)$, and X^d is the $nG \times Gk$ matrix given by

$$X^d = M(r)(I_G \otimes X). \tag{7.48}$$

As the first step in proving this, we need to write H^d in terms of X^d. To this end we consider

$$H = \text{diag}\{H_i\} = (I_G \otimes Q)A, \tag{7.49}$$

where $Q = (Y \; X)$. However, we can write $Q = (X\Pi_1 + V \; X) = XF + V(I_G \; O)$, so, from Eq. (7.49)

$$H = (I_G \otimes X)(I_G \otimes F)A + (I_G \otimes V)[I_G \otimes (I_G \; O)]A.$$

We can tidy this expression up by noting that

$$[I_G \otimes (I_G \; O)]A = \text{diag}\{(I_G \; O)A_i\} = \text{diag}\{W_i\} = W,$$

so

$$H = (I_G \otimes X)(I_G \otimes F)A + (I_G \otimes V)W$$

and, as $H^d = M(r)H$,

$$H^d = X^d(I_G \otimes F)A + M(r)(I_G \otimes V)W. \tag{7.50}$$

Our second step is to bring the $G^2 \times p^2G^2$ selection matrix $\mathcal{S}$ defined by Eqs. (7.39) and (7.41) into the picture. We do this by writing

$$M(r)(I_G \otimes V) = (I_G \otimes V) + (R \otimes I_n)C(I_G \otimes V) \tag{7.51}$$

[1] It is assumed that $p\lim X^{d'}\Phi^{-1}X^d/n$ exists.

and by noting that

$$C(I_G \otimes V) = \begin{pmatrix} I_G \otimes S_1 \\ \vdots \\ I_G \otimes S_p \end{pmatrix} (I_G \otimes V) = \begin{pmatrix} I_G \otimes V_{-1} \\ \vdots \\ I_G \otimes V_{-p} \end{pmatrix}$$

$$= \begin{pmatrix} I_G \otimes U_{-1} \\ \vdots \\ I_G \otimes U_{-p} \end{pmatrix} (I_G \otimes B^{-1}).$$

However, $U_{-j} = U_p \mathcal{S}_j'$ so

$$C(I_G \otimes V) = (I_{pG} \otimes U_p)\mathcal{S}'(I_G \otimes B^{-1})$$

and, from Eq. (7.51),

$$M(r)(I_G \otimes V) = (I_G \otimes V) + (R \otimes U_p)\mathcal{S}'(I_G \otimes B^{-1}). \qquad (7.52)$$

Note, by the same analysis, that we could write

$$X^d = M(r)(I_G \otimes X) = (I_G \otimes X) + (R \otimes X_p)\bar{\mathcal{S}}', \qquad (7.53)$$

where $X_p = (X_{-1} \cdots X_{-p})$, where $\bar{\mathcal{S}}$ is the $Gk \times Gkp^2$ selection matrix given by $\bar{\mathcal{S}} = (I_G \otimes \bar{\mathcal{S}}_1 \cdots I_G \otimes \bar{\mathcal{S}}_p)$ and $\bar{\mathcal{S}}_j$ is the $k \times kp$ selection matrix given by $\bar{\mathcal{S}}_j = (O \cdots I_k \cdots O)$, where each null matrix is $k \times k$.

The third step in the proof is to consider $H^{d'}\Phi^{-1}H^d$, which, by using Eqs. (7.50), we can write as

$$\begin{aligned} H^{d'}\Phi^{-1}H^d &= A'(I_G \otimes F')X^{d'}\Phi^{-1}X^d(I_G \otimes F)A \\ &\quad + W'(I_G \otimes V')M(r)'\Phi^{-1}X^d(I_G \otimes F)A \\ &\quad + A'(I_G \otimes F')X^{d'}\Phi^{-1}M(r)(I_G \otimes V)W \\ &\quad + W'(I_G \otimes V')M(r)'\Phi^{-1}M(r)(I_G \otimes V)W. \end{aligned} \qquad (7.54)$$

We consider each component in turn. First, from Eqs. (7.52) and (7.53),

$$\begin{aligned} (I_G \otimes V')M(r)'\Phi^{-1}X^d &= (I_G \otimes B^{-1'})[(\Sigma^{-1} \otimes U'X) \\ &\quad + (\Sigma^{-1}R \otimes U'X_p)\bar{\mathcal{S}}' + \mathcal{S}(R'\Sigma^{-1} \otimes U_p'X) \\ &\quad + \mathcal{S}(R'\Sigma^{-1}R \otimes U_p'X_p)\bar{\mathcal{S}}'], \end{aligned}$$

and, as X is strictly exogenous, $p\lim X'U/n = O$, $p\lim X_p'U/n = O$, and $p\lim X_p'U_p/n = O$.

Therefore

$$p\lim(I_G \otimes V')M(r)'\Phi^{-1}X^d/n = O. \qquad (7.55)$$

Next, from Eq. (7.52),

$$\begin{aligned}&(I_G \otimes V')M(r)'\Phi^{-1}M(r)(I_G \otimes V)\\&\quad = (I_G \otimes B^{-1'})[(\Sigma^{-1} \otimes U'U)\\&\qquad + (\Sigma^{-1}R \otimes U'U)\mathcal{S}' + \mathcal{S}(R'\Sigma^{-1} \otimes U_p'U)\\&\qquad + \mathcal{S}(R'\Sigma^{-1}R \otimes U_p'U_p)\mathcal{S}'](I_G \otimes B^{-1}).\end{aligned}$$

Now,

$$\begin{aligned}&U'U/n = (-RU_p' + E')(-U_pR' + E)/n \xrightarrow{p} R\Omega R' + \Sigma,\\&U'U_p/n \xrightarrow{p} -R\Omega,\end{aligned}$$

so

$$\begin{aligned}&(I_G \otimes V')M(r)'\Phi^{-1}M(r)(I_G \otimes V)/n \xrightarrow{p} (I_G \otimes B^{-1'})\\&\{[\Sigma^{-1} \otimes (R\Omega R' + \Sigma)] - (\Sigma^{-1}R \otimes R\Omega)\mathcal{S}' - \mathcal{S}(R'\Sigma^{-1} \otimes \Omega R')\\&\quad + \mathcal{S}(R'\Sigma^{-1}R \otimes \Omega)\mathcal{S}'\}(I_G \otimes B^{-1}).\end{aligned}$$

Putting our pieces together, we see from Eq. (7.54) that

$$\begin{aligned}p\lim H^{d'}\Phi^{-1}H^d/n = {}& A'(I_G \otimes F')p\lim X^{d'}\Phi^{-1}X^d/n(I_G \otimes F)A\\&+ W'(\Sigma^{-1} \otimes B^{-1'}\Sigma B^{-1})W + \mathcal{T},\end{aligned}$$

where $\mathcal{T}$ is given by Eq. (7.46). However, we have already seen that for the case in question we could write

$$I^{\delta\delta} = [p\lim H^{d'}\Phi^{-1}H^d/n - W'(\Sigma^{-1} \otimes B^{-1'}\Sigma B^{-1})W - \mathcal{T}]^{-1},$$

so our task is complete.

7.3.5. Statistical Inference from the Score Vector and the Information Matrix

7.3.5.1. Efficient Estimation of δ

1. **Case in which R is known:**
With R known, $M(r)$ is known. Consider the transformed equation

$$y^d = H^d\delta + \varepsilon, \tag{7.56}$$

where $y^d = M(r)y$ and $H^d = M(r)H$ are now known. Clearly this equation satisfies the assumptions of the LSE model in which the disturbances given by the vector ε are no longer subject to vector autoregression. It follows from Subsection 7.2.7 that the Cramer–Rao lower bound for an asymptotically efficient consistent estimator of δ is given by

$$I^{*\delta\delta} = [p\lim H^{d'}(\Sigma^{-1} \otimes P_z)H^d/n]^{-1}.$$

Comparing this expression with $I^{\delta\delta}$ given by Eq. (7.44), we see that $\mathcal{T}$ must represent the addition to the Cramer–Rao lower bound that comes about because R is unknown.

Moreover, as in the case of the basic LSE model discussed in Section 7.2, the several competing estimators collapse to the same efficient estimator. We consider each of these estimators in turn.

a. The 3SLS Estimator

Consider first a 3SLS estimator. Writing Eq. (7.56) as

$$y^d = H\delta + (R \otimes I_n)H_p^{\tau_l}\delta + \varepsilon,$$

we note that H is correlated with ε but $H_p^{\tau_l}$ is not. In forming a 3SLS estimator for δ we need an instrumental variable for H but not for $H_p^{\tau_l}$. As $p\lim Z'\varepsilon/n = 0$, all the predetermined variables in Z are available to form an instrumental variable for H. Regressing H on $(I_G \otimes Z)$, we would use

$$\hat{H} = (I_G \otimes P_z)H.$$

However, as $H_p^{\tau_l}$ involves variables in Z,

$$(I_{Gp} \otimes P_z)H_p^{\tau_l} = H_p^{\tau_l},$$

$$\hat{H}^d = (I_G \otimes P_z)H^d = \hat{H} + (R \otimes I_n)H_p^{\tau_l}.$$

Therefore, we can write the 3SLS estimator as

$$\tilde{\delta}_{3S} = [H^{d'}(\hat{\Sigma}^{-1} \otimes P_z)H^d]^{-1}H^{d'}(\hat{\Sigma}^{-1} \otimes P_z)y^d, \tag{7.57}$$

where $\hat{\Sigma} = \hat{E}'\hat{E}/n$ and $\hat{E}$ and the matrix formed from the 2SLS residual vectors after the 2SLS estimator has been applied to the individual equations making up Eq. (7.56), again by using Z to form instruments. Under our assumptions, standard asymptotic theory shows that $\sqrt{n}(\hat{\delta}_{3S} - \delta)$ has a limiting multivariate normal distribution with mean zero and covariance matrix $I^{*\delta\delta}$. Moreover, the analysis holds good regardless of whether X is strictly exogenous or X contains lagged endogenous variables.

b. The IV-GLS Estimator or White Estimator

Equation system (7.56) has two econometric problems associated with it, namely the nonspherical covariance matrix of the disturbance term ε and the correlation of right-hand variables with this disturbance term. Suppose we deal with the former problem first by premultiplying Eq. (7.56) by the nonsingular matrix $\mathcal{P}$, where $\mathcal{P}'\mathcal{P} = \Sigma^{-1} \otimes I_n$, to get

$$\mathcal{P}y^d = \mathcal{P}H^d\delta + \mathcal{P}\varepsilon. \tag{7.58}$$

In Eq. (7.58) the disturbances are now spherical but we are left with the second problem of right-hand variables, namely that $\mathcal{P}H$ is correlated to the disturbance term $\mathcal{P}\varepsilon$. We achieve an instrumental variable for $\mathcal{P}H$ by regressing this matrix on $\mathcal{P}(I_G \otimes Z)$ to give

$$\hat{\mathcal{P}H} = \mathcal{P}(I_G \otimes P_z)H.$$

However, as noted above, $(I_G \otimes P_z)(R \otimes I_n)H_p^{\tau_l} = (R \otimes I_n)H_p^{\tau_l}$, so in forming the White estimator we could use

$$\hat{\mathcal{P}H^d} = \mathcal{P}(I_G \otimes P_z)H^d$$

as an instrumental variable for $\mathcal{P}H^d$ in Eq. (7.58). Doing this and replacing the unknown Σ with $\hat{\Sigma}$ gives the estimator. However, a little work shows that this is identical to $\tilde{\delta}_{3S}$.

c. The IV-OLS Estimator

Consider again equation system (7.56), which we still write as

$$y^d = H\delta + (R \otimes I_n)H_p^{\tau_l}\delta + \varepsilon. \tag{7.59}$$

We have seen that H is correlated with ε. Suppose we attempt to break this correlation, at least asymptotically, by multiplying both sides of Eq. (7.59) by $I_G \otimes Z$ to obtain

$$(I_G \otimes Z)y^d = (I_G \otimes Z)H^d\delta + (I_G \otimes Z)\varepsilon. \tag{7.60}$$

Equation (7.60) still has a disturbance term whose covariance matrix is nonspherical, but we can deal with this by applying GLS estimation to the equation. Replacing the unknown Σ in this GLS estimator with $\hat{\Sigma}$ gives the IV-OLS estimator. However, a little work shows that this estimator is also identical to $\hat{\delta}_{3S}$.

2. Case in which *R* is Unknown

a. The Modified 3SLS Estimator $\tilde{\tilde{\delta}}_{M3s}$

For the more realistic case in which R is unknown, the Cramer–Rao lower bound $I^{\delta\delta}$ given by Eq. (7.44) must be the asymptotic covariance matrix of any consistent estimator purporting to be asymptotically efficient. Estimation is more complicated now as H^d and y^d are no longer observable. Moreover, the estimator $\hat{\Sigma}$ described above is no longer available. Suppose, however, that a consistent estimator $\tilde{R}$ can be obtained so we could form $M(\tilde{r})$, where $\tilde{r} = \operatorname{vec}\tilde{R}$, and thus we have the predictors $\tilde{H}^d = M(\tilde{r})H^d$ and $\tilde{y}^d = M(\tilde{r})y^d$ of H^d and y^d respectively. Suppose further that an alternative consistent estimator of Σ, $\tilde{\Sigma}$ say, could also be obtained. Then at first glance it may seem that a reasonable approach to obtaining an estimator of δ would be to replace H^d, y^d, and $\hat{\Sigma}$ in Eq. (7.57) with $\tilde{H}^d$, $\tilde{y}^d$, and $\tilde{\Sigma}$, respectively. However, a little thought will reveal that this approach is unacceptable. Recall that in forming $\tilde{\delta}_{3S}$, we agreed that with R known in Eq. (7.56) we needed an instrumental variable for H only and all the predetermined variables in Z qualify to form such an instrumental variable. However, with R unknown we are forced to work with $\tilde{y}^d$ and $\tilde{H}^d$, and these matrices are related by the equation

$$\tilde{y}^d = \tilde{H}^d\delta + M(\tilde{r})u = \tilde{H}^d\delta + \varepsilon + [M(\tilde{r}) - M(r)]u. \qquad (7.61)$$

In this artificial equation, we need an instrumental variable for $\tilde{H}^d$, and now all of Z is no longer available to us to form such an instrument.

The easiest case to handle is the one in which X is strictly exogenous and does not contain lagged endogenous variables. Then, as $p\lim X'u/n = 0$, X and X_p are still available to form instruments, but clearly Y_p is not. For the moment we restrict ourselves to this case. Suppose we drop Y_p from the instrument set and work with $Z_1 = (X\ X_p)$ instead of Z. Replacing H^d, y^d, and P_z in Eq. (7.57) with $\tilde{H}^d$, $\tilde{y}^d$, $\tilde{\Sigma}$, and $P_{z_1} = Z_1(Z_1'Z)^{-1}Z_1'$, respectively, we obtain the following estimator:

$$\tilde{\tilde{\delta}}_{\text{M3S}} = [\tilde{H}^{d'}(\tilde{\Sigma}^{-1} \otimes P_{z_1})\tilde{H}^d]^{-1}\tilde{H}^{d'}(\tilde{\Sigma}^{-1} \otimes P_{z_1})\tilde{y}^d. \qquad (7.62)$$

Before we discuss the asymptotic properties of this estimator, we need to outline the procedure for finding the consistent estimators $\tilde{R}$ and $\tilde{\Sigma}$.

b. Procedure for Obtaining Consistent $\tilde{R}$ and $\tilde{\Sigma}$

i. We apply three stage least squares to the original equation $y = H\delta + u$, ignoring the autoregressive disturbances and using the exogenous variables X to form the instrumental variables for H in this equation. Although the 3SLS estimator, $\hat{\delta}$ say, is not efficient, it is shown in Appendix 7.A that it is consistent.
ii. We form the 3SLS residual vectors $\hat{u} = y - H\hat{\delta}$. From $\hat{u}$, we form $\hat{U} = \text{devec}_n\, \hat{u}$ and $\hat{U}_p = S(I_p \otimes \hat{U})$.
iii. We compute $\tilde{R}' = -(\hat{U}_p'\hat{U}_p)^{-1}\hat{U}_p'\hat{U}$, $\tilde{E} = \hat{U} + \hat{U}_p\tilde{R}'$, and $\tilde{\Sigma} = \tilde{E}'\tilde{E}/n$.

In Appendix 7.A, it is shown that both $\tilde{R}$ and $\tilde{\Sigma}$ are consistent estimators. The analysis there makes it clear that any consistent estimator of δ would lead to consistent estimators of R and Σ. The 3SLS estimator is singled out as it is the estimator the econometrician has in hand when dealing with the LSE model.

With $\tilde{R}$ obtained, we form $\tilde{r} = \text{vec}\,\tilde{R}$, $M(\tilde{r})$, $\tilde{y}^d = M(\tilde{r})y$, and $\tilde{H}^d = M(\tilde{r})H^d$.

c. Consistency of $\tilde{\tilde{\delta}}_{\text{M3S}}$

We now show that $\tilde{\tilde{\delta}}_{\text{M3S}}$ is a consistent estimator. From Eqs. (7.61) and (7.62) we can write

$$\tilde{\tilde{\delta}}_{\text{M3S}} = \delta + [\tilde{H}^{d'}(\tilde{\Sigma}^{-1} \otimes P_{z_1})\tilde{H}^d]^{-1}\tilde{H}^{d'}(\tilde{\Sigma}^{-1} \otimes P_{z_1})\tilde{\varepsilon}, \qquad (7.63)$$

where

$$\tilde{\varepsilon} = \varepsilon + [M(\tilde{r}) - M(r)]u.$$

Recall from Subsection 7.3.1 that $M(r) = I_{Gn} + (R \otimes I_n)C$, so we can write

$$\tilde{\varepsilon} = \varepsilon + [(\tilde{R} - R) \otimes I_n]Cu, \tag{7.64}$$

$$\tilde{H}^d = H^d + [(\tilde{R} - R) \otimes I_n]H_p^{\tau_l}. \tag{7.65}$$

We wish to prove that the second vector on the right-hand side of Eq. (7.63) has a probability limit equal to the null vector. To this end, from Eq. (7.65) we have

$$\tilde{H}^{d'}(I_G \otimes Z_1)/n = H^{d'}(I_G \otimes Z_1)/n$$
$$+ [H_p^{\tau_l'}(I_{Gp} \otimes Z_1)/n][(\tilde{R} - R)' \otimes I_{k(1+p)}].$$

Under our asymptotic assumptions, $p \lim H^{d'}(I_G \otimes Z_1)/n$ and $p \lim H_p^{\tau_l'}(I_G \otimes Z_1)/n$ exists and, as $\tilde{R}$ is consistent,

$$p \lim \tilde{H}^{d'}(I_G \otimes Z_1)/n = p \lim H^{d'}(I_G \otimes Z_1)/n. \tag{7.66}$$

It follows then that

$$p \lim \tilde{H}^{d'}(\tilde{\Sigma}^{-1} \otimes P_{z_1})\tilde{H}^d/n = p \lim H^{d'}(\Sigma^{-1} \otimes P_{z_1})H^d/n. \tag{7.67}$$

Moreover, from Eq. (7.64),

$$(I_G \otimes Z_1')\tilde{\varepsilon}/n = (I_G \otimes Z_1')\varepsilon/n + [(\tilde{R} - R) \otimes I_{k(1+p)}]$$
$$\times (I_{Gp} \otimes Z_1')Cu/n.$$

As $p \lim(I_G \otimes Z_1')\varepsilon/n = 0$ and $p \lim(I_{Gp} \otimes Z_1')Cu/n$ exists,

$$p \lim(I_G \otimes Z_1')\tilde{\varepsilon}/n = 0. \tag{7.68}$$

From Eqs. (7.66)–(7.68) we have then that $\tilde{\tilde{\delta}}_{\text{M3S}}$ is consistent.

d. Asymptotic Efficiency of $\tilde{\tilde{\delta}}_{\text{M3S}}$

Having established that our modified 3SLS estimator is consistent, we now seek to prove that it is asymptotically efficient in that $\sqrt{n}(\tilde{\tilde{\delta}}_{\text{M3S}} - \delta)$ has a limiting multivariate normal distribution with a null vector mean and a covariance matrix equal to $I^{\delta\delta}$ given by Eq. (7.44). To do this we need to make the following simplifying assumption.

Assumption 7.1. Let $u_p = Cu = (u_{-1}' \cdots u_{-p}')'$ and $V = \mathcal{E}(u_p u_p')$. As n tends to infinity, the matrix $(I_{Gp} \otimes Z_1')V(I_{Gp} \otimes Z_1)/n$ tends to a positive-definite matrix.

This assumption is similar to the type of assumption used in discussing the asymptotic efficiency of a GLS estimator in a linear-regression framework with autoregressive disturbances and unknown autoregressive coefficients [see, for example, Theil (1971), Section 8.6]. Its importance for the discussion here is that it ensures that $(I_{Gp} \otimes Z_1')u_p/\sqrt{n}$ has a limiting distribution as n tends to infinity. We are still assuming that X contains no lagged endogenous variables, so this random vector has an expectation equal to the null vector. Under Assumption 1 its covariance matrix is bounded as n tends to infinity. Consider now

$$\sqrt{n}(\tilde{\tilde{\delta}}_{\text{M3S}} - \delta) = [\tilde{H}^{d'}(\tilde{\Sigma}^{-1} \otimes P_{z_1})\tilde{H}^d/n]^{-1}\{\tilde{H}^{d'}[\tilde{\Sigma}^{-1} \otimes Z_1(Z_1'Z_1])^{-1}]\} \times (I_G \otimes Z_1')\tilde{\varepsilon}/\sqrt{n}. \tag{7.69}$$

We have already established that the matrices in the square brackets and the curly braces have probability limits so we need to show that $(I_G \otimes Z_1')\tilde{\varepsilon}/\sqrt{n}$ has a limiting distribution. To this end, from Eq. (7.64) we can write

$$(I_G \otimes Z_1')\tilde{\varepsilon}/\sqrt{n} = (I_G \otimes Z_1')\varepsilon/\sqrt{n} + [(\tilde{R} - R) \otimes I_{k(1+p)}] \times (I_{Gp} \otimes Z_1')u_p/\sqrt{n}. \tag{7.70}$$

Under our assumption, $(I_{Gp} \otimes Z_1')u_p/\sqrt{n}$ has a limiting distribution, so the second term on the right-hand side of Eq. (7.70) has probability limit equal to the null vector, and so $(I_G \otimes Z_1')\tilde{\varepsilon}/\sqrt{n}$ has the same limiting distribution as that of $(I_G \otimes Z_1')\varepsilon/\sqrt{n}$, which is a multivariate normal distribution with a mean equal to the null vector and a covariance matrix $\Sigma^{-1} \otimes p\lim Z_1'Z_1/n$. Then, from Eqs. (7.67) and (7.69) we obtain

$$\sqrt{n}(\tilde{\tilde{\delta}}_{\text{M3S}} - \delta) \xrightarrow{d} N(0,\ V_M),$$

where $V_M = [p\lim H^{d'}(\Sigma^{-1} \otimes P_{z_1})H^d/n]^{-1}$. Having established the limiting distribution of $\tilde{\tilde{\delta}}_{\text{M3S}}$ it remains for us to show that $V_M \equiv I^{\delta\delta}$. Recall that $Z = (Z_1\ Y_p)$, so

$$M_z = M_{z_1} - M_{z_1}Y_p(Y_p' M_{z_1} Y_p)^{-1} Y_p' M_{z_1}, \tag{7.71}$$

where $M_{Z_1} = I_n - P_{z_1}$. However, from Eq. (7.29)

$$Y_p = X_p(I_p \otimes \Pi_1) + U_p(I_p \otimes B^{-1}) \tag{7.72}$$

and, as X_p is part of Z_1, $M_{z_1}X_p = O$, and

$$M_{z_1}Y_p = M_{z_1}U_p(I_p \otimes B^{-1}). \tag{7.73}$$

Substituting Eq. (7.73) into Eq. (7.71) gives

$$M_z = M_{z_1} - M_{z_1}U_p(U_p'M_{z_1}U_p)^{-1}U_p'M_{z_1}.$$

Now, with X containing no lagged endogenous variables, $p\lim X'U_p/n = O$, $p\lim X_p'U_p/n = O$, and $p\lim Z_1'U_p/n = O$. It follows then that

$$p\lim H^{d'}(\Sigma^{-1} \otimes M_{z_1})H^d/n$$
$$= p\lim H^{d'}\{\Sigma^{-1} \otimes [M_z + U_p(U_p'U_p)^{-1}U_p']\}H^d/n,$$

for Eq. (7.44), $V_M = I^{\delta\delta}$, as required.

In the preceding analysis we have assumed that X contains no lagged endogenous variables. When this is not the case we have seen that the Cramer–Rao lower bound remains at $I^{\delta\delta}$. However, now $p\lim X'U/n \neq O$, $p\lim X_p'U/n \neq O$, reduced-form equation (7.30) is no longer the final form, and we must specify which lagged endogenous variables enter which equations. All this makes the asymptotic analysis far more complex, and as a consequence it is left outside the scope of this present work.

7.3.5.2. Using X^d to Form Instrumental Variables

If X does not contain lagged endogenous variables, X^d is available to form instrumental variables. In this subsection we look at this possibility for both the case in which R is known and for the case in which R is unknown.

1. R IS KNOWN. Suppose again that R is known so y^d, H^d, and X^d are available to us. Consider again the transformed equation

$$y^d = H^d\delta + \varepsilon. \tag{7.74}$$

Now, we know from Eq. (7.30) that

$$y = (I \otimes X)\pi_1 + v,$$

where $\pi_1 = \text{vec}\,\Pi_1$, $v = \text{vec}\,V$, and $V = UB^{-1}$, so

$$y^d = X^d\pi_1 + M(r)v$$

may be regarded as the reduced-form equation for y^d. This being the case, we may be tempted to use X^d to form instrumental variables for H^d in Eq. (7.74). Suppose we form a IV-GLS type estimator. First, we would consider

$$\mathcal{P}y^d = \mathcal{P}H^d\delta + \mathcal{P}\varepsilon, \tag{7.75}$$

where we recall that $\mathcal{P}'\mathcal{P} = \Sigma^{-1} \otimes I_G$. We would then form an instrumental variable for $\mathcal{P}H^d$ in this equation by regressing $\mathcal{P}H^d$ on $\mathcal{P}X^d$ to get

$$\widehat{\mathcal{P}H^d} = \mathcal{P}X^d(X^{d'}\Phi^{-1}X^d)^{-1}X^{d'}\Phi^{-1}H^d.$$

Using $\mathcal{P}\hat{H}^d$ as an IV for $\mathcal{P}H^d$ in Eq. (7.75) and in the resultant estimator, replacing Φ with $\hat{\Phi} = \hat{\Sigma} \otimes I$ gives

$$\tilde{\delta}_d = [H^{d\prime}\hat{\Phi}^{-1}X^d(X^{d\prime}\hat{\Phi}^{-1}X^d)^{-1}X^{d\prime}\hat{\Phi}^{-1}H^d]^{-1}H^{d\prime}\hat{\Phi}^{-1}X^d \times (X^{d\prime}\hat{\Phi}^{-1}X^d)X^{d\prime}\hat{\Phi}^{-1}y^d.$$

We have assumed that $p\lim X^{d\prime}\hat{\Phi}^{-1}X^d/n$ exists. Standard asymptotic theory then reveals that $\tilde{\delta}_d$ is consistent and

$$\sqrt{n}(\tilde{\delta}_d - \delta) \xrightarrow{d} N(0, V_d),$$

where

$$V_d = [p\lim H^{d\prime}\Phi^{-1}X^d(X^{d\prime}\Phi^{-1}X^d)^{-1}X^{d\prime}\Phi^{-1}H^d/n]^{-1}.$$

From Eq. (7.50),

$$H^{d\prime}\Phi^{-1}X^d = A'(I_G \otimes F')X^{d\prime}\Phi^{-1}X^d + W'(I_G \otimes V')M(r)'\Phi^{-1}X^d,$$

and we have seen from Eq. (7.55) that

$$(I_G \otimes V')M(r)'\Phi^{-1}X^d/n \xrightarrow{p} O,$$

so

$$p\lim H^{d\prime}\Phi^{-1}X^d/n = A'(I_G \otimes F')p\lim X^{d\prime}\Phi^{-1}X^d/n.$$

We conclude that $V_d = I^{\delta\delta}$. We know that $I^{\delta\delta}$ is the Cramer–Rao lower bound for a consistent estimator of δ in which R is unknown. If R is known, as we are now assuming, the Cramer–Rao lower bound is $I^{*\delta\delta}$. We conclude then that $\tilde{\delta}_d$ is not an asymptotically efficient estimator of δ. Forming an IV as we have just done does not make the most efficient use of our knowledge of R.

2. R IS UNKNOWN. Now we look at the more realistic case in which R is unknown. Suppose we persevere with $\tilde{\delta}_d$, replacing H^d, X^d, and $\hat{\Phi}$ in this estimator with $\tilde{H}^d = M(\tilde{r})H^d$, $\tilde{X}^d = M(\tilde{r})(I_G \otimes X)$, and $\tilde{\Phi} = \tilde{\Sigma} \otimes I_n$, respectively, to obtain the estimator

$$\tilde{\tilde{\delta}}_d = [\tilde{H}^{d\prime}\tilde{\Phi}^{-1}\tilde{X}^d(\tilde{X}^{d\prime}\tilde{\Phi}^{-1}\tilde{X}^d)^{-1}\tilde{X}^{d\prime}\tilde{\Phi}^{-1}\tilde{H}^d]^{-1}\tilde{H}^{d\prime}\tilde{\Phi}^{-1}\tilde{X}^d \times (\tilde{X}^{d\prime}\tilde{\Phi}^{-1}\tilde{X}^d)^{-1}\tilde{X}^{d\prime}\tilde{\Phi}^{-1}\tilde{y}^d.$$

Consistency of $\tilde{\tilde{\delta}}_d$. Clearly,

$$\tilde{\tilde{\delta}}_d = \delta + [\tilde{H}^{d\prime}\tilde{\Phi}^{-1}\tilde{X}^d(\tilde{X}^{d\prime}\tilde{\Phi}^{-1}\tilde{X}^d)^{-1}\tilde{X}^{d\prime}\tilde{\Phi}^{-1}\tilde{H}^d]^{-1} \times \tilde{H}^{d\prime}\tilde{\Phi}^{-1}\tilde{X}^d(\tilde{X}^{d\prime}\tilde{\Phi}^{-1}\tilde{X}^d)^{-1}\tilde{X}^{d\prime}\tilde{\Phi}^{-1}\tilde{\varepsilon}, \tag{7.76}$$

where

$$\tilde{\varepsilon} = \varepsilon + [(\tilde{R} - R) \otimes I_n]Cu. \tag{7.77}$$

Now, in Subsection 7.3.3, Eq. (7.32), we saw that we could write

$$H^d = H + (R \otimes I_n)H_p^{\tau_l},$$

so

$$\tilde{H}^d = H^d + [(\tilde{R} - R) \otimes I_n] H_p^{\tau_l}.$$

Also, in Subsection 7.3.4, Eq. (7.53), we saw that we could write

$$X^d = (I_G \otimes X) + (R \otimes X_p)\bar{S}',$$

so

$$\tilde{X}^d = X^d + [(\tilde{R} - R) \otimes X_p]\bar{S}'. \tag{7.78}$$

Consider then

$$\begin{aligned}\tilde{H}^{d'}\tilde{\Phi}^{-1}\tilde{X}^d = {} & H^{d'}\tilde{\Phi}^{-1}X^d + H^{d'}(I_G \otimes X_p)[\tilde{\Sigma}^{-1}(\tilde{R} - R) \otimes I_{pk}]\bar{S}' \\ & + H_p^{\tau_l'}(I_{pG} \otimes X)[(\tilde{R} - R)'\tilde{\Sigma}^{-1} \otimes I_k] \\ & + H_p^{\tau_l'}(I_{pG} \otimes X_p)[(\tilde{R} - R)'\tilde{\Sigma}^{-1}R \otimes I_{pk}]\bar{S}' \\ & + H_p^{\tau_l'}(I_{pG} \otimes X_p)[(\tilde{R} - R)'\tilde{\Sigma}^{-1}(\tilde{R} - R) \otimes I_{pk}]\bar{S}'.\end{aligned}$$

We make the usual assumptions that $p\lim H_p^{\tau_l'}(I_{pG} \otimes X)/n$ and $p\lim H_p^{\tau_l'}(I_{pG} \otimes X_p)/n$ exist so, as $\tilde{R}$ is a consistent estimator of R,

$$\tilde{H}^{d'}\tilde{\Phi}^{-1}\tilde{X}^d/n \xrightarrow{p} p\lim H^{d'}\Phi^{-1}X^d/n.$$

In a like manner,

$$\tilde{X}^{d'}\tilde{\Phi}^{-1}\tilde{X}^d/n \xrightarrow{p} p\lim X^{d'}\Phi^{-1}X^d/n.$$
$$\tilde{X}^{d'}\tilde{\Phi}^{-1}\tilde{\varepsilon}/n \xrightarrow{p} 0.$$

We conclude that $\tilde{\tilde{\delta}}_d$ is a consistent estimator of δ.

Asymptotic Efficiency of $\tilde{\tilde{\delta}}_d$: From Eq. (7.76),

$$\begin{aligned}\sqrt{n}(\tilde{\tilde{\delta}}_d - \delta) = {} & \{[\tilde{H}^d\tilde{\Phi}^{-1}\tilde{X}^d(\tilde{X}^{d'}\tilde{\Phi}^{-1}\tilde{X}^d)^{-1}\tilde{X}^{d'}\tilde{\Phi}^{-1}\tilde{H}^d]^{-1}\tilde{H}^{d'}\tilde{\Phi}^{-1}\tilde{X}^d \\ & \times(\tilde{X}^{d'}\tilde{\Phi}^{-1}\tilde{X}^d)^{-1}\}\tilde{X}^{d'}\tilde{\Phi}^{-1}\tilde{\varepsilon}/\sqrt{n}.\end{aligned} \tag{7.79}$$

We have just shown that the term in the braces has a probability limit of

$$p\lim n[H^{d'}\Phi^{-1}X^d(X^{d'}\Phi^{-1}X^d)^{-1}X^{d'}\Phi^{-1}H^d]^{-1}H^{d'}\Phi^{-1}X^d(X^{d'}\Phi^{-1}X^d)^{-1}.$$

Now, using Eqs. (7.77) and (7.78), we can write

$$\begin{aligned}\tilde{X}^{d'}\tilde{\Phi}^{-1}\tilde{\varepsilon}/\sqrt{n} = {} & X^{d'}\tilde{\Phi}^{-1}\varepsilon/\sqrt{n} + [\tilde{\Sigma}^{-1}(\tilde{R} - R) \otimes I_k]\left(\frac{I_{pG} \otimes X'}{\sqrt{n}}\right)Cu \\ & + \bar{S}[R'\tilde{\Sigma}^{-1}(\tilde{R} - R) \otimes I_{pk}](I_{pG} \otimes X_p')Cu/\sqrt{n} \\ & + \bar{S}[(\tilde{R} - R)'\tilde{\Sigma}^{-1} \otimes I_{pk}](I_G \otimes X_p')\varepsilon/\sqrt{n} \\ & + \bar{S}[(\tilde{R} - R)'\tilde{\Sigma}^{-1}(\tilde{R} - R) \otimes I_{pk}](I_{pG} \otimes X_p')Cu/\sqrt{n}.\end{aligned}$$

Under Assumption 7.1, we have assumed that $(I_{pG} \otimes X')Cu/\sqrt{n}$ and $(I_{pG} \otimes X'_p)Cu/\sqrt{n}$ have limiting distributions. Clearly $(I_{pG} \otimes X'_p)\varepsilon/\sqrt{n}$ has a limiting distribution. Therefore, as $\tilde{R}$ is consistent, $\tilde{X}^{d'}\tilde{\Phi}^{-1}\tilde{\varepsilon}/\sqrt{n}$ has the same limiting distribution as that of $X^d\Phi^{-1}\varepsilon/\sqrt{n}$, which is a multivariate normal distribution with the null vector as mean and a covariance matrix $p\lim X^{d'}\Phi^{-1}X^d/n$. Returning now to Eq. (7.79) we see that

$$\sqrt{n}(\tilde{\tilde{\delta}} - \delta) \xrightarrow{d} N(0, V_d),$$

and, as we have seen that $V_d = I^{\delta\delta}$, the estimator $\tilde{\delta}_d$ achieves the Cramer–Rao lower bound and is therefore asymptotically efficient.

7.3.5.3. Maximum-Likelihood Estimator as Iterative Instrumental Variable Estimator

In the preceding analysis, we showed that efficient IVE involves finding the appropriate instrumental variable for the H part of H^d. In this section we show that the MLE has a similar IVE interpretation, although, as always, this interpretation is iterative.

Recall that the components of the score vector are

$$\begin{aligned}\frac{\partial l}{\partial \delta} &= -nW' \operatorname{vec} B^{-1'} + H^{d'}(\Sigma^{-1} \otimes I_n)\varepsilon,\\ \frac{\partial l}{\partial r} &= -K_{pG,G}(\Sigma^{-1} \otimes U'_p)\varepsilon, \qquad (7.80)\\ \frac{\partial l}{\partial \nu} &= \frac{D'}{2}(\operatorname{vec} \Sigma^{-1}E'E\Sigma^{-1} - n \operatorname{vec} \Sigma^{-1}).\end{aligned}$$

In equating $\partial l/\partial r$ to the null vector, we proceed as we did in Subsection 6.3.8.2 to obtain

$$\tilde{R}' = -(U'_p U_p)^{-1}U'_p U,$$

whereas $\partial l/\partial \nu = 0$ gives

$$\hat{\Sigma} = E'E/n.$$

In dealing with $\partial l/\partial \delta = 0$, we proceed in exactly the same manner as we did in Subsection 7.2.8.1 to obtain

$$\frac{\partial l}{\partial \delta} = [H^{d'} - W'(I_G \otimes B^{-1'}E')](\tilde{\Sigma}^{-1} \otimes I_n)\varepsilon.$$

Now,

$$H - (I_G \otimes EB^{-1})W = \bar{H} = \operatorname{diag}\{H_i - EB^{-1}W_i\},$$

where $H_i - EB^{-1}W_i = (Y_i, X_i) - EB^{-1}(\bar{W}_i, O)$. However, writing the reduced-form equation as

$$Y = Z\Pi + E\,B^{-1},$$

we see that

$$Y_i = Y\bar{W}_i = Z\Pi\bar{W}_i + EB^{-1}\bar{W}_i = Z\Pi_i + EB^{-1}\bar{W}_i,$$

so $Y_i - EB^{-1}\bar{W}_i$ gives the systematic part of the reduced form of Y_i, that is, the part that is left after the influence of the random disturbance matrix E has been removed. Thus,

$$\bar{H} = \text{diag}\{\bar{H}_i\}$$

with $\bar{H}_i = (Z\Pi_i \; X_i)$, and

$$H^d - (I_G \otimes E\,B^{-1})W = \bar{H} + (R \otimes I_n)H_p^{\tau_l} = \bar{H}^d$$

say, and

$$\frac{\partial l}{\partial \delta} = \bar{H}^{d\prime}(\tilde{\Sigma}^{-1} \otimes I_n)(y^d - H^d\delta).$$

Equating this derivative to the null vector and replacing the remaining parameters with their MLEs gives

$$\tilde{\bar{H}}^{d\prime}(\tilde{\Sigma}^{-1} \otimes I_n)(\tilde{y}^d - \tilde{H}^d\tilde{\delta}) = 0, \tag{7.81}$$

where

$$\tilde{\bar{H}}^d = \tilde{\bar{H}} + (\tilde{R} \otimes I_n)H_p^{\tau_l},$$

$$\tilde{\bar{H}} = \text{diag}\{Z\tilde{\Pi}_i \; X_i\},$$

$$\tilde{y}^d = M(\tilde{r})y,$$

$$\tilde{H}^d = H + (\tilde{R} \otimes I_n)H_p^{\tau_l},$$

and $\tilde{\delta}$, $\tilde{R}$, $\tilde{\Pi}_i$, and $\tilde{r} = \text{vec}\,\tilde{R}$ are the MLEs of δ, R, Π_i, and r, respectively. Solving Eq. (7.80) gives

$$\tilde{\delta} = [\tilde{\bar{H}}^{d\prime}(\tilde{\Sigma}^{-1} \otimes I_n)\tilde{H}^d]^{-1}\tilde{\bar{H}}^{d\prime}(\tilde{\Sigma}^{-1} \otimes I_n)\tilde{y}^d.$$

Although the interpretation is iterative, it clearly points to the estimation procedures outlined in the preceding subsections.

7.3.5.4. The Lagrangian Multiplier Test for H_0: $r = 0$

If the disturbances of the LSE model are not subject to a vector autoregressive process, then the estimation of δ is a far simpler affair. In place of $\tilde{\tilde{\delta}}_{M3S}$ we would use the 3SLS estimator obtained from $y = H\delta + u$ by using X to form instrumental variables for H, namely

$$\bar{\delta} = [H'(\bar{\Sigma}^{-1} \otimes P_x)H]^{-1}H'(\bar{\Sigma}^{-1} \otimes P_x)y,$$

where we form the estimator $\tilde{\Sigma}$ by using the 2SLS residual vectors (again using X to form instrumental variables) in the usual way. It is of interest to us then to develop a test statistic for the null hypothesis $H_0 : r = 0$ against $H_A : r \neq 0$. As with the SURE model, the most amenable test statistic is the LMT statistic, which is given by

$$T_1 = \frac{1}{n} \frac{\partial l}{\partial r}\bigg|_{\hat{\theta}}' I^{rr}(\hat{\theta}) \frac{\partial l}{\partial r}\bigg|_{\hat{\theta}},$$

where in forming $\hat{\theta}$ we put r equal to the null vector and evaluate all other parameters at the constrained MLEs, the MLEs we get for δ and ν after we set r equal to the null vector. The constrained MLE for δ in this context is the FIML estimator for δ discussed in Section 7.2. Asymptotically this estimator is equivalent to the 3SLS estimator $\bar{\delta}$.

We proceed as we did with the SURE model in Subsection 6.3.8.3. As in that model the actual test statistic itself will depend on the case before us. We have seen that if X is strictly exogenous then we can simplify I^{rr} so it is given by Eq. (7.47). With X containing lagged endogenous variables, we are stuck with the more complicated expression for I^{rr} given by Eq. (7.45). Of course, for both cases when $r = 0$, $M(r) = I_{nG}$, $\varepsilon = u$, $H^d = H, U = E$, $U_p = E_p$, $\lim E_p' E_p/n = p \lim U_p' U_p/n = I_p \otimes \Sigma$.

Consider now the simpler case in which X is exogenous. From Eq. (7.47) we have

$$I^{rr}(\theta)|_{r=0} = I_p \otimes \Sigma^{-1} \otimes \Sigma,$$

and, from Eq. (7.80) we have

$$\frac{\partial l}{\partial r}\bigg|_{r=0} = -K_{pG,G}(\Sigma^{-1} \otimes U_p')u. \tag{7.82}$$

Marrying these two components together, we can write the LMT statistic as

$$\begin{aligned} T_1' &= \frac{1}{n} u'(\Sigma^{-1} \otimes U_p) K_{G,pG}(I_p \otimes \Sigma^{-1} \otimes \Sigma) K_{pG,G}(\Sigma^{-1} \otimes U_p')u|_{\hat{\theta}} \\ &= \frac{1}{n} u'[\Sigma^{-1} \otimes U_p(I_p \otimes \Sigma^{-1})U_p']u|_{\hat{\theta}} \\ &= n\hat{u}'\{(\hat{U}'\hat{U})^{-1} \otimes \hat{U}_p[I_p \otimes (\hat{U}'\hat{U})^{-1}]U_p'\}\hat{u}, \end{aligned}$$

where $\hat{u}$ is the FIML residual vector, $\hat{U} = \text{devec}_n \, \hat{u}$, and $\hat{U}_p = S(I_p \otimes \hat{U})$. (An asymptotically equivalent test statistic would use the 3SLS residuals formed from $\bar{\delta}$). Under H_0, T_1' has a limiting χ^2 distribution with pG^2 degrees of freedom, the upper tail of this distribution being used to obtain the appropriate critical region.

Note that the form of the LMT statistic obtained here is exactly the same as that obtained for the SURE model in Subsection 6.3.8.3, although of course the residuals used differ in the two models. It follows then that the current LMT statistic before us has the same intuitive F test interpretation developed in Subsection 6.3.8.3.

Now for the more complicated case in which X contains lagged endogenous variables: For this case we have seen that I^{rr} is more complex now, being given by Eq. (7.45). Setting r equal to the null vector in this expression involves $I^{\delta\delta}|_{r=0}$, which, from Eq. (7.44), we can write as

$$I^{\delta\delta}(\theta)_{r=0} = p\lim\{H'[\Sigma^{-1} \otimes (P_z - P_p)]H/n\}^{-1},$$

where $P_p = U_p(U_p'U_p)^{-1}U_p'$. Thus,

$$I^{rr}(\theta)|_{r=0} = I_p \otimes \Sigma^{-1} \otimes \Sigma + K_{pG,G}\{p\lim n^2[I_G \otimes (I_p \otimes \Sigma^{-1})U_p'] \times HI^{\delta\delta}(\theta)_{r=0}H'[I_G \otimes U_p(I_p \otimes \Sigma^{-1})]\}K_{G,pG}.$$

Marrying this with $\partial l/\partial r|_{r=0}$ given by Eq. (7.82) and remembering that $K_{pG,G}^{-1} = K_{pG,G}' = K_{G,pG}$, we write the LMT statistic, ignoring the $p\lim$ as

$$T_1 = T_1' + nu'[\Sigma^{-1} \otimes U_p(I_p \otimes \Sigma^{-1})U_p']HI^{\delta\delta}(\theta)_{r=0} \times H'[\Sigma^{-1} \otimes U_p(I_p \otimes \Sigma^{-1})U_p']u|_{\hat{\theta}} \tag{7.83}$$

In evaluating this expression at $\hat{\theta}$, we put $\hat{u}$, $\hat{U}'\hat{U}/n$, and $\hat{U}_p$ in place of u, Σ, and U_p, respectively, where $\hat{u}$ is the FIML residual vector, $\hat{U} = \text{devec}_n\,\hat{u}$, and $\hat{U}_p = S(I_p \otimes \hat{U})$. For $I^{\delta\delta}$ we ignore the $p\lim$ and use

$$I^{\delta\delta}(\hat{\theta}) = \{H'[\hat{\Sigma}^{-1} \otimes (P_z - \hat{P}_p)]H/n\}^{-1},$$

where $\hat{P}_p = \hat{U}_p(\hat{U}'_p\hat{U}_p)^{-1}\hat{U}'_p$ or asymptotically equivalently, as $p\lim \hat{U}'_p\hat{U}_p = I_p \otimes \Sigma$,

$$I^{\delta\delta}(\hat{\theta}) = \{\hat{\Sigma}^{-1} \otimes [(P_z/n) - \hat{U}_p(I_p \otimes \hat{\Sigma}^{-1})U_p']\}.$$

Comparing the statistic with the equivalent statistic for the SURE model given by Eq. (6.14), we see that the two test statistics have the same format with one qualification concerning $I^{\delta\delta}(\hat{\theta})|_{r=0}$.

The matrix in the test statistics for the two models is

$$I^{\delta\delta}(\hat{\theta}) = \{X'[\hat{\Sigma}^{-1} \otimes (I_n - \hat{P}_p)]X/n\}$$

for the SURE model,

$$I^{\delta\delta}(\hat{\theta}) = \{H'[\hat{\Sigma}^{-1} \otimes (I_n - \hat{P}_p - M_z)]H/n\}^{-1}$$

for the LSE model.

The introduction of endogenous variables into the picture introduces the matrix $M_z = I_n - Z(Z'Z)^{-1}Z'$ into the expression for $I^{\delta\delta}(\hat{\theta})$.

There is one other asymptotically equivalent way of writing our test statistic. We saw in Eq. (7.43) that it is possible to write

$$I^{\delta\delta}(\theta) = \{p\lim H^{d'}[\Sigma^{-1} \otimes (M_E - P_p)]H^d/n\}^{-1},$$

so

$$I^{\delta\delta}(\theta)|_{r=0} = \{p\lim H'[\Sigma^{-1} \otimes (M_u - P_p)]H/n\}^{-1},$$

where $M_u = I_n - U(U'U)^{-1}U'$. Ignoring the $p\lim$ we could if we like use

$$I^{\delta\delta}(\hat{\theta}) = \{H'[\hat{\Sigma}^{-1} \otimes (\hat{M}_u - \hat{P}_p)H/n]\}^{-1} \tag{7.84}$$

in the expression for T_1, where $\hat{M}_u = I_n - \hat{U}(\hat{U}'U)^{-1}\hat{U}'$.

It is also possible to get some comparative insight into the Wald test by using the iterative solution of the MLE of R in much the same way as we did in Subsection 6.3.8.3. The detailed analysis is left to the reader.

7.4. THE LINEAR SIMULTANEOUS EQUATIONS MODEL WITH VECTOR MOVING-AVERAGE DISTURBANCES

7.4.1. The Model and Its Assumptions

In this final section, we consider a further extension of the LSE estimator by allowing the disturbances to be subject to a vector moving-average system of the order of p. We use same notation for the disturbance system as that used in Subsection 6.4.1. Replacing presample values with zero, we can write the model under consideration as

$$\begin{aligned} y &= H\delta + u, \\ u &= M(r)\varepsilon, \\ \varepsilon &\sim N(0, \Sigma \otimes I_n). \end{aligned}$$

Assuming invertability, we write

$$\varepsilon = M(r)^{-1}u.$$

As always, we assume no problems from unit roots that arise from lagged endogenous variables.

Alternatively, we can write the model as

$$\begin{aligned} YB + X\Gamma &= U, \\ U &= E_pR' + E, \end{aligned} \tag{7.85}$$

where the rows of the random matrix E are assumed to be independently, identically normally distributed random vectors with null vectors as means and covariance matrix Σ. Again E_p is the $n \times Gp$ matrix $(E_{-1} \cdots E_{-p})$, and if we replace presample values with zero we can write

$$E_p = S(I_p \otimes E),$$

where, S is the $n \times np$ shifting matrix

$$S = (S_1 \cdots S_p).$$

The reduced form of the model is

$$Y = X\Pi_1 + UB^{-1}, \tag{7.86}$$

with $U = E_p R' + E$. More will be said about this reduced-form later on in this section.

7.4.2. The Parameters of the Model, the Log-Likelihood Function, the Score Vector, and the Hessian Matrix

The parameters of the model are $\theta = (\delta' r' \nu')'$ and the log-likelihood function, apart from a constant, is

$$l(\theta) = n \log|\det B| - \frac{n}{2}\log\det\Sigma - \frac{1}{2}\varepsilon'(\Sigma^{-1} \otimes I_n)\varepsilon,$$

except now in this function we set ε equal to $M(r)^{-1}(y - H\delta)$, and we can write $\varepsilon = y^* - H^*\delta$, where $y^* = M(r)^{-1}y$ and $H^* = M(r)^{-1}H$.

The same comments can be made about the derivatives we now require as those made in Subsection 7.3.2. Derivatives with respect to r and ν that we need for both the score vector and for the Hessian matrix are the same as those derived in Subsections 6.4.4 and 6.4.5 with the proviso that we replace X^* with H^*. Derivatives involving δ but not r can be derived from those obtained in Subsections 7.2.4 and 7.2.5 with the proviso that H is now replaced with H^*, u with ε, and U with E. Finally, we obtain $\partial^2 l/\partial\delta\partial r'$ from the equivalent expression of Subsection 6.4.5 by replacing X^* with H^*.
Thus, we obtain the score vector and the Hessian matrix.

SCORE VECTOR

$$\frac{\partial l}{\partial \delta} = -nW' \operatorname{vec}(B^{-1'}) + H^{*'}(\Sigma^{-1} \otimes I_n)\varepsilon,$$

$$\frac{\partial l}{\partial r} = K_{pG,G}(I_G \otimes E_p')M(r)^{-1'}(\Sigma^{-1} \otimes I_n)\varepsilon,$$

$$\frac{\partial l}{\partial \nu} = \frac{D'}{2}(\operatorname{vec}\Sigma^{-1}E'E - n\operatorname{vec}\Sigma^{-1}).$$

HESSIAN MATRIX

$$\frac{\partial^2 l}{\partial\delta\partial\delta'} = -nW'K_{GG}(B^{-1'} \otimes B^{-1})W - H^{*\prime}(\Sigma^{-1} \otimes I_n)H^*,$$

$$\frac{\partial^2 l}{\partial\delta\partial r'} = -H^{*\prime}(\Sigma^{-1} \otimes I_n)M(r)^{-1}(I_G \otimes E_p)K_{G,pG}$$
$$- H^{*\prime}C'\{I_{pG} \otimes [M(r)^{-1}]^{\tau_n'}(I_G \otimes \text{vec}\, E\Sigma^{-1})\}.$$

$$\frac{\partial^2 l}{\partial\delta\partial v'} = -H^{*\prime}(\Sigma^{-1} \otimes E\Sigma^{-1})D,$$

$$\frac{\partial^2 l}{\partial r\partial r'} = -K_{pG,G}(I_G \otimes E_p')M(r)^{-1'}C'$$
$$\times\{I_{pG} \otimes [M(r)^{-1}]^{\tau_n'}(I_G \otimes \text{vec}\, E\Sigma^{-1})\}$$
$$- \{I_{pG} \otimes [I_G \otimes (\text{vec}\, E\Sigma^{-1})'][M(r)^{-1}]^{\tau_n}\}CM(r)^{-1}$$
$$\times(I_G \otimes E_p)K_{G,pG}$$
$$- K_{pG,G}(I_G \otimes E_p')M(r)^{-1'}(\Sigma^{-1} \otimes I_n)M(r)^{-1}$$
$$\times(I_G \otimes E_p)K_{G,pG}.$$

$$\frac{\partial^2 l}{\partial r\partial v'} = -K_{pG,G}(I_G \otimes E_p')M(r)^{-1'}(\Sigma^{-1} \otimes E\Sigma^{-1})D,$$

$$\frac{\partial^2 l}{\partial v\partial v'} = \frac{n}{2}D'(\Sigma^{-1} \otimes \Sigma^{-1})D - D'(\Sigma^{-1} \otimes \Sigma^{-1}E'E\,\Sigma^{-1})D.$$

7.4.3. The Information Matrix $I(\theta) = -p\lim\frac{1}{n}\partial^2 l/\partial\theta\partial\theta'$

The probability limits with reference to the derivatives of the Hessian matrix that involve r or v but not δ have already been evaluated in Appendix 6.A. The work that confronts us here is to evaluate the probability limits that refer to the derivatives of the Hessian matrix that involve δ. Before we do this it is expedient for us to return to the properties of $M(r)^{-1}$ discussed in Subsection 6.4.2. In that subsection we saw that

$$M(r)^{-1} = \begin{bmatrix} M^{11} & \cdots & M^{1G} \\ \vdots & & \vdots \\ M^{G1} & \cdots & M^{GG} \end{bmatrix},$$

where each submatrix is $n \times n$ and M^{ii} is a lower-triangular matrix with ones down its main diagonal whereas $M^{ij} i \neq j$ is strictly lower triangular. In fact, we saw that each M^{ii} is a Toeplitz matrix of the form

$$I_n + a_1 S_1 + \cdots + a_{n-1} S_{n-1}$$

for suitable a_is that are functions of the elements of $M(r)$, whereas each M^{ij}, $i \neq j$, is of the form

$$b_1 S_1 + \cdots + b_{n-1} S_{n-1}$$

again for suitable b_js that are functions of the elements of $M(r)$. It follows that we can write

$$M(r)^{-1} = I_{Gn} + \begin{bmatrix} N^{11} & \cdots & N^{1G} \\ \vdots & & \vdots \\ N^{G1} & \cdots & N^{GG} \end{bmatrix} = I_{Gn} + \mathcal{N}$$

say, where $N^{ij} = M^{ij}, i \neq j$, and $N^{ii} = M^{ii} - I_n$.

Therefore, each $n \times n$ submatrix N^{ij} is a strictly lower-triangular Toeplitz matrix of the form

$$b_1 S_1 + \cdots + b_{n-1} S_{n-1}.$$

Recall that we have written

$$M(r)^{-1'} = \begin{bmatrix} \mathcal{M}_{11} & \cdots & \mathcal{M}_{1G} \\ \vdots & & \vdots \\ \mathcal{M}_{G1} & \cdots & \mathcal{M}_{GG} \end{bmatrix}.$$

Here it is convenient also to write

$$M(r)^{-1'} = I_G + \mathcal{N}' = I_{Gn} + \begin{bmatrix} N^{11'} & \cdots & N^{G1'} \\ \vdots & & \vdots \\ N^{1G'} & \cdots & N^{GG'} \end{bmatrix}$$
$$= I_{Gn} + \begin{bmatrix} \mathcal{N}_{11} & \cdots & \mathcal{N}_{1G} \\ \vdots & & \vdots \\ \mathcal{N}_{G1} & \cdots & \mathcal{N}_{GG} \end{bmatrix}$$

say, where each $n \times n$ matrix $\mathcal{N}_{ij}$ is strictly upper-triangular Toeplitz and of the form

$$b_1 S_1' + \cdots + b_{n-1} S_{n-1}'.$$

Using the notation we have just introduced, we can write

$$H^{*\prime}(I_G \otimes E) = H' M(r)^{-1'}(I_G \otimes E) = H'(I_G \otimes E) + H'\mathcal{N}(I_G \otimes E).$$

Now,

$$H'(I_G \otimes E) = \operatorname{diag}\{H_i' E\} = \operatorname{diag}\begin{Bmatrix} Y_i' E \\ X_i' E \end{Bmatrix}. \tag{7.87}$$

Regardless of the nature of X, $p\lim$, $X'E/n = O$, and so $p\lim X_i'E/n = O$. Also, from reduced-form equation (7.86),

$$Y_i' E = \bar{W}_i' Y' E = \bar{W}_i' \Pi_1' X' E + \bar{W}_i' B^{-1'} R E_p' E + \bar{W}_i' B^{-1'} E' E.$$

However, $p\lim E_p' E/n = O$, so $p\lim Y_i' E/n = \bar{W}_i' B^{-1'}\Sigma$, and returning to Eq. (7.87) we see that

$$p\lim H'(I_G \otimes E)/n = W'(I_G \otimes B^{-1'}\Sigma),$$

regardless of whether X is strictly exogenous or contains lagged endogenous variables. We now wish to show that $p\lim H'\mathcal{N}'(I_G \otimes E)/n = O$. To do this, we write

$$H'\mathcal{N}'(I_G \otimes E) = \begin{bmatrix} H_1'\mathcal{N}_{11}E & \cdots & H_1'\mathcal{N}_{1G}E \\ \vdots & & \vdots \\ H_G'\mathcal{N}_{G1}E & \cdots & H_G'\mathcal{N}_{GG}E \end{bmatrix},$$

$$H_i'\mathcal{N}_{ij}E = A_i' \begin{pmatrix} Y'\mathcal{N}_{ij}E \\ X'\mathcal{N}_{ij}E \end{pmatrix},$$

where A_i is the selection matrix given by

$$A_i = \begin{bmatrix} \bar{W}_i & O \\ O & \bar{T}_i \end{bmatrix} = \begin{pmatrix} W_i \\ T_i \end{pmatrix}$$

and the selection matrices $\bar{W}_i$, W_i, $\bar{T}_i$, and T_i are defined in Subsection 7.2.3. Now $Y'\mathcal{N}_{ij}E$ and $X'\mathcal{N}_{ij}E$ are $G \times G$ and $k \times G$ matrices whose (r, s) elements are $y_r'\mathcal{N}_{ij}\varepsilon_s$ and $x_r'\mathcal{N}_{ij}\varepsilon_s$, respectively. It follows that, as $\mathcal{N}_{ij}$ is strictly upper triangular,

$$p\lim y_r'\mathcal{N}_{ij}\varepsilon_s/n = 0, \qquad p\lim x_r' N_{ij}\varepsilon_s/n = 0,$$

regardless of whether X is strictly exogenous or contains lagged endogenous variables, so $p\lim H_i' N_{ij} E/n = O$, and we have achieved our aim. We have then that

$$p\lim H^{*\prime}(I_G \otimes E)/n = W'(I_G \otimes B^{-1'}\Sigma), \tag{7.88}$$

regardless of the nature of X.

We now wish to prove that $p\lim H^{*\prime}C'(I_{pG} \otimes a^{\bar{\tau}_n})/n$ is the null vector, where we recall that a is the $nG \times 1$ vector given by

$$a = M(r)^{-1'} \operatorname{vec} E\Sigma^{-1}$$

and, from the properties of the devec operator,

$$a^{\bar{\tau}_n} = [M(r)^{-1}]^{\bar{\tau}_n}(I_G \otimes \operatorname{vec} E\Sigma^{-1}).$$

The analysis here is the same as that conducted in Appendix 6.A, except that we now have H in place of X. Following that appendix, we write

$$H^{*\prime}C'(I_{pG} \otimes a^{\bar{\tau}_n}) = H^{*\prime}(I_G \otimes S_1'a^{\bar{\tau}_n} \cdots I_G \otimes S_p'a^{\bar{\tau}_n}),$$

$$H^{*\prime}(I_G \otimes S_j'a^{\bar{\tau}_n}) = \begin{bmatrix} H_1'\mathcal{M}_{11}S_j'a^{\bar{\tau}_n} & \cdots & H_1'\mathcal{M}_{1G}S_j'a^{\bar{\tau}_n} \\ \vdots & & \vdots \\ H_G'\mathcal{M}_{G1}S_j'a^{\bar{\tau}_n} & \cdots & H_G'\mathcal{M}_{GG}S_j'a^{\bar{\tau}_n} \end{bmatrix}$$

for $j = 1, \ldots, p$. Now recalling how we wrote $a^{\bar{\tau}_n}$, we have

$$H_i'\mathcal{M}_{il}S_j'a^{\bar{\tau}_n} = H_i'\mathcal{M}_{il}S_j'(\mathcal{M}_1 \text{ vec } E\Sigma^{-1} \cdots \mathcal{M}_G \text{ vec } E\Sigma^{-1}) \tag{7.89}$$

for $i, l = 1, \ldots, G$. We consider the typical matrix on the right-hand side of Eq. (7.89)

$$\begin{aligned} H_i'\mathcal{M}_{il}S_j'\mathcal{M}_k \text{ vec } E\Sigma^{-1} &= H_i'\mathcal{M}_{il}S_j'\mathcal{M}_k(\Sigma^{-1} \otimes I_n)\varepsilon \\ &= H_i'\mathcal{M}_{il}S_j'\left(\sum_{r=1}^{G}\sum_{s=1}^{G} \sigma^{rs}\mathcal{M}_{ks}\varepsilon_r\right) \end{aligned}$$

for $k = 1, \ldots, G$ and where $\Sigma^{-1} = \{\sigma^{rs}\}$.

Therefore, in evaluating $p \lim H^{*\prime}C'(I_{pG} \otimes a^{\bar{\tau}_n})/n$ we are typically looking at $p \lim H_i'\mathcal{M}_{il}S_j'\mathcal{M}_{kr}\varepsilon_s/n$.

Above we noted that $\mathcal{M}_{ii}$ is upper triangular and $\mathcal{M}_{ij}$, $i \neq j$, is strictly upper triangular so from the properties of shifting matrices $S_j'\mathcal{M}_{kr}$ is strictly upper triangular and therefore so is $\mathcal{M}_{il}S_j'\mathcal{M}_{kr}$. As such, $p \lim H_i'\mathcal{M}_{il}S_j'\mathcal{M}_{kr}\varepsilon_s/n$ is the null vector even if X_i contains lagged dependent variables. We conclude that, regardless of the nature of X,

$$p \lim H^{*\prime}C'(I_{pG} \otimes a^{\bar{\tau}_n})/n = O.$$

With these probability limits in hand and using those derived in the equivalent SURE model, we are now in a position to write the information matrix. Let

$$I(\theta) = \begin{bmatrix} I_{\delta\delta} & I_{\delta r} & I_{\delta v} \\ I_{r\delta} & I_{rr} & I_{rv} \\ I_{v\delta} & I_{vr} & I_{vv} \end{bmatrix};$$

then

$$\begin{aligned} I_{\delta\delta} &= W'K_{GG}(B^{-1\prime} \otimes B^{-1})W + p \lim H^{*\prime}(\Sigma^{-1} \otimes I_n)H^*/n, \\ I_{\delta r} &= p \lim \frac{1}{n}H^{*\prime}(\Sigma^{-1} \otimes I_n)M(r)^{-1}(I_G \otimes E_p)K_{G,pG}, \qquad (7.90) \\ I_{\delta v} &= W'(\Sigma^{-1} \otimes B^{-1\prime})D, \\ I_{rv} &= O, \end{aligned}$$

$$I_{rr} = p\lim \frac{1}{n} K_{pG,G}(I_G \otimes E'_p)M(r)^{-1'}(\Sigma^{-1} \otimes I_n)M(r)^{-1} \times (I_G \otimes E_p)K_{G,pG},$$

$$I_{vv} = \frac{1}{2} D'(\Sigma^{-1} \otimes \Sigma^{-1})D.$$

Comparing this information matrix with that obtained for the corresponding SURE model given in Subsection 6.4.6 we see that the former is considerably more complex than the latter. The matrix in the block (1,1) position has an extra term in it, namely $W'K_{GG}(B^{-1'} \otimes B^{-1})W$. Also the matrix in the block (1, 3) position is now nonnull.

In fact, this information matrix, unlike all previous ones considered in this work, does not lend itself to further simplification when we restrict ourselves to the case in which X is strictly exogenous. Consider $I_{\delta r}$. Then, following an analysis similar to that conducted at the end of Appendix 6.A, we see that evaluating the probability limit, that is, $I_{\delta r}$, involves our looking at

$$p\lim H_i' \mathcal{M}_r(\Sigma^{-1} \otimes I_n)\mathcal{M}'_s S_k \varepsilon_j / n = p\lim \frac{1}{n} \sum_{x=1}^{G} \sum_{y=1}^{G} \sigma^{xy} H_i' \mathcal{M}_{rx} \mathcal{M}'_{sy} S_k \varepsilon_j$$

for $i, j, r, s = 1, \ldots, G, k = 1, \ldots, p$. It is the complicated nature of the matrix $\mathcal{M}_{rx}\mathcal{M}'_{sy}S_k$ that prevents further evaluation. All we know of this matrix is that from the properties of the shifting matrix S_k the last k columns of the matrix are all $n \times 1$ null vectors. Fortunately, assuming that such p lims exists and leaving $I_{\delta r}$ in the form given by Eq. (7.90) suffices for our purposes.

7.4.4. The Cramer–Rao Lower Bound $I^{-1}(\theta)$

For one last time we invert the information matrix to obtain the Cramer–Rao lower bound. As always, we let

$$I^{-1}(\theta) = \begin{bmatrix} I^{\delta\delta} & I^{\delta r} & I^{\delta v} \\ I^{r\delta} & I^{rr} & I^{rv} \\ I^{v\delta} & I^{vr} & I^{vv} \end{bmatrix}.$$

Then

$$\begin{aligned} I^{\delta\delta} = \{ & W'K_{GG}(B^{-1'} \otimes B^{-1})W + p\lim H^{*\prime}(\Sigma^{-1} \otimes I_n)H^*/n. \\ & - 2W'(\Sigma^{-1} \otimes B^{-1'})D[D'(\Sigma^{-1} \otimes \Sigma^{-1})D]^{-1}D'(\Sigma^{-1} \otimes B^{-1})W \\ & - p\lim \frac{1}{n} H^{*\prime}(\Sigma^{-1} \otimes I_n)M(r)^{-1}(I_G \otimes E_p)K_{G,pG}[K_{pG,G} \\ & \times (I_G \otimes E'_p)M(r)^{-1'}(\Sigma^{-1} \otimes I_n)M(r)^{-1}(I_G \otimes E_p)K_{G,pG}]^{-1} \\ & \times K_{pG,G}(I_G \otimes E'_p)M(r)^{-1'}(\Sigma^{-1} \otimes I_n)H^*\}^{-1}. \end{aligned}$$

In Subsection 7.3.4, we saw that we could write the third matrix in this inverse as

$$-W'(\Sigma^{-1} \otimes B^{-1'}\Sigma B^{-1})W - W'K_{GG}(B^{-1'} \otimes B^{-1})W$$

and, as we have shown that $p\lim H^{*\prime}(I_G \otimes E)/n = W'(I_G \otimes B^{-1'}\Sigma)$,

$$W'(\Sigma^{-1} \otimes B^{-1'}\Sigma B^{-1})W = p\lim H^{*\prime}(I_G \otimes P_E)H^*/n,$$

where $P_E = E(E'E)^{-1}E'$. If we now let

$$\mathcal{F} = (\Sigma^{-1} \otimes I_n)M(r)^{-1}(I_G \otimes E_p),$$

we can write

$$I^{\delta\delta} = \{p\lim H^*(\Sigma^{-1} \otimes M_E)H^*/n - p\lim \frac{1}{n} H^{*\prime}\mathcal{F} \\ \times [\mathcal{F}'(\Sigma \otimes I_n)\mathcal{F}]^{-1}\mathcal{F}'H^*\}^{-1},$$

where $M_E = I_n - P_E$.

The other components of the Cramer–Rao lower bound are

$$I^{\delta r} = -I^{\delta\delta} p\lim H^{*\prime}\mathcal{F}[\mathcal{F}'(\Sigma \otimes I_n)\mathcal{F}]^{-1}K_{G,pG},$$

$$I^{\delta v} = -2I^{\delta\delta}W'(I_G \otimes B^{-1'}\Sigma)NL',$$

$$I^{rr} = p\lim n K_{pG,G}[\mathcal{F}'(\Sigma \otimes I_n)\mathcal{F}]^{-1} \\ \times [\mathcal{F}'(\Sigma \otimes I_n)\mathcal{F} - \mathcal{F}'H^*I^{\delta\delta}H^{*\prime}\mathcal{F}][\mathcal{F}'(\Sigma \otimes I_n)\mathcal{F}]^{-1}K_{G,pG},$$

$$I^{rv} = 2K_{pG,G}\, p\lim[\mathcal{F}'(\Sigma^{-1} \otimes I_n)\mathcal{F}]^{-1}\mathcal{F}'H^*I^{\delta\delta} \\ \times W'(I_G \otimes B^{-1'}\Sigma)NL',$$

$$I^{vv} = 2LN[\Sigma \otimes \Sigma + 2(I_G \otimes \Sigma B^{-1})WI^{\delta\delta}W'(I_G \otimes B^{-1'}\Sigma)]NL'.$$

Consider the case in which δ is the vector of parameters of primary interest. If the nuisance parameters given by the vector r were known, then the Cramer–Rao lower bound for a consistent estimator of δ would be

$$I^{*\delta\delta} = \{p\lim H^{*\prime}[\Sigma^{-1} \otimes (I_n - P_E)]H^*/n\}^{-1}.$$

It follows that

$$T = p\lim \frac{1}{n} H^{*\prime}\mathcal{F}[\mathcal{F}'(\Sigma \otimes I_n)\mathcal{F}]^{-1}\mathcal{F}'H^*$$

represents an addition to the Cramer–Rao low bound for δ that comes about because r is unknown.

7.4.5. Maximum-Likelihood Estimator of δ

We return now to the reduced-form equation

$$Y = X\Pi_1 + UB^{-1}.$$

As $U = E_p R' + E$, we can write this equation as

$$Y = X\Pi_1 + E_p R' B^{-1} + E B^{-1}.$$

Now, from Eq. (7.85)

$$E = YB + X\Gamma - E_p R',$$

so

$$E_{-1} = Y_{-1}B + X_{-1}\Gamma - E_{p,-1}R',$$
$$E_{-2} = Y_{-2}B + X_{-2}\Gamma - E_{p,-2}R',$$

and so on, where

$$E_{p,-i} = [E_{-(1+i)} \cdots E_{-(p+i)}]$$

for $i = 1, \ldots, n - 1 + p$. It follows that if we replace presample values with zero we must be able to write the reduced-form equation as

$$Y = \bar{Z}\bar{\Pi} + E B^{-1}, \qquad (7.91)$$

where $\bar{Z} = (X\ X_{n-1}\ Y_{n-1})$, $X_{n-1} = [X_{-1} \cdots X_{-(n-1)}]$ and $Y_{n-1} = [Y_{-1} \cdots Y_{-(n-1)}]$.

There is a crucial difference between this equation and the reduced-form equation of the previous model given by Eq. (7.30). The latter involved only $Z = (X\ X_p\ Y_p)$ and hence in forming instrumental variables we need consider only values of the Xs and the Ys that were lagged p periods. In the asymptotic analysis of the previous model, we could make the assumption that $p \lim Z'Z/n$ exists. Now, regardless of the value of p, Y, through Eq. (7.91) is linked to variables that are lagged in $n - 1$ periods. This prevents us from forming the type of IVEs considered in the previous model. The problem is that, unlike Z, both dimensions of the matrix $\bar{Z}$ are dependent on n, so no assumptions about the existence of $p \lim \bar{Z}'\bar{Z}/n$ can be made. However, such an assumption is crucial in forming IVEs.

The same point can be made a different way if y^d is compared and contrasted with y^*. Recall that

$$y^d = M(r)y = y + (R \otimes I_G)Cy,$$

where R is a $G \times Gp$ matrix whose elements are constants (not depending on n) and

$$C = \begin{pmatrix} I_G \otimes S_1 \\ \vdots \\ I_G \otimes S_p \end{pmatrix}.$$

If we partition R so $R = (R_1 \ldots R_p)$, where each R_j is $G \times G$, we have

$$y^d = y + (R_1 \otimes I_G)y_{-1} + \cdots + (R_p \otimes I_G)y_{-p},$$

where, as always, $y_{-j} = (I_G \otimes S_j)y$ refers to the vector whose elements are those of y lagged j periods, $j = 1, \ldots, p$. Let $r_i^{j'}$ refer to the ith row of the matrix R_j. Then the $n \times 1$ vector in the ith block position of y^d, y_i^d can be written as

$$y_i^d = y_i + \left(r_i^{1'} \otimes I_G\right)y_{-1} + \cdots + \left(r_i^{p'} \otimes I_G\right)y_{-p}. \tag{7.92}$$

We consider the tth element of this vector. From Eq. (7.92)

$$\begin{aligned} y_{ti}^d &= y_{ti} + \left(r_{i1}^1 y_{t-11} + \cdots + r_{iG}^1 y_{t-1G}\right) \\ &\quad + \cdots + \left(r_{i1}^p y_{t-p1} + \cdots + r_{iG}^p y_{t-pG}\right), \end{aligned}$$

that is, in forming y_{ti}^d we use y_{ti} plus a linear combination of the $t-1$, $t-2 \ldots t-p$ values of all the endogenous variables. We form current values of y^d by using the corresponding current values of y plus linear combinations of lagged values of all the endogenous variables, lagged down p periods. If we introduce the notation $\mathbf{y}_t^d$ and $\mathbf{y}_t$ for the $G \times 1$ vectors containing the tth values of y^d and y, respectively, then we have

$$\mathbf{y}_t^d = \mathbf{y}_t + R_1\mathbf{y}_{t-1} + \cdots + R_p\mathbf{y}_{t-p}.$$

The fact that we consider only variables lagged p periods in our autoregressive systems has practical implications for our asymptotic theory. Consider $p\lim(R \otimes A_n)$, where A_n is a $K \times K$ matrix, say, whose probability limit exists. Then, seeing that the elements of R are constants that do not depend on n and that the dimensions of R do not depend on n, we can write

$$p\lim(R \otimes A_n) = (R \otimes I_K)(I_G \otimes p\lim A_n).$$

This greatly simplifies our asymptotic analysis.

Now, in Subsection 6.4.2 we saw that it is possible to write

$$M(r)^{-1} = I_{nG} + (\bar{R} \otimes I_n)\bar{C}, \tag{7.93}$$

where $\bar{R}$ is a $G \times G(n-1)$ matrix whose elements are products of the elements of R and $\bar{C}$ is the $Gn(n-1) \times Gn$ matrix given by

$$\bar{C} = \begin{pmatrix} I_G \otimes S_1 \\ \vdots \\ I_G \otimes S_{n-1} \end{pmatrix}.$$

It follows that we can write

$$y^* = M(r)^{-1}y = y + (\bar{R} \otimes I_G)\bar{C}y.$$

Conducting an analysis similar to the preceding one, we see that

$$\mathbf{y}_t^* = \mathbf{y}_t + \bar{R}_1\mathbf{y}_{t-1} + \cdots + \bar{R}_{n-1}\mathbf{y}_{t-(n-1)},$$

that is, in forming current values of y^* we use the corresponding current values of y plus linear combinations of all the endogenous variables lagged right down to the beginning of our sample period. (In fact, if we did not agree to set presample values to zero they would be infinitely lagged).

The practical implications of these for our asymptotic theory is that we cannot isolate $\bar{R}$ in the way we isolated R above. As the dimensions of $\bar{R}$ depend on n, this matrix blows up as n tends to infinity. This makes the asymptotic analysis for the moving average system far more complicated than that for the autoregressive system.[2]

In this subsection then, we content ourselves with the insights into the MLE of δ that we obtain from an iterative interpretation of this estimator. We proceed as we did in Subsection 7.3.5.3. Equating $\partial l/\partial v$ to the null vector gives

$$\tilde{\Sigma} = E'E/n,$$

and we write

$$\frac{\partial l}{\partial \delta} = [H^{*\prime} - W'(I_G \otimes B^{-1\prime}E')](\tilde{\Sigma}^{-1} \otimes I_n)\varepsilon.$$

Writing $M(r)^{-1}$ as we did in Eq. (7.93) we have

$$H^* = H + (\bar{R} \otimes I_n)\bar{C}H.$$

Consider then

$$H - (I_G \otimes EB^{-1})W = \operatorname{diag}\{H_i - EB^{-1}W_i\},$$
$$H_i - EB^{-1}W_i = (Y_i - EB^{-1}\bar{W}_i \; X_i).$$

Clearly $\bar{Y}_i = Y_i - EB^{-1}\bar{W}_i$ is that part of Y_i left after the influence of the disturbance matrix E has been removed. Let

$$\bar{H} = \operatorname{diag}\{H_i\} \text{ with } \bar{H}_i = (\bar{Y}_i \; X_i),$$
$$\bar{H}^* = \bar{H} + (\bar{R} \otimes I_n)\bar{C}H.$$

Then $\bar{H}^*$ represents that part of H^* purged of the influence of E and therefore of $\varepsilon = \operatorname{vec} E$, and our derivative can be written as

$$\frac{\partial l}{\partial \delta} = \bar{H}^{*\prime}(\tilde{\Sigma}^{-1} \otimes I)(y^* - H^*\delta).$$

Equating this derivative to the null vector and replacing the remaining parameters with their MLEs gives

$$\tilde{\bar{H}}^{*\prime}(\tilde{\Sigma}^{-1} \otimes I_n)(y^* - \tilde{H}^*\tilde{\delta}) = 0,$$
$$\tilde{\delta} = [\tilde{\bar{H}}^{*\prime}(\tilde{\Sigma}^{-1} \otimes I_n)\tilde{H}^*]^{-1}\tilde{\bar{H}}^{*\prime}(\Sigma^{-1} \otimes I_n)\tilde{y}^*,$$

[2] Suppose $\hat{r}$ is a consistent estimator of r. Let $\hat{y}^* = M(\hat{r})^{-1}y$, $\hat{H}^* = M(\hat{r})^{-1}H^*$, $\hat{X}^* = M(\hat{r})^{-1}(I_G \otimes X)$. One suspects that the estimator $\tilde{\tilde{\delta}}^* = [\hat{H}^{*\prime}\hat{\Phi}^{-1}\hat{X}^*(\hat{X}^{*\prime}\hat{\Phi}^{-1}\hat{X}^*)^{-1}\hat{X}^{*\prime}\hat{\Phi}^{-1}\hat{H}^*]^{-1}\hat{H}^{*\prime}\hat{\Phi}^{-1}(\hat{X}^{*\prime}\hat{\Phi}^{-1}\hat{X}^*)^{-1}X^{*\prime}\hat{\Phi}^{-1}\hat{y}^*$ is asymptotically efficient.

where

$$\tilde{\tilde{H}}^* = \tilde{H}^* - (I_G \otimes \tilde{E}'\tilde{B}^{-1})W,$$
$$\tilde{H}^* = M(\tilde{r})^{-1}H,$$
$$\tilde{y}^* = M(\tilde{r})^{-1}y,$$
$$\tilde{\Sigma} = \tilde{E}'\tilde{E}/n.$$

Thus, we see that the MLE of δ has an iterative IVE interpretation in which we obtain the instrumental variable for H^* by purging H of the influence of ε.

7.4.6. The Lagrangian Multiplier Test Statistic for $H_0 : r = 0$

We have seen in the previous subsection that forming IVEs for δ for the LSE model with vector moving-average disturbances is a lot more difficult than for the model with vector autoregressive disturbances. It is imperative then that we obtain a classical test statistic for the null hypothesis $H_0 : r = 0$ for the model before us. As always, the LMT statistic is the most amenable, and in this section we show that the LMT statistic for the LSE model with vector moving-average disturbances is the same statistic as that developed for the preceding LSE model with vector autoregressive disturbances. As in this linear-regression model and in the SURE model, the LMT statistic is incapable of distinguishing between the two disturbance systems.

We do this by noting that with $r = 0$, $M(r) = I_{nG}$, $H^* = H^d = H$, $U = E$, $u = e$, $U_p = E_p$, $p\lim E_p'E_p/n = p\lim U_p'U_p/n = I_p \otimes \Sigma$ and $\mathcal{F} = \Sigma^{-1} \otimes U_p$, so for both models

$$\left.\frac{\partial l}{\partial r}\right|_{r=0} = \pm K_{pG,G}(\Sigma^{-1} \otimes U_p')u,$$

$$I^{\delta\delta}(\theta)|_{r=0} = \{p\lim H'[\Sigma^{-1} \otimes (M_u - P_p)]H/n\}^{-1},$$

$$I^{rr}(\theta)|_{r=0} = I_p \otimes \Sigma^{-1} \otimes \Sigma + K_{pG,G}\{p\lim[I_G \otimes (I_p \otimes \Sigma^{-1})U_p'] \times HI^{\delta\delta}(\theta)|_{r=0}H'[I_G \otimes U_p(I_p \otimes \Sigma^{-1})]\}K_{G,pG}.$$

It follows then that the LMT statistic for $H_0 : r = 0$ is the same for both models, for both the case in which X is exogenous and for the case in which X contains lagged endogenous variables.

APPENDIX 7.A. CONSISTENCY OF $\tilde{R}$ AND $\tilde{\Sigma}$.

Write the model as $YB + X\Gamma = QA = U$, where $Q = (YX)$ and $A = (B'\ \Gamma')'$. Consider $\hat{U} = Q\hat{A} = U + Q(\hat{A} - A)$, where $\hat{A}$ is some consistent estimator of A. As $-p\lim(U_p'U_p)^{-1}U_p'U = R'$, it follows that $\tilde{R}' = -(\hat{U}_p'\hat{U}_p)\hat{U}_p'\hat{U}$, where $\hat{U}_p' = S(I_p \otimes \hat{U})$ is a consistent estimator of R' as long as $\hat{A}$ is a consistent estimator of A. Similarly, as $p\lim E'E/n = \Sigma$, $\tilde{\Sigma} = \tilde{E}'\tilde{E}/n$ with $\tilde{E} = \hat{U} + \hat{U}_p\tilde{R}'$ will also be consistent, provided $\hat{A}$ is consistent. The estimator $\hat{A}$ used in our analysis is formed from the 3SLS estimator we obtain by ignoring the autoregression and by using X to form the instrumental variable for H in $y = H\delta + u$ in the usual manner. To establish the consistency of $\tilde{R}$ and $\tilde{\Sigma}$ then it suffices to show that such an estimator is consistent.

The first step in obtaining the 3SLS estimator is to apply a 2SLS estimator to each equation. Write the 2SLS estimator for the ith equation, $y_i = H_i\delta_i + u_i$, as

$$\tilde{\delta}_i = \delta_i + \left(\frac{H_i' P_x H_i}{n}\right)^{-1} \frac{H_i' X}{n} \left(\frac{X'X}{n}\right)^{-1} \frac{X'u_i}{n}, \tag{7.A.1}$$

where $P_x = X(X'X)^{-1}X'$. Our assumptions ensure that the p lims exist for all the matrices on the right-hand side of Eq. (7.A.1) Moreover, we have assumed that X is strictly exogenous so $p \lim X'u_i/n = 0$. It follows that the 2SLS estimators are consistent estimators and that $p \lim \hat{u}_i \hat{u}_j/n = p \lim u_i' u_j/n$, where $\hat{u}_i$ is the 2SLS residual vector (the latter p lim is assumed to exist).

The next step in applying the 3SLS estimator is to form the matrix $\hat{\mathcal{V}} = \{\hat{u}'\hat{u}/n\}$. Clearly $p \lim \hat{\mathcal{V}} = \{p \lim u_i' u_j/n\} = \mathcal{V}$, say. The 3SLS estimator in this is asymptotically equivalent to

$$\delta^* = \delta + \left[\frac{H'(\mathcal{V}' \otimes P_x)H}{n}\right]^{-1} \frac{H'(I \otimes X)}{n}$$
$$\times \left[\mathcal{V}^{-1} \otimes \left(\frac{X'X}{n}\right)^{-1}\right] \frac{(I \otimes X')u}{n}. \tag{7.A.2}$$

Again, our assumptions ensure that the p lims of all the matrices on the right-hand side of Eq. (7.A.2) exist. Moreover, with X strictly exogenous, $p \lim(I \otimes X')Xu/n = 0$, and it follows that the 3SLS estimator of δ is consistent.

References and Suggested Readings

Bowden, R. J. and Turkington, D. A., 1984. *Instrumental Variables*, Econometric Society Monograph in Quantitative Economics 8. Cambridge University Press, New York.

Bowden, R. J. and Turkington, D. A., 1990. *Instrumental Variables*, paperback edition, Cambridge University Press, New York.

Breusch, T. S., 1978. Testing for Autocorrelation in Dynamic Linear Models. *Australian Economic Papers* **17**, 334–335.

Breusch, T. S. and Pagan, A. R., 1980. The Lagrange Multiplier Test and its Applications to Model Specification in Econometrics. *Review of Economic Studies* **47**, 239–254.

Cramer, J. S., 1986. *Econometric Applications of Maximum Likelihood Methods*. Cambridge University Press, Cambridge, U. K.

Davis, P. J., 1979. *Circulant Matrices*. Wiley, New York.

Dhrymes, P. J., 1978. *Mathematics for Econometrics*. Springer, New York.

Durbin, J., 1988. Maximum Likelihood Estimation of the Parameters of a System of Simultaneous Regression Equations. *Econometric Theory* **4**, 159–170.

Dwyer, P. S., 1967. Some Applications of Matrix Derivatives in Multivariate Analysis. *Journal of the American Statistical Association* **26**, 607–625.

Dwyer, P. S. and MacPhail, M. S., 1948. Symbolic Matrix Derivatives. *Annals of Mathematical Statistics*, **19**, 517–534.

Godfrey, L. G., 1978a. Testing Against General Autoregressive and Moving Average Error Models when the Regressors Include Lagged Dependent Variables. *Econometrica* **46**, 1293–1302.

Godfrey, L. G., 1978b. Testing for Higher Order Serial Correlation in Regression Equations when the Regressors Include Lagged Dependent Variables. *Econometrica* **46**, 1303–1310.

Godfrey, L. G., 1988. Misspecifications Tests in Econometrics, Econometric Society Monograph in Quantitative Economics 16. Cambridge University Press, New York.

Godfrey, L. G. and Breusch T. S., 1981. A Review of Recent Work on Testing for Autocorrelation in Dynamic Economic Models. In: D. Currie, R. Nobay, and D. Peel (eds.), *Macro-Economic Analysis*.

Graham, A., 1981. *Kronecker Products and Matrix Calculus with Applications*. Ellis Horwood, Chichester, U. K.

Hadley, G., 1961. *Linear Algebra*. Addison-Wesley, Reading, MA.

Hausman, J. A., 1975. An Instrumental Variable Approach to Full Information Estimates for Linear and Certain Non-Linear Econometric Models. *Econometrica* **43**, 727–738.

Henderson, H. V. and Searle, S. R., 1979. Vec and Vech Operators for Matrices, with Some Uses in Jacobians and Multivariate Statistics. *Canadian Journal of Statistics* **7**, 65–81.

Henderson, H. V. and Searle, S. R., 1981. The Vec-Permutation Matrix, the Vec Operator, and Kronecker Products: A Review. *Linear and Multilinear Algebra* **9**, 271–288.

Koopmans, T. C., Hood, W. C., 1953. The Estimation of Simultaneous Linear Economic Relationships. In: W. C. Hood and T. C. Koopmans (eds.), *Studies in Econometric Methods*. Cowles Commission Monograph 14, Wiley, New York, pp. 112–199. Reprint Yale University Press, New Haven, CT, 1970.

Koopmans, T. C., Rubin, H., and Leipnik, R. B., 1950. Measuring the Equation Systems of Dynamic Economics. In: T. C. Koopmans (ed.), *Statistical Inference in Dynamic Economic Models*. Cowles Commission Monograph 10, Wiley, New York, pp. 53–237.

Lutkepohl, H., 1996. *Handbook of Matrices*. Wiley, New York.

MacDuffee, C. C., 1933. *The Theory of Matrices*. Reprinted by Chelsea, New York.

Magnus, J. R. 1985. *Matrix Differential Calculus with Applications to Simple, Hadamard, and Kronecker Products*, Journal of Mathematical Psychology, 474–492.

Magnus, J., 1988. *Linear Structures*. Oxford University Press, New York.

Magnus J. R. and Neudecker, H., 1979. The Commutation Matrix: Some Properties and Applications. *Annals of Statistics* **7**, 381–394.

Magnus, J. R. and Neudecker, H., 1980. The Elimination Matrix: Some Lemmas and Applications. *SIAM Journal on Algebraic and Discrete Methods*, 422–449.

Magnus, J. R. and Neudecker, H. 1985. Matrix Differential Calculus with Applications to Simple, Hadamard, and Kronecker Products. *Journal of Mathematical Psychology* **29**, 474–492.

Magnus, J. R. and Neudecker, H., 1986. Symmetry, 0–1 Matrices and Jacobians: A Review. *Econometric Theory* **2**, 157–190.

Magnus, J. R. and Neudecker, H., 1988. *Matrix Differential Calculus with Applications in Statistics and Econometrics*. Wiley, Chichester, U. K.

Magnus J. R. and Neudecker, H., 1999. *Matrix Differential Calculus with Applications in Statistics and Econometrics*. Revised edition, Wiley, Chichester, U. K.

McDonald, R. P. and Swaminathan, H., 1973. A Simple Matrix Calculus with Applications to Multivariate Analysis. *General Systems* **18**, 37–54.

Muirhead, R. J., 1982. *Aspects of Multivariate Statistical Theory*. Wiley, New York.

Neudecker, H., 1967. On Matrix Procedures for Optimising Differential Scalar Functions of Matrices. *Statistica Neerlandica* **21**, 101–107.

Neudecker, H., 1969. Some Theorems on Matrix Differentiation with Special References to Kronecker Matrix Products. *Journal of the American Statistical Association* **64**, 953–963.

Neudecker, H., 1982. On Two Germane Matrix Derivatives. *The Matrix and Tensor Quarterly* **33**, 3–12.

Neudecker, H., 1985. Recent Advances in Statistical Application of Commutation Matrices. In: W. Grossmann, G. Pflug, I. Vineze and W. Wertz (eds.), *Proceedings of the Fourth Pannonian Symposium on Mathematical Statistics*. Reidel, Dordrecht, The Netherlands, Vol. B, pp. 239–250.

Pagan, A. R. 1974. *A Generalised Approach to the Treatment for Autocorrelation, Australian Economic Papers* **13**, 267–280.

Phillips, A. W., 1966. The Estimation of Systems of Difference Equations with Moving Average Disturbances. Paper presented at the Econometric Society Meetings, San Francisco, 1966.

Pollock, D. S. G., 1979. *The Algebra of Econometrics*. Wiley, New York.

Rogers, G. S., 1980. *Matrix Derivatives*. Marcel Dekker, New York.

Rothenberg, T. J., 1973. *Estimation with A Priori Information*, Cowles Foundation Monograph 23, Yale University Press, New Haven, U. S.

Rothenberg, T. J. and Leenders, C. T., 1964. Efficient Estimation of Simultaneous Equation Systems. *Econometrica* **32**, 57–76.

Searle, S. R., 1979. On Inverting Circulant Matrices. *Linear Algebra and Its Application* **25**, 77–89.

Theil, H., 1971. *Principles of Econometrics*. Wiley, New York.

Tracy, D. S. and Dwyer, P. S., 1969. Multivariate Maxim and Minima with Matrix Derivatives. *Journal of the American Statistical Association* **64**, 1574–1594.

Tracy, D. S. and Singh, R. P., 1972. Some Modifications of Matrix Differentiation for Evaluating Jacobians of Symmetric Matrix Transformations. In: D. Tracy (ed.), *Symmetric Functions in Statistics*. University of Windsor, Ontario, Canada.

Turkington, D. A., 1989. Classical Tests for Contemporaneously Uncorrelated Disturbances in the Linear Simultaneous Equations Model. *Journal of Econometrics* **42**, 299–317.

Turkington, D. A., 1998. Efficient Estimation in the Linear Simultaneous Equations Model with Vector Autoregressive Disturbances. *Journal of Econometrics* **85**, 51–74.

Turkington, D. A., 2000. Generalised Vec Operators and the Seemingly Unrelated Regression Equations Model with Vector Correlated Disturbances. *Journal of Econometrics* **99**, 225–253.

White, H., 1984. *Asymptotic Theory for Econometricians*. Academic Press, New York.

Wise, J., 1955. The Autocorrelation Function and the Special Density Function. *Biometrika* **42**, 151–159.

Wong, C. S., 1980. Matrix Derivatives and its Applications in Statistics. *Journal of Mathematical Psychology* **22**, 70–81.

Zellner, A., 1962. An Efficient Method of Estimating Seemingly Unrelated Regressions and Tests for Aggregation Bias. *Journal of the American Statistical Association* **57**, 348–368.

Zellner, A. and Theil, H. 1962. Three-Stage Least Squares: Simultaneous Estimation of Simultaneous Equations. *Econometrica* **30**, 54–78.

Index

P

Q

R

S